US FIGHTERS
OF WORLD WAR TWO

This early Mustang wears American-style camouflage and national insignia, together with the British serial FX883 and the RAF fin flash. The aircraft was in fact supplied to the RAF under Lend-Lease as a Mustang III in a batch which included both P-51Bs and P-51Cs. (North American)

US FIGHTERS
OF WORLD WAR TWO

ROBERT F. DORR

ARMS AND
ARMOUR

Arms and Armour Press
A Cassell Imprint
Villiers House, 41-47 Strand, London WC2N 5JE.

Distributed in the USA by Sterling Publishing Co. Inc.,
387 Park Avenue South, New York, NY 10016-8810.

Distributed in Australia by Capricorn Link (Australia) Pty.
Ltd., P.O. Box 665, Lane Cove, New South Wales 2066.

British Library Cataloguing in Publication Data
Dorr, Robert F. *1939–*
US Fighters of World War Two.
1. United States. World War 2. Fighter aircraft
I. Title
623.74640973
ISBN 1-85409-073-9

Jacket illustrations: North American P-51D-5NA Mustang on
an early flight test. The first few hundred 'D' models were
built without the dorsal fin fillet and were flown in combat.
Field modification kits were supplied for those aircraft that
came off the production lines without this important aid to
vertical stability. (North American via Jerry Scutts)

Designed and edited by DAG Publications Ltd. Designed by
David Gibbons; edited by David Dorrell; layout by Anthony A.
Evans, typeset by Typesetters (Birmingham) Ltd, Warley,
West Midlands; camerawork by M&E Reproductions, North
Fambridge, Essex; Quality printing by The Bath Press,
Lower Bristol Road, Bath, BA2 3BL.

Acknowledgments: Any errors in this volume are the
sole responsibility of the author. The book would
have been impossible, however, without the gener-
osity of many who helped.

Assistance was provided by the US Department of
Defense. I am especially grateful to Lt Col Don Black,
Bob Bockman and Ken Carter in the Pentagon. I also
want to thank:

Among those who fly and fight: Robert V. Brulle,
who flew a P-47 Thunderbolt with the call-sign 'Relic
Yellow 2' with the 390th Fighter Squadron; Will
Carroll who ferried shiny new F6F Hellcats with
VFR-1; Michael Curphey, who may know more about
the F4U Corsair than anybody; Robin Olds, who has
more than a passing acquaintance with Lightnings
and Thunderbolts; and Kemal Saied, who flew
P-47Ds with the 404th Fighter Group and is the
author of *Thunderbolt Odyssey* (Stonewood Press,
Tulsa, 1989).

Among the fraternity: Hal Andrews, Rick Burgess,
Bill Crimmins, George Cully, Larry Davis, Lou
Drendel, Jeffrey Ethell, Harry Gann, Dan Hagedorn,
Joseph G. Handelman, M. J. Kasiuba, Jon Lake,
Ernest R. McDowell, David R. McLaren, David W.
Menard, David Ostrowski, Alain Pelletier, Norman
Polmar, Joshua Stoff, Jim Sullivan, and Norman
Taylor. And, as always, the Grumman History Center,
Lois Lovisolo, Peter Kirkup, Bill Barto.

The views expressed in this book are mine and
do not necessarily reflect those of the United States
Air Force.

Robert F. Dorr

Contents

Introduction

To take command of the air. These simple words describe the job of the fighter pilot from the earliest days of aerial warfare. An ace in the First World War, Baron Manfred von Richthofen, characterized the fighter pilot's mission in equally simple terms. 'Fighter pilots,' he said, 'have to rove in the area allotted to them in any way they like, and when they spot an enemy they attack and shoot him down; anything else is rubbish.'

The importance of fighter aircraft has been proved again and again. Had Luftwaffe fighters been able to wrest control of the skies during the 1940 battle which meant Britain's life or death, the outcome of the war would amost certainly have been different. The brilliant Japanese surprise attack against Pearl

Buried beneath a stack of three P-51Ds and nearly obscured by them, Los Angeles-built P-51B 42-106811 with the flush canopy of an early Mustang chugs along, keeping up nicely with its more graceful wingmates. The 'E2' code on the fuselage of these fighters identifies them as belonging to the 375th Fighter Squadron, 361st Fighter Group. 'E2C' was being piloted by Lt Col Tom J. J. Christian, 'E2S' by Lt Urban Drew, who later shot down a Messerschmitt Me 262 jet fighter. The wartime caption states that these North American fillies were about to peel off to lose altitude for landing in England following an uneventful bomber escort mission. An October 1943 policy decision by the USAAF eliminated the requirement for factory-applied camouflage, although the P-51B, if not its fellow 'D' models, was probably camouflaged at some point in the past. (US Army)

Seen from a transport, this formation of five US Marine Corps Grumman F6F-5 Hellcats is winging over the Western Pacific. These deceptively calm waters were the backdrop for what one officer called the battle of the century, between Grumman's pride and the Mitsubishi A6M5 'Zeke 52' – the vaunted 'Zero'. The victor in battle after battle, the F6F Hellcat had been so well designed that it scarcely needed a flight test programme before reaching the Fleet. It went into production smoothly and at such volume that in one month alone (March 1945) Grumman produced over 600 Hellcats. Late-model F6F-5s lacked a small window behind the canopy found on earlier -3 and -5 models. The 150(US)gal centre-line fuel tank shown here was parallel to, and 61.25in below, the engine thrust line and was used on F6F-3, F6F-3N, F6F-5 and F6F-5N models. (USMC via Lou Drendel)

Harbor succeeded in part because the Hawaiian islands were defenceless, lacking fighters to blunt the assault. When the latent power of the United States was finally unleashed and the Allies turned the tide of the war, their first step was to use fighters to seize control of the sky.

The US Army called them pursuit ships. The US Navy faced the added challenge of making them operate from aircraft-carrier decks. Marine Corps pilots flew them at Guadalcanal, a very special hell where merely living was a challenge and fighting was an ordeal. The American fighters of the Second World War – most of them well advanced in the design stage before Pearl Harbor – rose to the occasion to make their contribution to the Allied effort. Many served in the Royal Air Force, and it was British initiative that led to the best of them, the P-51 Mustang. But it was the untapped potential of the American industrial giant that rose to the final

needs of the war, turning out just a few dozen less than 100,000 fighters in three and a half years. When it was over, American fighters had absolute command of the air over Tokyo and Berlin.

The war was a period of trial and triumph. For every Mustang, Thunderbolt or Hellcat, there were a dozen fighter designs which enhanced knowledge, spurred progress, and ended up not winning the ultimate prize of a large-scale production order. Few today can dredge up a sharply focused memory of the XP-46, the F2M-1, or the XP-75, but like the more important fighters, they, too, made a contribution.

Beginning in a state of almost total unpreparedness for war, the people who designed, built, and flew American fighters had acquitted themselves superbly by VJ-Day. There would never again be any question about the importance of the fighter aircraft or its role in deciding the course of a conflict.

P-38 Lightning

When it was the newest thing in the air, the Lockheed P-38 Lightning was also the hottest. If any twin-engined fighter in the world at that time was faster, more powerful or more heavily armed, it wore a nameplate from Messerschmitt. In the Allied world, until the advent of the de Havilland Mosquito, the P-38 Lightning was unmatched. And no other aircraft (except for the Mosquito) seemed able to fulfil so many roles – fighter, bomber, night fighter, reconnaissance aircraft, air ambulance, torpedo-bomber, even glider tug.

In 1940 – when toys were made of iron – a thoughtful Dad could pop into Woolworth's or Kresge's and, for an exorbitant one dollar seventeen cents, purchase for his air-minded youngster a magnificent 12in Buddy-L replica of the twin-boom P-38 Lightning. It was a glorious toy, too expensive for most amid the Depression, and in all its sheer glory the toy proclaimed that the Lockheed P-38 Lightning touched the heart. Long after the Lightning was no longer new, when Thunderbolts, Mustangs and Hellcats were flying, eager-eyed young men still looked at the P-38 Lightning with that special glint in their eyes and wanted to fly it. At one training base as late as 1945, long after Mustangs had appeared over Berlin, a slot in the cockpit of the P-38 Lightning remained the first choice of new flight cadets.

The ravages of time have not been kind to the original negative of Lockheed's best-known view of the XP-38 Lightning prototype, so this likeness provided by the company's ever-helpful Eric Schulzinger is perhaps the best that can be made in a darkroom today. Not evident from this study of the prototype (37-457) is the stunning effect of sun-splattered natural silver interrupted only by pre-war national insignia on the wings and Army stripes on the vertical tail. This prototype, ironically, was lost when it undershot a landing at Mitchel Field after the type's first transcontinental flight in February 1939. (Lockheed)

Stamped on the back of this early study of the P-38 Lightning was a stern warning: 'Under letter of July 2, 1940, signed by [Lockheed President] Robert E. Gross; Army Regulations 380-5; the Espionage Act of January 12, 1938; and Presidential Proclamation of March 22, 1940, this photograph may not be released or shown to any unauthorized person . . .' Restrictions were later eased and the shape of the P-38 became familiar to the public. (Lockheed via M. J. Kasiuba)

It appears that this flight was followed by an unexpected set-down! Date and location are not known but this unintended seaplane version of the Lightning, 41-2257, was a Burbank-built 'G' Model. It is understood that this was one of 524 P-38E and P-38G models earmarked for the RAF with serials AF221–AF744 but never delivered to Britain. (USAF)

In California mountains, P-38J Lightning 42-67183 leads F-5B photo ship 42-67332 through a sunless sky. Both aircraft wear the post-1943 American national insignia with a thin red/orange surround which was employed only briefly. The P-38J (foreground) wears camouflage which was standard for US Army Air Forces (as the Army Air Corps was renamed on 20 June 1941), while the reconnaissance F-5B (background) is adorned in synthetic haze paint. Briefly the standard camouflage for high-altitude reconnaissance aircraft, haze paint was Sky Base Blue with a light shadow of shading of Flight Blue. (Lockheed via M. J. Kasiuba)

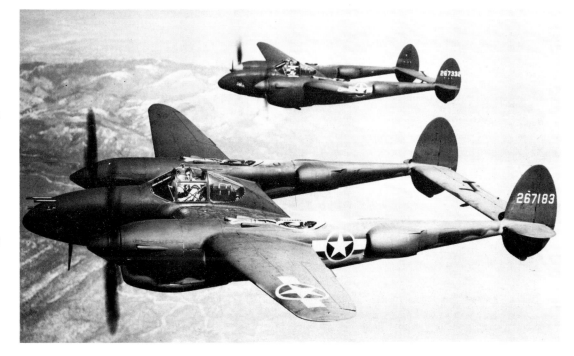

Many pursuit ships looked impressive in the sky. Only the P-38 Lightning could halt your breath, chill your spine, while still on the ground. Being run up on the flight line, before it moved an inch, the P-38 was slender and streamlined. Its engines emitted a throaty message of power. Other pursuit ships became better known, others toted up fine performance figures, but the P-38 Lightning inspired the mind and fired the spirit; the P-38 was majestic.

The P-38 produced the top-ranking American air ace of all time. The P-38 killed the Japanese admiral who had been the architect of Pearl Harbor, Isoroku Yamamoto. The P-38 bored through the blue accompanied by legends drummed up by Public Relations hype, one being that the Germans feared it enough to call it 'Der gabelschwanz Teufel' (the fork-tailed devil) – which was about half right. Perhaps it did not evoke fear, not in the way the publicity hounds claimed, but the P-38 with its distinctive twin-boomed shape certainly was a devil of sorts. As late as VJ-Day, when it was older than other American fighters, it still had to be taken seriously. The P-38 remained in production throughout the war.

Design

The twin-engined fighter of the future seemed, in 1936, to be the Bell XFM-1 Airacuda, which had won a design competition that year and was a veritable flying fortress with a multi-man crew and numerous guns pointing in various directions. The ungainly Bell design was, in fact, just about everything but a genuine fighter. Concluding that the Bell design did not meet its needs for a high-altitude interceptor, the US Army Air Corps opened Competition X-608 to Boeing, Consolidated, Curtiss, Douglas and Vultee as well as Lockheed.

Contrary to some accounts, the competition called from the beginning for a twin-engined aircraft. The configuration, however, was not specified. A design team under H. L. Hibbard, which included a young Clarence L. (Kelly) Johnson – given broad marching orders by chief executive Robert E. Gross – began studying various configurations. The team had not designed a military aircraft before. To some, the team seemed hardly likely to succeed when Johnson came up with a radical twin-boom configuration. But Lockheed won the contract to produce a prototype.

Johnson took the initiative and arrived at the twin-boom layout only after studying more orthodox arrangements. At one stage a preliminary design had twin booms with engines fore and aft of the cockpit in a central nacelle; another had the pilot sitting in an enclosed cockpit astride one of the booms.

Once decided upon, the final twin-boom arrangement bestowed numerous advantages, such as accommodation of engines, main landing gear, superchargers and radiators, as well as providing the benefits of endplate effect on the tailplane with twin vertical surfaces. Although this configuration left the nose free for armament, the foreshortened central nacelle was over time to prove rather useless as a place to put additional equipment. Nor was the design, now known as the Lockheed Model 22, any lightweight: the original gross weight of 14,800lb (6,713kg) was higher than that of most contemporary American light bombers.

With four 0.50in (12.7mm) machine-guns and a single 20mm cannon, the P-38 Lightning could put out a withering volley of fire – as long as it was not out-manoeuvred by smaller, more nimble fighters. P-38J 43-28859 is firing its guns on a low-level flight over water. (via M. J. Kasiuba)

Flight Test

On 27 January 1939 at March Field in Riverside, California, the prototype XP-38, serial number 37-457 (the system employed by the Air Corps made this the 457th aircraft ordered for purchase in fiscal year 1937), took off on its maiden flight with Lieutenant Benjamin S. Kelsey at the controls. The prototype, powered by 960hp Allison V-1710-11/15 engines driving inward-rotating propellers, was brought out of secrecy for an 11 February 1939 transcontinental speed dash, crossing the United States in 7hr 2min with two refuelling stops. Alas, this superb long-distance flight was marred when 37-457 undershot the runway at Mitchel Field, New York, on approach, crashed, and was destroyed.

In general, early tests of the P-38 Lightning were trouble-free and boded well for the chequered career the pursuit ship would have during the war years. Minor changes occurred as new variants of the Lightning were developed (see later) but the basic design was sound. As has been noted, the twin-boom configuration freed the Lightning's nose for unsynchronized guns and produced a broad, sturdy warplane with respectable range, able to carry 4,000lb (1,814kg) of underwing ordnance. So effective was the design that major changes did not occur until the definitive P-38J model, when the intakes under the engines were enlarged to house core-type intercoolers, the curved windscreen was replaced by a flat panel, and the boom-mounted radiators were enlarged. The 'J' model eventually achieved a combat range of 2,300 miles (3,700km). Although the Lightning did not escort heavy bombers all the way to their targets in the latter stages of the war, this range made possible penetration flights deep into Hitler's 'Fortress Europe', as well as combat missions over the vast expanses of the Pacific.

Variants

Beginning with Lieutenant Kelsey's pre-war mount, the P-38 Lightning underwent continuous changes over the war years, just as most fighter types did. The

Another study of the Lightning in natural metal which, if anything, made it appear more streamlined than ever. P-38L 42-68008 on an early acceptance flight over California. (Lockheed)

Lightning pilots. There was no luxury in New Guinea but there was spirit, attested by the slogan above the portal. These Lightning pilots, assumed to be members of the 475th Fighter Group, are (left to right): Lt Robert H. Adams, Lt John L. Jones and Lt Jess E. Gidley. In two days of action, 21–23 July 1943, their squadron accounted for 17 Japanese fighters, Adams scoring four. (USAF via M. J. Kasiuba)

twin-boom pursuit ship existed in these versions:

XP-38. Lockheed Model 022-64-01 prototype (the company's initial model number for each variant appears in parentheses in entries below). Allison V-1710-C9 engines, one radiator. One built.

YP-38. (122-62-02) pre-production service test aircraft. V-1710-F2 engines with radiators in each boom; rotation of propellers changed. Thirteen built.

P-38. (222-62-02) armed with 37mm gun. V-1710-F2 engines. 30 built.

RP-38. This designation was assigned to some two-seat conversions from the P-38.

XP-38A. (622-62-10). One aircraft converted with a pressurized cockpit. V-1710-F2 engines. The designations P-38B and P-38C were not used.

XP-49. (522-66-07). Experimental test version. V-1430 engines. Two built.

P-38D. (222-62-08). First production variant. V-1710-F2 engines. 36 built.

P-38E. (222-62-09). Armed with 20mm gun, 210 built.

P-38F. (222-60-09). V-1710-F5 engines. Improved systems, 527 built.

P-38G. (322-68-19), minor changes. V-1710-F10 engines. 1,082 built.

P-38H. (422-81-20), increased load and improved superchargers. V-1710-F17 engines. 601 built, 123 converted to F-5C.

THROUGH THESE PORTALS PASS THE HOTTEST PILOTS IN THE WORLD

Wearing 'plane in group' number 24, the ship taking the lead in this formation of four Lightnings is P-38H 42-66605. This appears to be a stateside flight. Once camouflage was no longer applied at the factory, camouflaged and natural-metal Lightnings appeared together in the same squadrons. (USAF)

Another view of the waterlogged P-38 [see page 9]. (USAF)

P-38J. (422-81-14), able to carry two 380(US)gal (1,362-litre) drop tanks. V-1710-F17 engines. 2,970 built, some converted to F-5E, F-5F.

P-38K. (422-85-22). Test aircraft with enlarged propellers. V-1710-F15 engines. One built.

P-38L. (422-87-23). Principal production conversion, Allison V-1710-111 engines. 3,923 built including 113 by Vultee at Nashville. Some converted to TP-38L two-seat trainers, 74 to P-38M two-seat night fighters.

P-38M. (522-87-23). Two-seat night fighter conversion. V-1710-111 engines.

F-4. (222-60-13). First reconnaissance version. V-1710-F4 engines. 20 built.

F-5A. (222-68-16). Reconnaissance version. V-1710-F4 engines. 181 built, one converted to XF-5D.

F-5B. (422-81-21). Reconnaissance version. V-1710-F17 engines. 200 built.

F-5C. (422-81-20). Reconnaissance version. V-1710-F17 engines. 123 converted from P-38H.

XF-5D. (222-68-16). Experimental reconnaissance conversion from F-5A. V-1710-F10 engines. One built.

F-5E. (422-81-22). Reconnaissance version. V-1710-F17 engines. 705 converted from P-38J/P-38L.

F-5F. (422-81-22). Reconnaissance version. V-1710-F17 engines. Conversions from P-38J.

F-5G. (422-87-23). Reconnaissance version. V-1710 engines. Conversions from P-38L.

Combat

Although no P-38s were at Oahu when Pearl Harbor was attacked, Lightning squadrons were in position along the west coast of the USA where many Americans expected the next Japanese attack to come. The 1st Fighter Group was the first to take the twin-boom Lightning on charge but the first 'action' belonged to the 55th Fighter Group at Paine Field, Washington, which began patrolling with its P-38s in readiness for an enemy invasion that never came. Even further north, where bold Japanese leaders struck at American soil, Lightning pilots shot down two enemy flying-boats near Adak, Alaska, on 4 August 1942.

As the American war machine swung into gear – awkwardly, at first – P-38s demonstrated their ability to make the long northern flight to Great Britain. Strategy against the Reich called for transforming the British Isles into a 'giant aircraft-carrier' to mount campaigns over occupied Europe. The P-38 deliveries marked the first time pursuit ships reached the British Isles under their own power. During a prolonged stop-over in Iceland, which permitted Lightning pilots to hunt for Focke-Wulf Fw 200 Condors, Lieutenant Elza Shahan achieved a dramatic first, shooting down one of the four-engined Luftwaffe patrol bombers on 15 August 1942.

Some men who first took the P-38 to war, even lowly lieutenants, had pulled garrison duty in the Air Corps long enough to know the snappy P-12 biplane, the nimble P-26 'Peashooter' monoplane, and lacklustre pre-war pursuit ships like the P-39 Airacobra. Others, the less mature breed in the new ranks of citizen-soldier swollen by the demands of a new war, flew the P-38 as their first and only aircraft. So unique was the P-38 that the many hours' flight experience of its mature pilots was perhaps not much help in mastering the Lightning.

Men in Lightning cockpits discovered, as they always do, that any fighter plane is always a series of compromises. The good news about the P-38 was its speed and heavy weapons capability. The bad news was that the Lightning was big, complex, not always easy to maintain, and not the best fighter to fly if the enemy ambushed you. 'You want the smallest effective fighter for the job you want to do,' says an aeronautical engineer. 'You want to roll very rapidly if the other guy gets you into a dogfight. But with two engines with high inertia, the Lightning was hard to roll and could not accelerate and roll.' If you were bounced by a 'Zero' or Messerschmitt, you were in serious trouble. But if you were smart enough to anticipate the other guy's actions before he could bounce you, the Lightning's superior speed and armament made it unbeatable.

The 1st Fighter Group was in action in the Mediterranean Theatre shortly after the November 1942 Allied landing known as Operation 'Torch'. The 14th and 82nd Fighter Groups followed. The men flew and fought under difficult conditions but there were high moments. On 5 April 1943 twenty-six P-38s got the jump on a formation of Junkers Ju 52 transports with fighter escort. The 1st Fighter Group shot down sixteen German aircraft, including eleven of the transports.

As the Allies secured North Africa and turned to push back German forces in Sicily and Italy, the 37th Fighter Group joined the fray with P-38F and P-38H models. Now, Lightning pilots began encountering the Focke-Wulf Fw 190. The Fw 190 quickly proved to be another enemy who would always have the upper hand as long as he enjoyed the advantage of surprise.

In due course, the P-47 Thunderbolt and P-51 Mustang became more decisive in Europe, but only after considerable numbers of Germany's best pilots had fallen to the fork-tailed Lightning.

In the Pacific the commander of Allied Air Forces, Major General George C. Kenney, was enthusiastic about the P-38, and especially about its long range – and used strong language to ask for more of them. The 35th Fighter Group brought sixteen factory-new Lightnings to Port Moresby, New Guinea, in August 1942. Several of the group's pilots, including Lieutenant Richard I. Bong, soon transferred to the 49th Fighter Group as the war raged across New Guinea and moved from island to island.

On 18 April 1943 Lightnings flew one of the most unusual missions of the war. Having broken Japanese codes even before the outbreak of the war in the Pacific, American officers learned that the architect of the Pearl Harbor attack, Admiral Isoroku Yamamoto, was to make an inspection trip to Bougainville and other bases. With its long range, the P-38 had the capability to intercept Yamamoto. Major John Mitchell, a P-38 squadron commander, drew the perilous task of planning to ambush the admiral.

Eighteen P-38 Lightnings took off from Henderson Field – won at such terrible price in the fighting at Guadalcanal – and navigated 435 miles (700km),

Particularly in the long-distance Pacific war, the twin-engined reliability offered by the Lightning's pair of Allisons was always a solid 'plus' for pilots who wanted to fight hard and still get home safely. P-38L Lightning 44-23856 is demonstrating its 'one engine out' capability, flying with one propeller feathered. (USAF)

aiming for the spot where Yamamoto's Mitsubishi G4M 'Betty' was predicted to intersect their path. The Lightnings arrived with perfect timing just as the Japanese formation appeared.

Mitchell sent four P-38s, led by Lieutenant Thomas Lanphier, to attack the two 'Betty' bombers carrying Yamamoto and his deputy. Escorting 'Zero' fighters dropped their belly tanks and a melee ensued. But the Americans had the advantage of surprise. Three 'Bettys' and three 'Zeros' fell in the fight, while one P-38 was lost. 'I fear we have only awakened a sleeping giant,' Yamamoto had warned his countrymen following the triumph at Pearl Harbor. The 'Betty' carrying Yamamoto crashed, taking the admiral to his death. While Lanphier is usually credited with the kill, exact details of that historic fight remain in dispute to this day.

Not well known is the fact that the Lightning had some success in the Pacific as a night fighter. The 418th Night Fighter Squadron found the P-70 Havoc inadequate. But with a mixed collection of P-70s and P-38H Lightnings the squadron devised tactics which worked well to intercept enemy bombers. These Lightnings were day fighters with no radar and the P-38 pilots were forced to wait for the enemy to appear in ground searchlights. The 6th Fighter Squadron tackled the problem by fitting at least two P-38Gs with a second seat and an SCR-540 radar mounted in a drop tank. In due course the specialized P-38M night fighter was developed, but although the all-black P-38M was both impressive-looking and highly effective, it appears that only four 'M' models reached the Philippines before VJ-Day.

The importance of the Lightning in the Pacific is underscored by the aerial victory totals of Captain Richard I. Bong (40) and Captain Thomas McGuire (38). Both were awarded the Medal of Honor. Major Charles H. MacDonald of the 475th Fighter Group began his victory string in New Guinea, flew a P-38L nicknamed 'Putt Putt Maru', and downed 27 Japa-

The Lockheed XP-49, a one-off experimental fighter which was outwardly almost indistinguishable from the P-38 – although powered by supercharged Continental V-1430 engines. The XP-49, or company Model 522, was used for stratospheric research above 40,000ft (12,192m). Considered a secret at the time, the XP-49 was flown extensively but no in-flight photo of it is known to survive. (Lockheed)

A formation of P-38H Lightnings in the bank over southern California, exuding the clean lines and awesome power which made the Lightning so memorable. (USAF)

nese aircraft. An F-5, one of the photo-reconnaissance variants of the Lightning, became the first Allied aircraft to land in Japan after the surrender.

Flying the P-38

The pilot of the P-38 Lightning sat in a roomy, spacious cockpit with the 'feel' of a very large aeroplane all around him. It was an unforgiving machine, and it was unkind to maintenance men who had to labour overtime to keep it in the air, especially in the appalling conditions found in the Pacific. Once in the air, the pilot enjoyed a sensational feeling of speed and power. He also had some idiosyncracies to contend with. More than one P-38 pilot found himself in a raging dogfight when his windshield frosted up, a problem to which the Lockheed fighter was prone. The word 'energy' was not part of the fighter pilot's vocabulary in those days, but any pilot who allowed his energy to drain off was inevitably going to lose the edge.

When it was not dogfighting, the P-38 Lightning did a little of everything else, helped by innovative 'wrench-twisters' who contrived all sorts of local modifications. One invention in the field – so dangerous that it might not have been approved had it gone to higher headquarters for scrutiny – was a drop-tank with a glass nose used to carry combat photographer David Douglas Duncan, lying prone in a very cramped state, to take pictures. Had the Lightning got into trouble, Duncan would have had no way out.

Test pilots made extensive use of the basic P-38 design, as well as the XP-49 and XP-58 offshoots of the Lightning, to advance knowledge of aviation in general and to write up recommendations for improved aircraft and weapons as the war progressed. The XP-49 was a pressurized pursuit ship outwardly almost identical to the P-38 but used for stratospheric research above 40,000ft (12,192m). The XP-58 Chain Lightning, sometimes called the 'Destroyer', was a larger aircraft based only generally on the P-38 design and intended for heavy cannon armament in the nose. The XP-58 was strongly influenced by Elliott Roosevelt's wartime efforts to develop a 'convoy fighter' – a heavily armed aircraft which would accompany bombers to their targets. The advent of the long-range P-51D Mustang rendered the concept questionable, but not before Hughes and Republic had also submitted designs.

Units

The principal P-38 fighter groups (with some of their fighter squadrons shown in parentheses) included the: 1st (27 FS, 71 FS, 94 FS); 4th (333 FS, 334 FS, 335 FS); 8th (35 FS, 36 FS, 80 FS); 14th (37 FS, 48 FS, 48 FSD, 49 FS); 18th; 20th (55 FS, 77 FS, 79 FS); 35th (39 FS); 49th (7 FS, 8 FS, 9 FS); 55th (54 FS, 38 FS, 338 FS, 343 FS); 56th; 78th; 80th (459 FS); and 82nd (95 FS, 97 FS, 98 FS). Some of these groups used the Lightning only briefly; the 56th Fighter Group, for example, is better remembered for the P-47D Thunderbolt. Others never had more than one P-38 squadron.

Fighter group designations in the 100 and 200 ranges were, theoretically, allocated for Reserve and Air National Guard use, so the roster of Lightning groups continued with the: 343rd (54 FS); 347th; 364th (383 FS, 384 FS, 385 FS); 367th (392 FS, 393 FS, 394 FS); 370th (401 FS, 402 FS, 485 FS); 474th (428 FS, 429 FS, 430 FS); 475th; and 479th (434 FS, 435 FS, 436 FS).

Most of the 143 Lightning Mk. Is (based on the P-38E) ordered for the Royal Air Force in March 1940 were rejected after tests with AF105 and AF106 at Boscombe down and handed back to the USAAF,

which used them as trainers under the designation P-322. A batch of 524 Lightning IIs (equivalent to the P-38G) was ordered for the RAF in August 1942, but this contract was also cancelled and these machines were diverted to the USAAF.

With the liberation of Paris, the French air arm was rapidly reconstituted and a few Lightnings were delivered to the Armée de l'Air. The F-5B photo-reconnaissance version equipped a French group serving on Corsica in 1944–45. Other air forces did not make use of the P-38 Lightning until after VJ-Day, and then only in limited numbers.

Post-war

Some leaders of the war effort had been badly informed about the P-38's performance from the beginning, Eighth Air Force chief General Ira C. Eaker being one. The result was that the P-38 made its bones in the Pacific while being regarded less favourably by commanders in other theatres. It is possible that, had an accurate picture of P-38 capabilities been available to Eaker, Lieutenant General James H. Doolittle and others, the eventual production total might have exceeded the 9,942 built.

In the final year of the war, leaders, pilots and mechanics used their imagination to produce various 'field mods' of the P-38 in addition to the drop-tank/photography modification already mentioned – and to exploit other capabilities which did not require modifications. Casualty evacuation was also performed, making use of drop-tanks with

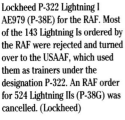

Lockheed P-322 Lightning I AE979 (P-38E) for the RAF. Most of the 143 Lightning Is ordered by the RAF were rejected and turned over to the USAAF, which used them as trainers under the designation P-322. An RAF order for 524 Lightning IIs (P-38G) was cancelled. (Lockheed)

transparent nose sections, each of which reportedly could hold not one but two litters. A P-38J was tested with rectractable ski landing gear for possible use in the Aleutians, an idea whose time never came. As a glider tug, the versatile P-38 could tow three fully laden light assault gliders.

The Lockheed P-38 Lightning did not enjoy a long post-war career, as did the P-47 and P-51. Although it shared with the B-17 Fortress the special status of being in production throughout the entire period of the war, the Lightning's job was essentially finished when the surrender came. The type left front-line squadron use in 1946 and was officially declared surplus to military requirements in 1949.

A few Lightnings reached the world's smaller air forces. Some actually fought in brief spasms of turmoil in Latin America. In general, though, the P-38 was just too big, too costly, and too difficult to fly for a second-line air arm to make effective use of it.

Survivors

In the 1950s there were still more than a few P-38 and F-5 Lightnings on the American civil register, being used for practical duties in the days before 'warbird' air shows. No fewer than fifteen examples of this spectacular pursuit aircraft remain in museums and on display today.

Interestingly, a P-38M Lightning night fighter (44-53097) is among the Lightning airframes that still survive today and, after a zigzag career which

included brief service in Honduras, became the first twin-engined fighter to join Doug Champlin's Fighter Aces Museum in Mesa, Arizona.

The US Air Force Museum at Dayton, Ohio, is the proud owner of P-38L Lightning 44-53232, which is immaculately restored in wartime markings. The Confederate Air Force's 'Ghost Squadron' still flies its Lightning, perhaps the only machine of the type which is regularly accessible to air show audiences.

Reunions

For those who were not a part of it, it is no easy task to feel the awe that a generation of Americans – fighter pilots included – bestowed on the P-38 Lightning. All aircraft types have their devotees, and the men who flew most of the principal types still get together regularly to re-live their experiences – so participation at reunions may not be a fair measure of the regard in which the Lightning is held. Still, it has to be noted that a glance at a single veterans' journal recently disclosed reunion plans on the part of no fewer than six different P-38 and F-5 Lightning fighter groups!

The P-38 National Association, which boasted 1,300 members by February 1990, was holding periodic reunions for 'pilots, crews, those who were protected by it in combat, those who built it, and fans of this, the greatest pursuit aircraft of World War II'. Information is understood to be available from the P-38 National Association, P.O. Box 1816, Burbank, California 91507.

Based on the P-38, the Lockheed XP-58 Chain Lightning (also called the 'Destroyer') was intended as a giant 'convoy fighter', able to carry four 37mm or one 75mm cannon in its nose. The very powerful XP-58 was successful in tests but did not win a production order. (Lockheed)

'Droop snoot' version of the P-38 Lightning served as a pathfinder for high-altitude precision bombing missions. Some of these modifications for a glass nose to hold a bomb-aimer were made in the field. Having the extra crew member apparently had no effect on the aircraft's performance. (Lockheed)

The P-38 Lightning was not around in large numbers after the war, but a few found civil uses and a couple still fly today. Lockheed F-5G Lightning photo ship c/n. 8187 (ex P-38L 44-27182) had worn the civil registration N62441 before becoming N501MH. Seen at Santa Maria, California, in 1959, this Lightning was owned by the Mark Hurd Company. (Robert F. Dorr)

Doomed from the Start

The United States was unprepared for the Second World War. Long after Spitfires and Hurricanes had been making their valiant stand against intruders adorned with swastikas, Americans still felt protected by vast oceans. When war came, its coming was sudden, traumatic. To many, black smoke billowing from the battleship USS *Arizona* (BB-39) at Pearl Harbor became a heart-wrenching symbol of what it meant to be unarmed and unready.

There was another image of defeat and despair but it was not photographed – Seversky P-35 fighters caught on the ground at Clark Field, in the Philippines, on 8 December 1941. About 50 P-35s belonging to Lieutenant Joseph H. Moore's 20th Pursuit Squadron were transformed into burning wrecks almost the instant fighting began. Speaking of slipping into war with such antiquated equipment, the first man in Moore's squadron to die in battle, Lieutenant Max Louk, had written home, 'We are doomed from the start . . .'

It was a sad denouement for the peppy, attractive pursuit ship which was the US Army Air Corps' first fighter to feature all-metal construction and a retractable undercarriage. In pre-war years the P-35 seemed a modern monoplane fighter and was popular with crews. It also inspired fine, stainless steel children's toys at a time when not everything was plastic.

The P-35 was the first important product of Alexander Kartveli, chief engineer of the Seversky (later Republic) company at Farmingdale, Long Island – the man and manufacturer behind the later Thunderbolt. Kartveli was an ex-artillery oficer, a Russian immigrant like his boss, Alexander P. Seversky, and a veteran of unsuccessful ventures with two previous aircraft manufacturers. Although

Seversky relinquished the company's presidency to William Kellet in a 1939 financial crisis, Kartveli was solidly on board and was crafting a series of solid, sturdy monoplanes.

The company's SEV-2XP, a two-seat model of the forthcoming P-35, was being evaluated by the US Army Air Corps in June 1935 when it was damaged sufficiently to need factory repair. This inspired Kartveli to introduce partly retractable main gear and a single seat, creating the prototype SEV-1XP – one of a number of monoplane fighters flown as pursuit prototypes and racers in the 1930s by Seversky, Jacqueline Cochran, and others. The SEV-1XP was powered by an 850hp Wright R-1820-G5 Cyclone, which proved wholly inadequate.

With a new engine and the company designation SEV-7 (later AP-1), the P-35 pursuit ship was chosen in preference to the Curtiss Hawk 75 (later P-36) for a 16 June 1936 US Army purchase of 77 aircraft (serials 36-354 to 36-430). The new powerplant was the 950hp Pratt & Whitney R-1830-9 Twin Wasp 14-cylinder radial engine. With a wing span of 36ft, gross weight of 6,723lb, and four forward-firing fixed machine-guns (two 0.30in and two 0.50in), the P-35 was substantially larger than its Air Corps predecessors and could attain a maximum speed of 310mph. At the time, Americans did not know of a Messerschmitt fighter which was bigger, more heavily armed, and faster.

P-35 Tests

In July 1937 the first P-35 was delivered to Wright Field, Ohio, for tests. The remaining 76 went initially to the 1st Pursuit Group at Selfridge Field, Michigan. There the P-35 was greeted with enthusiasm, which

In the pre-war years Americans did not realize that the very attractive Seversky P-35 was inadequate to cope with fighters from Messerschmitt and Mitsubishi. In 1940 the 'PA' code signified the 1st Pursuit Group at Selfridge Field. This P-35 basking in a rare sunny day belonged to the Group's 94th Pursuit Squadron. (via Clyde Gerdes)

This Seversky AP-1 was a civil-registered racer variant of the P-35 fighter. The streamlined propeller spinner reportedly did not improve the aeroplane's maximum speed of around 280mph (450km/h). (Republic)

Ground view of a Seversky P-35A on 8 November 1940. On 10 October 1940 President Franklin D. Roosevelt embargoed fighter exports to Sweden and this company model EP-106 became a P-35A with the US Army Air Corps. (Republic)

persisted even after six aircraft were lost in accidents in 1938.

Under the manufacturer's designation EP-106, the pursuit ship was sold to Sweden, which rescued the financially troubled Seversky firm with its 1939 order for 120 aircraft. Designated J 9 in Sweden's Flyg-vapen (Air Force), half of these had been delivered by 18 June 1940 when Roosevelt embargoed the remainder of the sale. The second batch of 60 EP-106s were impressed into US service as the P-35A.

At least 48 of these 60 P-35As were assigned to the Philippines. The 8 December 1941 Japanese assault on the Philippines (7 December in the West) came with the same stunning swiftness as the strike on Pearl Harbor. It is easy to forget today, but the entire Far East seemed to collapse all at once – almost immediately, Japanese forces commanded the air. In the Philippines, a rag-tag force of P-26s, P-35s and P-40s was overwhelmed as if by a tidal wave.

Some of the low-wing, silvery P-35As diverted from the Swedish purchase – these belonged to the 17th Pursuit Squadron, 24th Pursuit Group, at Nichols Field – were still wearing Swedish markings as they struggled vainly to get aloft to fight 'Zeros' overhead. All but eight of the 48 P-35As at Nichols, like the bulk of the P-35s at Clark, were wiped out in the first 48 hours of Japanese attacks.

There was little enthusiasm left for the P-35. Now, as the world saw better fighters which would dominate the war years – the introduction of the Mitsubishi A6M 'Zero-sen' was especially painful to the Allies – it became plain that the P-35 had had faults all along. Among them were poor stability, inadequate armament, and the lack of self-sealing fuel tanks and armour protection for the pilot.

A single P-35 emerged from the production line as the sole Republic XP-41, equipped with a turbo-supercharger for its R-1830 engine but little-changed otherwise. The XP-41 was tested briefly at Wright Field. By then development work on the more advanced P-43 Lancer and P-47 Thunderbolt were well under way, so there was no need to proceed with the XP-41 design.

Republic conceived a two-seat version of the P-35A, designated 2-PA, as a dive-bomber for the Swedish Air Force. All but two of the 50 ordered by Sweden were diverted to US service as the AT-12 Guardsman advanced trainer.

And what of the twelve P-35As out of the batch of 60 which apparently did not go to the Philippines? Many books state that these P-35A fighters went to Ecuador. In fact, as researcher Dan Hagedorn has learned, Ecuador never received this shipment of new P-35 pursuit ships, but did, years later, operate four P-35s which were former racers.

The Seversky P-35 had an exceptionally clean shape and at the time of its debut seemed to reflect the latest and best in aeronautical knowledge. In the Philippines on 8 December 1941 it was hopelessly outclassed. (via Roger F. Besecker)

The final airframe to begin on the production line as a P-35 (serial 36-430) ended up becoming the sole XP-41, a test aircraft which had the same engine as the P-35 but was equipped with a turbo-supercharger. The XP-41 was tested briefly at Wright Field, Ohio, but its performance was soon exceeded by the Republic P-43 Lancer and other types, and the machine was scrapped. (Republic)

▷ Perhaps the best known photograph of a P-35 shows the aircraft devoid of distinctive markings on the flatlands near Farmingdale, Long Island, where Republic manufactured fighters for so many years. Hamilton Standard's emblem appears on the three-bladed propeller. (Republic)

If American pilots really were doomed from the start by the outdated aircraft the US taxpayer had given them, another reason was the Curtiss P-36, more familiar to non-American readers as the Hawk 75, or in RAF service as the Mohawk. The P-36 was in many ways a fine aircraft, but it typified pre-war engineering at a time when British and German fighters were years ahead.

A monoplane low-wing pursuit ship with a retractable undercarriage, the private-venture Hawk 75 aroused little interest when first studied by the US Army in May 1935, although Curtiss won permission to market the aircraft to foreign buyers.

Originally powered by a 900hp Wright XR-1670-5 radial, the aircraft became the Model 75B when re-engined with an 850hp Wright R-1820 Twin Wasp radial. Studied again by the US Army in 1936, it lost a production order to the Seversky P-35.

The Army did, however, place an order for three Y1P-36 service-test aeroplanes (serials 37-68 to 37-70) and took delivery of these machines from February 1937 onwards. Following tests at Wright Field, Ohio, which are reported to have included a 575mph power dive (almost certainly an exaggeration), a decision was made to order 210 P-36As. This was the largest US fighter contract since the First World War.

In addition, overseas contracts began to fill Curtiss's order book. China ordered 112 export Hawk 75Ms. Twelve Hawk 75Ns went to Thailand and 29 Hawk 75Os went to Argentina, with a further 20 being assembled in the latter country. These machines all had a fixed undercarriage. Norway ordered 24 Hawk 75A-6s and 36 Hawk 75A-8s, but only nineteen had been delivered before the German invasion in April 1940.

French Hawks

The principal foreign customer was France, which purchased 200 Hawk 75A-1 fighters with four 7.5mm (0.30in) machine-guns and the first pilot armour to appear on a modern US fighter type. In September 1939, one of these claimed the first Luftwaffe fighter to be shot down over French skies. A few eventually fell into Vichy French hands, which resulted in aircraft of this type confronting each other in combat. Others, captured by the Germans in Norway and France, were sold to Finland. Subsequent French orders for 630 aeroplanes were not fulfilled, but 227 of them were diverted to the Royal Air Force, which first used the Mohawk name and operated the type in India with forgettable results.

The sole P-36B (38-20), a converted 'A' model,

The Curtiss P-36 Mohawk was a very clean and functional aircraft, if markedly inferior to the fighters being developed by the Axis. This machine wears markings which were in use at Chanute Army Airfield, Illinois, although signs on hangars in the background appear to mark the location as a civil airstrip, in about 1939. (via David W. Menard)

Fine study of an all-silver Curtiss P-36 Mohawk of the US Army Air Corps in flight near Wright Field, Ohio, circa 1939. (USAF)

was powered by a 1,000hp Pratt & Whitney R-1830-25 radial. The XP-36D was tested with two cowling-mounted 0.50in and four wing-mounted 0.30in guns. The sole XP-36F had two under-wing 23mm Madsen cannon and two nose machine-guns. Production shifted to 31 examples of the P-36C with engine improvements. The 36 Hawk 75A-8s intended for Norway were diverted into US service as P-36Gs.

The US Army Air Corps dispersed its fleet of 243 P-36s widely. The 20th Pursuit Group flew the type at Barksdale Field, Louisiana, while the 1st Pursuit Group at Selfridge Field, Michigan, entered a dozen P-36Cs in the National Air Races in Cleveland in September 1939, each painted in an elaborate, one-of-a-kind camouflage scheme. The XP-36D, XP-36E and XP-36F appeared in an exhibition of 'modern' fighters (another exaggeration) at Bolling AFB, Washington, DC, in January 1940.

At Pearl Harbor, 1st Lieutenant Lewis M. Sanders, Commander of the 46th Pursuit Squadron at Wheeler Field, got aloft with a brace of four P-36As and led his men in shooting down three of the attackers. 2nd Lieutenant George H. Sterling, killed in the action, was one of the first American fatalities of the war.

Dimensions of the P-36G were characteristic for the type and included: wing span 37ft, length 28ft 6in, height 9ft 3in and wing area 236sq ft. The 'G' model, powered by a 1,200hp Wright R-1820-205A Cyclone radial, was said to be capable of a maximum speed of 322mph at 15,200ft. The aircraft could climb to 15,000ft in six minutes. Range was 650 miles and service ceiling 32,350ft.

From the initial order for 210 P-36s, one airframe was later completed as the XP-40 and another became the sole XP-42 – two more fighters which

Curtiss P-36 Mohawks on the line at Ladd Field, Alaska (now Fort Wainwright), in about 1940. Even the most experienced Army Air Corps pursuit pilots found that during the lean pre-war years their flying hours were severely rationed. (via David W. Menard)

Ground view of the first service-test Curtiss YP-37 (serial 38-472), apparently taken at Wright Field. This development of the P-36 had a complicated undercarriage, a simplified version of which was retained on the P-40 Warhawk. (via Dave Ostrowski)

Perhaps the most-photographed aeroplane among one XP-37 and thirteen YP-37 airframes, service-test YP-37 38-472 shows its rakish lines in flight, apparently from the Curtiss plant in Buffalo. (via M. J. Kasiuba)

were not yet up to the standard of what Germany and Britain were producing.

The P-36 Mohawk design also led to yet another 'almost ran' as the US entered the war. The long-nosed Curtiss XP-37 (like the XP-40 to follow) was designed for higher speeds by dispensing with the drag-inducing radial engine and using, instead, a liquid-cooled, in-line powerplant.

Curtiss's Donovan R. Berlin used the P-36 air-frame to create the re-engined XP-37. The XP-37's Allison V-1710-11, equipped with a General Electric turbo-supercharger, was rated at 1,000hp, a hefty figure in the pre-war years. Ambitious engineers at Curtiss promised the US Army Air Corps that this in-line-powered offspring of the P-36 would attain a level speed of 340mph.

Landing the aeroplane was not in the contract, however. To attain increased speed, the designers moved the cockpit of the XP-37 (known to the company as the Hawk 75I) far back on the spine of the fuselage. At a normal angle of attack, the pilot literally could not see over the nose and wing in order to have a view of the runway! Aircraft were forgiving in those pre-war years and pilots apparently solved the problem by banking and peering down.

After the first machine had been tested in 1938, an effort was made to improve pilot visibility in thirteen service-test YP-37 airframes (serials 38-472 to 38-484) by lengthening the fuselage by 22in (to 32ft 10in). The lengthened proboscis remained an impediment to seeing out, however. The YP-37s were powered by the slightly modified V-1710-21 engine.

The YP-37s went through extensive testing at Wright Field, Dayton, Ohio, including gunnery trials. The US Army's Pursuit Projects Office at Wright Field, under 1st Lieutenant Benjamin Kelsey, was sorely undermanned and under-funded, and the YP-37s had to vie for attention with such promising types as the XP-38 Lightning and XP-39 Airacobra. Visibility remained a problem and the YP-37s were not as stable as Army pilots wanted.

YP-37 Figures

The YP-37 had a wing span of 37ft 4in. Height was 9ft 6in, and wing area 236sq ft. Empty weight was 5,723lb, maximum take-off weight 7,718lb. The aircraft actually reached 331mph (not the promised 340mph) at 20,000ft. It cruised at 305mph and landed (when the pilot could see) at 85mph. Service ceiling was a respectable 34,000ft and range 540 miles.

The XP-37 and YP-37 were rather outlandish for their day, but Berlin, Kelsey and Air Corps procurement chief Colonel Oliver Echol soon lost interest in it when they saw flight results from another development of the P-36 design, the XP-40 Tomahawk (P-40A to P-40C variants), later developed still further as the Warhawk (P-40D to P-40Q). The P-40 did not exactly achieve greatness in the war years which came all too soon but more than 14,000 were built, making it the third most numerous American fighter of the war. A subsequent Curtiss test aircraft, the XP-46, produced data which was made available to North American in the design of the immortal P-51 Mustang.

Airacobra

The Bell P-39 Airacobra is one pursuit ship which, however much it illustrates American lack of preparedness for war, nevertheless played a significant role in the conflict. It could not have been comforting to be a young American pilot in the cockpit of a P-39 at the time of Pearl Harbor, but by that time several hundred of these machines had already been delivered.

The P-39 was a utilitarian workhorse. It was also the first production aircraft from Larry Bell's new manufacturing firm in Buffalo, New York. It made a contribution, beyond doubt. Yet the point must be repeated that, like so many other American fighters

on the eve of fighting, the P-39 was unable to cope with its competitors from Messerschmitt and Mitsubishi.

First flown on 6 April 1939, the P-39 was outwardly conventional in appearance, but its engine was located behind the pilot. It was the first US Army single-seat fighter with a retractable tricycle undercarriage and the first to carry a cannon (that is, a weapon firing an explosive shell) rather than a machine-gun (which fires bullets). Indeed, it was the location of the American Armament Corporation T9 37mm cannon in the propeller spinner, together with two synchronized, cowling-mounted 0.50in (12.7mm) Browning machine-guns, which made it

Early Bell XP-39B Airacobra on a test flight near the maker's plant in Buffalo, New York. XP-39B was a 'rebuild' of the original XP-39 and was powered by a 1,090hp Allison V-1710-37 in-line engine. (Bell)

Flying high over Foster Field, Texas, in 1943, 41-7324 is a P-39F Airacobra, identical to the P-39D except for an Aeroproducts propeller replacing the Curtiss product. The P-39F was said to be capable of reaching 368mph (592km/h) at 13,800ft (4,200m). (USAF)

necessary to locate the 1,200hp Allison V-1710 in-line engine within the fuselage above the rear half of the low-set monoplane wing. The propeller was driven by an extension shaft which passed beneath the cockpit floor.

This was far from a conventional layout but it was retained, together with a side door for entry/exit to and from the raised, braced-canopy cockpit, throughout the long production run of 9,589 Airacobras (8,914 with USAAF funding). Nearly half the production run, 4,779 aircraft, went via Lend-Lease to the Soviet Union, which used the type mainly for ground-attack – a sensible disposition for a fighter never able to hold its own against the Axis in aerial combat.

The sole XP-39 test ship (38-326) was evaluated at Wright Field, Ohio. Twelve service-test YP-39s (40-27 to 40-39) followed, while the prototype was returned to the manufacturer to be rebuilt as the sole XP-39B with fairing doors for its mainwheel units, a lowered canopy, and two additional 0.30in (7.62mm) nose machine-guns.

When the US Army Air Corps ordered 20 production machines on 10 August 1939, they were designated P-45s but were renamed P-39Cs before flying. These were equipped with bullet-resistant windshields and self-sealing fuel tanks. They were followed by the first major production version, the P-39D, of which 923 were ordered in 1940–41. The 'D' model received two further 0.30in (7.62mm)

Seen after a take-off accident at Ladd Field, Alaska, on 13 June 1943, 42-18594 is a P-39N Airacobra, of which 2,095 were built during the war years. Most of these aircraft were ferried to the Soviet Union under the Lend-Lease agreement, but this P-39N apparently got only part of the way. Soviet red star appears to have been covered over with paint or mud. (USAF)

guns, for a total of four in the wing leading edges, and also had provision for a 500lb (227kg) bomb or a 75(US)gal centre-line drop tank. At a time when Britain was sending purchasing delegations all over the United States to order every weapon they could lay hands on, 675 examples of the lacklustre P-39D won an August 1941 contract for the RAF as the Airacobra Mk. I. These differed from the American version in having an armament of one Hispano Suiza M1 20mm nose cannon and six 0.303in (7.7mm) machine-guns.

Except for thirteen pre-production specimens, the P-39 lacked a turbo-supercharger. One RAF pilot who flew the Airacobra at Buffalo recalls 'some trepidation' about the aircraft. Only about 65 Airacobras in fact saw service with No 601 Squadron, the RAF's sole user, and their inadequate climb and poor high-altitude performance soon led to their replacement by Spitfires in March 1942.

Ex-British Airacobras, designated P-400 by the USAAF, went to New Guinea and Guadalcanal. There and in Europe, the P-39 was quickly removed from the air-to-air combat arena and assigned to other duties. A few were modified in the field to become TP-39F and RP-39Q two-seat familiarization trainers.

The three XP-39Es (41-19501, 41-19502 and 42-71464) were test-beds with 1,510hp Allison V-1710-47 engines, laminar-flow wings, and heightened vertical tails. These features were later incorporated in the P-63 Kingcobra, which was very much a new and different aeroplane.

P-39F, P-39J, P-39K, P-39L and P-39M fighters were all similar with but minor changes and most were kept in the United States for training duties. Together with a few P-39Ds, the P-39N and P-39Q versions were built in significant numbers for the Soviet Union, most being delivered by USAAF pilots via Alaska. The P-39Q carried the same nose armament as other USAAF machine but the four wing 0.30in (7.62mm) machine-guns were deleted and replaced by two 0.50in (12.7mm) guns in under-wing fairings with 600 rounds. From the P-39Q-21-BE block onwards, a four-bladed propeller was fitted. No fewer than 4,905 Airacobras were of the P-39Q model. Further production of the Airacobra under the new designation P-76 was planned in 1942 but did not materialize.

The P-39D was capable of 335mph (539km/h) when flown at 5,000ft (1,525m) at a weight of 7,650lb (3,473kg). Range at maximum cruise power was 350 miles (563km). Maximum take-off weight of the P-39D was 8,850lb (4,018kg).

Dimensions of the Bell P-39D Airacobra included: wing span 34ft (10.37m), length 30ft 2in (9.21m) and height 11ft 10in (3.60m).

P-39 Action

Of the relatively few American-operated Airacobras which served abroad, two fighter groups (81st, 350th) were in the Middle East by 1942 to assist with the Operation 'Torch' landings in North Africa. These groups provided protection for Allied shipping in the Mediterranean, covered convoys landing troops in Sicily, and supported Allied landings at Anzio.

The US Navy had tested a tailwheel undercarriage variant as the XFL-1 Airabonita and acquired seven P-39s for use as target drones under the designation F2L-1K.

P-39s also saw service in Portugal and with the Free French and Co-belligerent Italian air arms. The Royal Australian Air Force received 22 Airacobras as emergency reinforcements during the dark days when a Japanese invasion seemed imminent. Some ex-Soviet examples may have reached North Korea in the late 1940s. Although it served worldwide, the P-39 Airacobra never knew the touch of greatness. Only a handful survive today, including a preserved P-39Q (44-3887) which is displayed as a P-39D at the US Air Force Museum, Dayton, Ohio.

The bottom line for the Airacobra, alas, is the language of an official report which describes the

P-39 as '. . . especially disappointing, with a low ceiling, slow rate of climb, and relative lack of manoeuvrability [which] put its pilots at a decided disadvantage'.

Warhawk

As mentioned previously, the Curtiss line of fighters led eventually to the P-40 Warhawk. Like the Seversky P-35 and the Bell P-39, the Curtiss aeroplanes stand as symbols of an American nation which refused to see that war was coming, remained certain of its own invincibility, and isolated itself, thinking of the Atlantic and Pacific as solid barriers against Hitler and Hirohito.

The P-40 Warhawk may have been an improvement on earlier Curtiss fighters, but not by much. Like the Airacobra, it eventually served in the war in vast numbers. Also like the Airacobra, it was all but useless in air-to-air combat. Nevertheless, some 13,800 airframes were manufactured, making the P-40 the third most numerous of American fighters, after the Mustang and Thunderbolt.

The P-40 began life, as noted, as little more than a P-36 Mowhawk redesigned with the Allison V-1710 liquid-cooled in-line engine, offering better aerodynamics, more power, and better fuel consumption than air-cooled radial engines of similar size.

The Allison powerplant was, however, ineffective at altitude. With other fighter designs showing more promise, the P-40 was not deemed worth improving by retrofitting with a turbo-supercharger. Thus the P-40 was inferior to just about all Axis fighters, even older ones, above 15,000ft (4,572m). Nevertheless, the P-40 fought in every theatre and is remembered with fondness as a tough and reliable mount, able to absorb and inflict punishment, and always effective in the air-to-ground role.

The sole XP-40 (38-10) first flew in late 1938 and, as noted earlier, was actually the tenth production P-36A airframe re-engined with the 1,000hp Allison V-1710-19 in-line powerplant. After being awarded a May 1939 contract for production – which was then the largest ever issued by the US Army – the prototype was modified by having its coolant radiator moved from under the rear fuselage to the nose, and the basic configuration of the P-40 series was then established.

As production of P-40s and P-40Bs progressed, the latter introducing armour protection for the pilot and self-sealing fuel tanks, hundreds of export machines known as Tomahawks Mk. I, IA, IB and II, were sold to the RAF. One hundred were diverted to China for use by General Claire Chennault's

American Volunteer Group (AVG), the 'Flying Tigers'. RAF machines were armed with 0.303in (7.7mm) Browning wing machine-guns instead of the 0.30in (7.62mm) guns employed on American P-40s. The RAF in due course employed Tomahawks with Nos 2, 4, 16, 26, 73, 94, 112, 168, 171, 208, 231, 239, 241, 250, 268, 349, 400, 403, 414, 430 and 613 Squadrons. Some Tomahawk IIs were shipped to the Soviet Union after having American machine-guns re-installed.

P-40Bs were among the first American casualties at Pearl Harbor and Clark Field, Philippines. Second Lieutenant George S. Welch of the 47th Pursuit Squadron went aloft in a P-40B during the Pearl Harbor raid to shoot down four Japanese aircraft, later ending the war with sixteen aerial victories.

Improved self-sealing fuel tanks were introduced, starting in 1941 with the first P-40C (41-13328), of which 193 were delivered to the USAAF. The P-40D model with 1,150hp Allison V-1710-39 engine was used only in token numbers by the USAAF, but 560 reached the RAF as the Kittyhawk Mk. I. The P-40E, of which 2,320 were built for the USAAF and several hundred for the RAF as the Kittyhawk Mk. IA, introduced a standard armament of six wing-mounted 0.50in (12.7mm) machine-guns, an increased gross weight of 8,840lb (4,009kg) and a fuel capacity of 201(US)gal.

The 'E' model in this series also had a centre-line hardpoint for a fuel tank, a 500lb (227kg) bomb, or other ordnance up to 700lb (318kg). The P-40E replaced P-40Bs with the AVG in China, which accounted for 286 Japanese aircraft with the loss of but eight pilots in air-to-air combat. The 'E' model was the mount of Robert H. Neale, top-scoring AVG ace with sixteen victories.

By 1943, P-40Es and Kittyhawk IAs were fighting in the Pacific, North Africa, and Sicily. P-40Es were also flown by Australian, Canadian, New Zealand, and South African pilots.

A milestone in the P-40's career came in 1941 when a British Rolls-Royce Merlin 28 engine (soon to be manufactured in the US as the Pakcard V-1650) was installed in the sole XP-40F. The Merlin was rated at 1,120hp initially. It gave the XP-40F a speed of 373mph (600km/h). Although it must be said once again that this pursuit ship was no match for its Axis opponents, the new engine gave the P-40 a lengthened lease on life.

P-40F Warhawk

The production P-40F, powered by the Packard-built Merlin V-1650-1, had a gross weight of nearly 10,000lb (4,535kg). 1,311 were ordered by the

Publicity photo of an early P-40 Warhawk blasting away with six 0.30in (7.62mm) machine-guns appears to show the pursuit ship swooping down out of the night but may, in fact, have been taken while the P-40 was tethered on the ground. In reality, the P-40's bite was not quite as fearsome as Curtiss and the Army proclaimed, and it was not very effective in the air-to-air role during the war. (via M. J. Kasiuba)

Best known user of the Curtiss P-40 Warhawk was General Claire Chennault's American Volunteer Group (AVG), the famous 'Flying Tigers', whose aircraft wore Chinese insignia and shark's teeth markings, as shown. Superior pilot skill was the main reason AVG pilots were able to prevail over Japanese fliers during the fighting in China. (via M. J. Kasiuba)

Curtiss P-40N Warhawk fighters from the 110th Tactical Reconnaissance Squadron, Missouri Air National Guard, seen from a B-24 Liberator over the South Pacific. (via M. J. Kasiuba)

USAAF, which now introduced the widely known Warhawk name. This name has later come into general use to apply to all aircraft in the P-40 series, even though the P-40F itself was officially the Kittyhawk II in RAF service.

The only P-40G (39-221) was a P-40 modified to carry what eventually became the standard armament – six 0.50in (12.7mm) guns. The P-40J was a proposal to improve the performance of the Allison V-1710 powerplant with a turbo-supercharger but, as noted earlier, was not proceeded with. The XP-40K was a modified airframe in the P-40K series although not a prototype for the P-40K model. Development of Allison-powered Warhawks continued despite the superiority of the Merlin, and the P-40K was

powered by the 1,200hp Allison V-1710-73. In addition, the production P-40K eventually employed both the extended fuselage and taller tail fin which distinguished late-model P-40s.

A 'stripped' variant of the Packard V-1650 Merlin-powered Warhawk was introduced as the P-40L. This had two of the usual six 0.50in (12.7mm) guns removed and incorporated weight-saving changes. Although 700 were delivered to the USAAF, the hoped for improvement in performance for short-range combat was marginal. Most P-40Ls had the extended fuselage typical of late Warhawks.

The P-40M, known as the Kittyhawk Mk. III and IV in RAF service, reverted to the 1,200hp Allison V-1710-81, a more advanced version of the familiar

Another wartime publicity shot, intended to show US Army Air Corps pursuit pilots at the ready (and thought to be previously unpublished); it appears to have been posed. These P-40s wear the original national insignia used by the USA on entry into the war, complete with red circle in the centre of the star – which was too often confused with Japan's red 'meatball'. (Curtiss)

Fascinating picture of the American war machine gearing up: a brace of Curtiss P-40 fighters is loaded aboard a small escort carrier, apparently the USS *Chenango* (CVE-28), a converted oiler. Aircraft closest to camera is 41-14305, a P-40F. The P-40 was never carrier-capable but was sometimes transported across oceans in this manner. (USN)

A refreshing example of a well-preserved historical aircraft is this Curtiss P-40 Warhawk at the US Air Force Museum, Dayton, Ohio, in 1966. Although painted as an American Volunteer Group machine, it is actually a P-40E which served with the RAF as AK987. (USAF)

powerplant intended for improved performance at higher altitude. Six hundred were built and, apart from the USAAF, the P-40M served with the South African Air Force.

The P-40N (Kittyhawk Mk. IV in the RAF) was the most numerous variant of this prolific fighter, no fewer than 5,219 being built by three Curtiss plants. The weight-saving effort begun with the 'L' model was continued, although most P-40Ns were eventually built with the full armament of six 0.50in (12.7mm) guns. Late P-40Ns had the 1,200hp Allison V-1710-99. A few of these were converted to two-seat TP-40N trainers. The P-40N, many of which reached the Soviet Union, had new radio and oxygen equipment and flame-damping exhausts.

The XP-40Q, three of which were converted and powered by the 1,425hp Allison V-1710-121, looked like a totally new design (and much like the air racers of the post-war era), with its clipped wingtips, four-bladed propeller, and a bubble canopy. The XP-40Q, although visually attractive and despite significant improvement in performance, was still no match for the Mustang and Thunderbolt, and was not mass-produced. The final designation in this series, P-40R, went to some 300 P-40F and P-40L airframes completed with Allison engines during a shortage of Merlins.

To use the very numerous P-40N model as representative of the series, the aircraft had these dimensions: span 37ft 4in (11.38m), length 33ft 4in (10.16m), height 12ft 4in (3.76m), and wing area 236sq ft (21.92m^2).

The P-40N had a maximum speed of 343mph (552km/h) at 15,000ft (4,570m); initial rate of climb was 2,800ft (853m) per minute; service ceiling 31,000ft (9,450m); and range with auxiliary fuel 1,080 miles (1,738km). All these figures, of course, like all those applied to every aeroplane in this volume, are approximations. Actual performance varied according to temperature, altitude, and other factors.

The P-40N weighed 6,200lb (2,812kg) empty and 8,850lb (4,014kg) fully loaded. Dimensions were: span 37ft 4in (11.38m), length 33ft 4in (10.16m), height 12ft 4in (3.76m), wing area 236sq ft. The typical 'N' model was armed with six 0.50in (12.7mm) machine-guns and could carry up to 1,500lb (680kg) of bombs.

With 12,043 airframes built, the P-40 was one of the most numerous aircraft of the war. Despite sheer numbers and considerable press-coverage – P-40s with the AVG and elsewhere were often depicted wearing 'shark's teeth' markings – the P-40 remains in history a second-rank fighter, one flown by as many victims as heroes, a classic in some respects but never a candidate for greatness. A number of flyable P-40s can still be seen at air shows in the USA and Europe.

F4F Wildcat

At Pearl Harbor, Wake Island, and especially on Guadalcanal, some of the toughest flying of the war was done by US Marine Corps fighter pilots who faced an enemy flushed with victory and attacking in overwhelming numbers. To withstand this onslaught, Americans had to struggle not with just one enemy but with many. To the pilot of a Grumman F4F Wildcat taxiing at Guadalcanal's Henderson Field in a torrential downpour, struggling through geysers of water and mud, the list of enemies included bad weather, corrosion, primitive conditions, even tropical disease. Marine fliers sometimes needed a roll of toilet paper or a protective bunker – or a hot meal – as much as anything else. It was hard to stay ready to repel the next wave of Japanese bombers when you had to spend time plucking leeches from your skin with a bayonet, or running to the latrine to disgorge the foul water and poor food.

It was a difficult war, in those days in the Pacific. It was made more difficult by the Japanese Mitsubishi 'Zero' fighter.

Marine fliers who fought early in the Pacific were well trained and highly experienced but so, too, were their opponents. Although Guadalcanal was intended as an American offensive, the Japanese initially had air superiority, which had to be wrested from them, battle by battle. It was possible to engage 'Zeros' in a dogfight during the afternoon and limp home only to find the airfield under attack at night by Japanese bombers. As will become evident later, the need for a night fighter persisted throughout the early fighting on those Pacific islands. In the meantime the Americans had to fight with what they had.

The Grumman F4F Wildcat is best remembered as a portly but nimble fighter which was almost good enough to fight in the same sky as the Mitsubishi 'Zero'. This F4F-4 wears the revised national insignia adopted on 15 May 1942 which dispensed with the red centre circle inside the star, too often confused with the red hinomaru, the circle painted on Japanese aircraft. (via M. J. Kasiuba)

The prototype Wildcat, Grumman XF4F-2 (Bureau number 0383) on the ramp at the manufacturer's plant at Bethpage, Long Island. The rotund Wildcat did not initially compete well with the Brewster F2A-1 Buffalo, but its design was sound and in due course the Wildcat replaced the Buffalo to become the principal carrier-based fighter of the early war period. (Grumman)

The Wildcat was no 'Zero'. The Japanese fighter was light and fast and had cannon instead of machine-guns. The American fighter was sturdier and gave its pilot a much better chance of surviving if he was hit. As they gained experience, Marines (and the Navy fliers who fought in the Wildcat) learned how to coax greater manoeuvrability from their fighter. They learned how to make better gunnery compensate for the lesser killing power of their guns. And because their aircraft was tough, they stayed in the fight, day after day. The Hellcat and Corsair came along in time to give hard-pressed pilots a better machine in their hands; but before that the Grumman F4F Wildcat became, in the process, one of the near-great fighters of the war. This was no small feat, for the history of the Wildcat goes back to more than half a decade before America entered the conflict.

Wildcat Heritage

To meet a 1936 requirement for a carrier-based fighter, Leroy Grumman's well-established manufacturing company gave the US Navy its proposal for its Design 16 (company model G-16), or XF4F-1, a biplane fighter which built upon the technical advances attained by Grumman's FF-1, F2F-1, and F3F-1 biplane fighters already delivered to the Fleet.

Even before Grumman grew into its Bethpage, Long Island facility on 8 April 1937, the Navy made it known that it wanted the Brewster XF2A-1 Buffalo

instead. Why? Because the F2A-1 was a monoplane.

With war clouds still gathering, the Navy had decided that the monoplane was the wave of the future. As insurance against failure of the Brewster design, the Navy authorized one prototype of Grumman's XF4F-1 biplane, but this was later shelved.

The XF4F-1 drew 'a little less than a yawn', as one company employee remembers. But the Brewster design, whatever its merits, did not have the 'stretching' potential to accommodate add-ons that came with the war – armour, drop-tanks, self-sealing fuel tanks – and did not survive long as the Fleet's premier fighter. Grumman engineers wisely scrapped the XF4F-1 in its entirety and went back to the drawing-board. With a completely fresh start, they were able to win a contract for a prototype monoplane fighter, the XF4F-2, to become known as the Wildcat.

'The big thing that made the Wildcat what it was,' recalls a Bureau of Aeronautics engineer, 'was that Grumman threw away the XF4F-1. It was important that the company shifted to a monoplane. But more important were that the new aircraft had (1) a bigger wing; (2) a different engine with an improved supercharger system'. When war came, bringing with it the need for armour, pylons, self-sealing tanks, and other added features, the Wildcat had the growth potential to remain competitive.

First flown by company pilot Robert L. Hall on 2 September 1937 – and almost immediately moved to NAS Anacostia, Washington, DC, for tests – the

Grumman F4F-4 Wildcat, also at the manufacturer's Bethpage plant. The F4F-4 introduced folding wings for carrier stowage. (Grumman)

Guadalcanal. At Henderson Field, where Marines fought valiantly against Japanese intruders, an early F4F Wildcat taxies with a fuel tank visible under its starboard wing. This Wildcat is operating from pierced-steel planking, but other F4Fs had trouble with 'The Canal's' crushed coral runways and taxi strips. (US Marine Corps)

Another view of an F4F-4 Wildcat operating under difficult conditions at Henderson Field, Guadalcanal, this one on 2 February 1943. The wartime caption indicated that this Wildcat was credited with shooting down 19 Japanese aircraft (note flags) while flown by several pilots. (USMC)

XF4F-2 (company model G-18) was powered by a 1,050hp Pratt & Whitney R-1830-66 Twin Wasp engine and attained a maximum speed of 290mph (467km/h). The XF4F-2 fighter (Bureau Number 0383) was clearly a winner, yet there were to be pointed and prolonged difficulties with its power-plant. In particular, there were repeated crankshaft failures. A visiting French delegation made known its preference for the Wright Cyclone, but the decision to turn to the Cyclone – the 'different engine' – was to be a little longer in coming.

The Wildcat's general appearance was now estab-lished, although the XF4F-2 had a short-span wing with rounded tips, rounded tail surfaces, and belly windows to facilitate the pilot's downward view – all later abandoned. Of all-metal construction with a riveted monocoque fuselage, its cantilever wing set in mid-position on the fuselage and equipped with retractable tailwheel landing gear, the XF4F-2 brought some satisfaction to engineers Leroy Grum-man, Bill Schwendler and others when it proved marginally faster than the Brewster product in 1938 evaluations at Anacostia and Dahlgren, Maryland. It also easily outperformed the Seversky XFN-1, a navalized version of the P-35. The Brewster fighter remained in favour, however, and was ordered into production on 11 June 1938.

Design Progress

In October 1938 an order was placed for an XF4F-3 with a wing having an area of 260sq ft (24.15m^2) – the 'bigger wing' – as well as revised tail surfaces and a Pratt & Whitney R-1830-76 Twin Wasp engine with a two-stage supercharger that produced 1,050hp on take-off and greater power at high altitude. New armament included two 0.30in (7.62mm) guns in the fuselage and two 0.50in (12.7mm) guns in the outer wings.

On 11 April 1938 the first machine crashed and sustained severe damage. It was rebuilt as the XF4F-3 (company model G-36), still with the Bureau Number 0383. Although considerably heavier in its new configuration, the XF4F-3 reached an impres-sive 333mph (536km/h) and showed excellent man-oeuvrability, as well as a service ceiling of 33,500ft (10,372m). First flown on 12 February 1939, again by Bob Hall, the XF4F-3 was modified with a rede-signed tail unit in which the tailplane was moved higher up the fin and the profile of the vertical tail was altered. In this final form, the XF4F-3 was found to have good handling characteristics and man-oeuvrability. Stability problems persisted, and minor changes in configuration were made. Finally, con-vinced that it was looking at the best carrier fighter

now available, the Navy on 8 August 1939 ordered 54 F4F-3 production aircraft (BuNos 1844–1897). In due course 185 F4F-3s and 95 lower-powered F4F-3As (originally designated F4F-6) were built.

With war seemingly imminent in Europe, Grum-man offered the company G-36A design for export, receiving orders for 81 and 30 aircraft from the French and Greek Governments respectively. The first aircraft for France's Aéronautique Navale (Naval Air Arm), powered by a 1,000hp Wright R-1820 Cyclone G205A, flew on 10 May 1940 – by which time France was being overrun. The British Purchas-ing Commission agreed to take these aircraft, calling them Martlet Mk I, later increasing the order to 90. Ten were lost aboard a ship torpedoed by a German submarine, but the first Martlets began to reach the UK in July 1940, after the first five off the line had been delivered to Canada. These initially equipped No 804 Squadron of the Fleet Air Arm, then based at Hatston in the Orkneys. Originally to have been armed with four to six 7.5mm Darne machine-guns for French use, the first Martlets ended up with two 0.50in (12.7mm) Colt Browning guns in each wing and no nose guns.

The name 'Wildcat' was in use from 1 October 1941. The first F4F-3 Wildcat for the US Navy was flown on 20 August 1940. At the beginning of December the type began to equip US Navy squadrons VF-4 and VF-7 aboard the USS *Wasp* (CV-7) and USS *Ranger* (CV-4) respectively. Some of these aircraft operated in the Atlantic on Neu-trality Patrol in 1940. The 95 F4F-3As (originally F4F-6s) ordered by the US Navy were powered by the R-1830-90 engine with a single-stage super-charger, and deliveries began in 1941. Thirty of these machines were diverted to Greece but, en route when Greece fell, ended up in British service as the Martlet III.

The F4F-3P designation went to at least ten Wildcats converted to armed photo-reconnaissance aircraft. The conversion consisted of a 30in (0.77m) focal-length aerial camera installed in the lower starboard fuselage with a pulley-operated trap-door covering the camera opening.

An XF4F-4 prototype (BuNo 1897) was flown on 15 April 1941 and incorporated refinements which resulted from British combat experience, including six-gun armament, armour, self-sealing tanks, and (most important) folding wings. The hydraulically operated 'sto-wings' were intended to increase by some 150 per cent the number of aircraft that could be embarked in a carrier. This prototype was assigned to squadron VF-42 at NAS Norfolk, Virginia.

The designation F4F-4 went to 1,168 production

Wildcats whose wings folded manually, powered by the 1,200hp Wright R-1830-36 Cyclone radial. Delivery of F4F-4 fighters began in November 1941. Carrier trials were conducted by VF-3 aboard the USS *Saratoga* (CV-3) on 6–7 January 1942 in the wake of the Japanese attack on Pearl Harbor. A number of US Navy and Marine squadrons were already equipped with earlier Wildcats as the slow pace of peacetime development, now that war had arrived, grew frenetic.

A number of F4F-4 variants were proposed by Grumman. The F4F-4A was a proposed engine change, reverting to the Pratt & Whitney R-1830-90, but was never built. The F4F-4B was an export designation for Wildcats supplied under Lend-Lease to the Fleet Air Arm as the Martlet IV. The F4F-4P photo-reconnaissance aircraft joined the series by the time 1,169 'dash four' aeroplanes had been produced.

The XF4F-5 and XF4F-6 designations went to experimental variants of the Wildcat, the latter first flying on 11 October 1940 and eventually being redesignated F4F-3A.

Final Variants

The F4F-7 (company model G-52) was one answer to the need for intelligence in the vast distances of the Pacific war. The aircraft was, very simply, a long-range photo-reconnaissance ship. The wing folding mechanism and all armament were removed and the wing was sealed to serve as a fuel tank capable of holding 555(US)gal of fuel. The camera was installed in the fuselage behind the cockpit with the camera window located in the belly.

Flown on 30 December 1941, the F4F-7 aroused much interest and at one point Grumman were instructed to complete 21 F4F-4 airframes (BuNos 5263–5283) as F4F-7s. It is not clear whether all were delivered, but one showed off its long range with an 11-hour non-stop flight across the United States for delivery to NAS San Diego. At least two F4F-7s reached the fighting on Guadalcanal.

The XF4F-8 designation went to a pair of Wildcats (BuNos 12228 and 12229) built as lightweight fighters for operation from escort carriers. The XF4F-8 was powered by an experimental 1,300hp single-stage, two-speed supercharged XR-1820-56 Cyclone driving an 'uncuffed' Hamilton Standard constant-speed propeller. This version of the Cyclone was both lighter and more powerful than its predecessors. Although no production order was placed for the 'dash eight' model, these aircraft were tested with various items of equipment and one of them flew with the large tail surfaces adopted for the General Motors FM-2.

At the beginning of 1942 the US Navy saw that Grumman were going to be exceedingly busy with the number and variety of warplanes they were producing. Not only was the firm building the F4F-4 Wildcat, TBF Avenger, J2F Duck, and J4F Widgeon, but plans were well advanced for the production of the F6F Hellcat fighter. General Motors, who had stopped making private motor cars in order to divert resources to the war effort, were available to pick up some of the overload. Under

Flying from an aircraft-carrier could be a dangerous business, and operating from the deck of a very small escort carrier was especially risky. The wartime caption for this photo states that the F4F Wildcat is 'going off the deck after the tail had torn off'. The national insignia appears to be bordered by an outer circle of yellow, evidence that the aircraft was part of Operation 'Torch', the invasion of North Africa. (USN)

Preparing to launch from a very narrow space, this F4F-4 Wildcat belongs to squadron VGF-29 and is about to take off from the auxiliary carrier USS Santee (ACV-29). VGF squadrons had the unusual task of using fighters to spot gunfire for battleships and cruisers during shore bombardments. (USN)

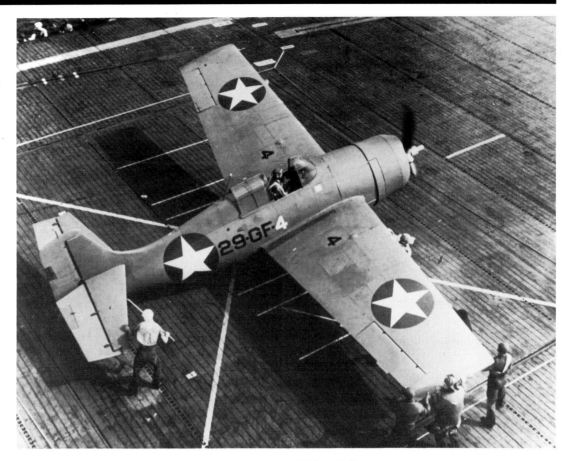

wartime pressures, all five GM plants were reorganized and the car-maker's Eastern Aircraft Division was created.

The FM-1 Wildcast, resulting from an 18 April 1942 contract, was identical to the F4F-4 except for an armament change and was built by three Eastern plants in New Jersey with final assembly taking place in Linden. The FM-1 was armed only with four wing-mounted 0.50in (12.7mm) machine-guns with 1,720 rounds (compared with six guns but only 1,440 rounds in the F4F-4). Although the change in armament reflected a difference between the US Navy (which felt that a four-gun fighter could be designed with more effective folding wings) and the British (who were adamant about the need for a six-gun platform), 312 aeroplanes in the FM-1 series reached Britain as Martlet Vs (serials JV325 to JV636). In all, 909 FM-1 aircraft were built.

The FM-2 was a General Motors improvement of the basic Wildcat with the tall fin and rudder tested on the XF4F-8 and a production 1,350hp Wright R-1820-56W engine with water injection. Production of the FM-2 eventually reached 4,777 aircraft, or about 40 per cent of the 7,251 Wildcats built by both manufacturers. 370 of these went to Britain as the Wildcat VI, the only anglicized versions which never wore the Martlet name.

Glider fighter

One of the more intriguing tests involving the Wildcat was a 1942 effort in Philadelphia to evaluate the idea of fighters being towed by bombers, to serve as long-range escorts while conserving fuel. In one form or another, this idea was to recur until well into the post-war period, although it was never tried in combat. The Wildcat was an ideal candidate to be towed because its three-bladed Curtiss Electric propeller could be easily feathered and the engine re-started in flight.

A hook-on and break-off system was devised, enabling the Wildcat to be towed, glider-fashion, from an attachment point beneath the wing, the Wildcat pilot having the option to connect and disconnect at will. In May 1942 an F4F was towed by a Douglas BD-1 (the US Navy version of the A-20 Havoc) and later two Wildcats were towed by a B-17 Fortress over a 1,200-mile (1,930km) 8-hour course.

Like many of the ingenious wartime experiments of which few or no surviving photographs exist, this hybrid arrangement worked quite well. The Wildcat pilot could remain idle while his aircraft flew effectively as a glider, its range being limited only by the endurance of the two aircraft.

With Commander Leroy G. Simpler at the controls, this F4F Wildcat begins its take-off roll using jet-assisted boost on 18 March 1944. The name of the ship and its location are not known. JATO (jet-assisted take-off), using jettisonable propellant bottles, became a standard method of take-off for heavier aircraft in the post-war years. (USN)

Formation of Wildcats in flight. (USN)

Another experimental version of the Wildcat was, in effect, a copy of Japan's seaplane adaptation of the 'Zero', the Mitsubishi A6M2, code-named 'Rufe' by the Allies. At one time, the US Navy placed orders for no fewer than one hundred F4F-3S fighters equipped with a pair of Edo single-step floats and tailplane-mounted auxiliary fins. The only example which actually flew (BuNo 4038) was taken aloft on 28 February 1943 by T. F. (Hank) Kurt from the East Rivet at College Point.

In due course the float-equipped Wildcat moved to Naval Air Station Anacostia alongside the Potomac River in Washington, in its day one of the Navy's most important and most secretive test centres. Trials on the Potomac confirmed Kurt's finding that directional control was far from satisfactory and the aircraft was fitted with a large ventral fin to enhance yaw control. On 6 June 1943 the machine was transferred to Norfolk, Virginia, for rough-water tests. The Wildcat did not agree well with wave crests of 2ft (0.61m) or higher.

The seaplane version of the Wildcat was, at best, capable of 206mph (332km/h). One hopeful writer has raised this figure to 241mph (388km/h), perhaps having in mind an uncontrolled nose dive. The F4F-3S Wildcat's Japanese counterpart was not exactly a speed demon either; perhaps more important, the conditions of battle were such that the two types were never likely to meet each other in combat, while both could be slaughtered by conventional fighters not burdened with bulky floats. Moreover, the need for water-based operations seemed less pressing when it became apparent, during the Pacific island-hopping campaign, that Navy Construction Battalions (Seabees) were talented at quickly carving out airfields, complete with paved or coral runways, where none had existed before.

The seaplane Wildcat inevitably became known as the Wildcatfish, a mouthful to say the least. The US Navy decided not to pursue the idea further.

Flying the F4F

Being the pilot of a Wildcat was an unforgettable experience. The aircraft's narrow-track stalky landing gear gave it dubious ground-handling characteristics. It could be 'mushy' when manoeuvrability counted most. There was a violent draught if the cockpit hood was slid open in flight and there was

In 1939 the French Purchasing Commission ordered 81 Wildcats under the Grumman export designation G-36A. After only seven had been built, France fell to the Nazi onslaught and the remaining aircraft in this series went to Britain as the Martlet I. This machine was one of the first to be build for France's Aéronavale. (IWM)

A formation of F4F-4 Wildcats showing the 'interim' national insignia with red surround adopted on 29 June 1943 and used only until October 1943. Unfortunately, the red border for this marking perpetuated a problem which had existed earlier – causing American aircraft to be mistaken for Japanese. (USN)

The Wildcat was manufactured by the Eastern Division of General Motors under the designation FM-2. This pair of FM-2s is operating from the USS *White Plains* (CVE-66) on 24 June 1944 during strikes on Japanese facilities at Rota in the Marianas. (USN)

no provision for jettisoning the hood in an emergency. The pilot's seat was cramped and too low relative to the location of his head and his need for visibility. In short, much as pilots were to praise it, the Wildcat could be tricky and unforgiving.

However, by dint of its time and place, the Wildcat was the fighter in which American Marines and naval officers made their stand against the Mitsubishi A6M 'Zero'; and while the Japanese fighter enjoyed numerous advantages in its performance and capabilities, the Wildcat achieved a measure of greatness in part due to circumstance, in part because some exceptional men flew it.

Fighting the 'Zero' was not a task to be envied. Marines and Navy men learned early in the war not to dogfight with the more nimble 'Zero' if the contest could be resolved in some other fashion. Where possible, they sought to break through a screen of Mitsubishis and attack the enemy's big bombers directly. At times, a brace of 'Zeros' could be lured into an overshoot, making it easier to break through to the bombers.

Foster Hailey, correspondent for the *New York Times*, summed up the results in 1943: 'The Grumman Wildcat, it is no exaggeration to say, did more than any single instrument of war to save the day for the United States in the Pacific.'

Fighting in the F4F

A Martlet I of No 802 Squadron, Royal Navy, was the first American-built fighter in British service to destroy a German fighter in combat. The Grumman fighter is best remembered in the hands of outnum-bered American pilots pitted against the Mitsubishi 'Zero' in 1942–43, but first blood was drawn when a British pilot of No 802 Squadron operating from the small escort carrier HMS *Audacity* shot down a four-engined Focke-Wulf Fw 200 Condor near Gibraltar on 20 September 1941. Later versions of the Martlet/Wildcat served with Nos 802, 804, 805, 806, 881, 882, 888, 890, 892, 893, 894, 896 and 898 Squadrons, mostly aboard small escort carriers, in the Atlantic and elsewhere.

When Wildcats first went into US service, they equipped squadrons aboard the carriers USS *Ranger* (CV-4), USS *Enterprise* (CV-6), USS *Hornet* (CV-12), and USS *Saratoga* (CV-3).

But it was the Marines who received early attention. The first Wildcat pilot to win the Medal of Honor belonged to Marine squadron VMF-211, which lost nine F4F-3s on the ground during the 7 December 1941 attack on Pearl Harbor and seven more on the ground at Wake Island the next day. The battered defenders of Wake fought on against overwhelming odds and on 9 December 1941 two VMF-211 pilots teamed up to shoot down a Japanese bomber, the first American Wildcat kill. Before Wake was overrun, Captain Robert McElrod achieved a direct hit on a Japanese destroyer with a bomb dropped from his Wildcat, sinking the ship and losing his life but winning the Medal of Honor posthumously.

The first American Wildcat kills seem to have been a pair of twin-engined Mitsubishi G3M2 bombers downed by Lieutenant David S. Kliever and Tech Sgt William Hamilton of VMF-211, flying from Wake on 9 December 1941.

This General Motors FM-2 Wildcat has suffered a disabling mishap and is about to be jettisoned overboard by crew members of the USS *Nehenta Bay* (CVE-74) on 18 June 1944. Figures give perspective to the very small size of the island on an escort carrier. (USN)

A General Motors FM-2 Wildcat of squadron VC-13 operating from the escort carrier USS *Hoggatt Bay* (CVE-75) during the late war years. Barely visible is the nickname 'Judy' applied to the nose cowling of this Wildcat in white paint. (USN)

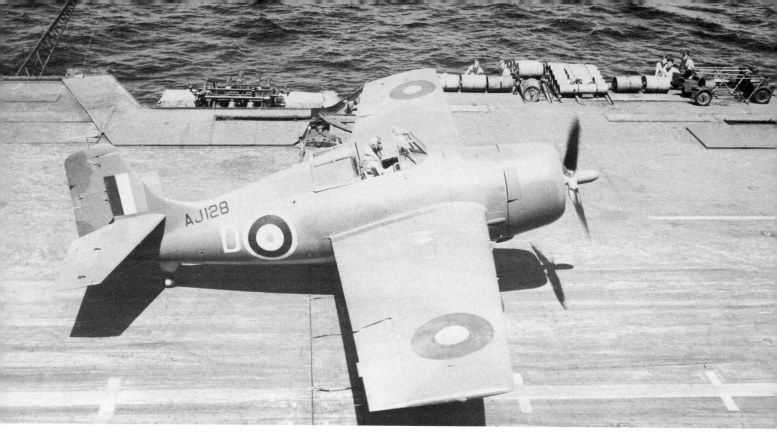

A Grumman Martlet II (AJ128) ready for take-off from a British aircraft-carrier in late 1942. Many of the Martlet IIs were shipped to India where they were assembled and put into action over the Indian Ocean. (IWM/Robert F. Dorr)

Grumman Martlet IV FN142 of No 893 Squadron launches from HMS *Formidable* in the Mediterranean in 1943. This is the 43rd example of the Mk IV version, which first came off Grumman's production line on 27 February 1942. (IWM/ Robert F. Dorr)

During the defence of Wake Island, Marines kept their Wildcats flying by cannibalizing wrecked aircraft, improvising tools, and hand-making some parts. When the Japanese attempted their first landings on Wake early in the morning of 11 December 1941, four Wildcats attacked the invasion force with 100lb (45kg) bombs and 0.50in (12.7mm) machine-gun fire. During the fighting the Japanese destroyer *Kisaragi* was sunk and a number of other ships were damaged by the Wildcats, forcing the Japanese invasion fleet to retire.

It was a temporary respite. On 21 December 1941 the Japanese returned, reinforced by carrier aircraft, for the final assault on Wake. The two surviving Wildcats attacked a 39-aircraft raid from the Japanese carriers *Soryu* and *Hiryu*. One Wildcat was quickly shot down by escorting 'Zeros', but the other shot down two of the raiders before its pilot, Captain Herb Frueler, was wounded. Frueler struggled back to the island where he crash-landed, wrecking Wake's last Wildcat. The island fell to the Japanese onslaught two days later.

The Wildcat was the fighter used by Lieutenant Edward (Butch) O'Hare of squadron VF-42 from the USS *Lexington* (CV-2), who shot down five Mitsubishi G4M bombers in five minutes near Rabaul on 20 February 1942, becoming the Navy's first ace of the war and winning the Wildcat's second Medal of

Another view of a Martlet IV operating from a British carrier. (IWM/Robert F. Dorr)

Honor. O'Hare survived, got the Medal from President Roosevelt, and had a Chicago airport named after him.

In the strategically significant Coral Sea battle of early May 1942 – the first fought between opposing carrier forces – 22 F4F-3s of VF-2 operated from the USS *Yorktown* and 20 of VF-42 flew from the deck of the ill-fated *Lexington*. During an attack on the two US carriers, nine of 27 Japanese aircraft were shot down for a loss of two F4Fs. The following day while escorting TBD Devastator torpedo-bombers, Wildcats downed a dozen defending 'Zeros'.

Wildcats achieved conspicuous success in the Battle of Midway and in operations at Guadalcanal. The Wildcat really earned its spurs not on pitching, heaving carrier decks but in the heat, stench, and muck at Henderson Field on Guadalcanal where, slowly, the tide began to turn and Americans mounted the first offensive action of the Pacific conflict.

During the initial landings on Guadalcanal, known as Operation 'Watchtower', 94 F4F-4s were embarked in *Enterprise, Saratoga* and *Wasp* to provide air cover. Early on 7 August 1942, VF-71 pilots destroyed twelve A6M2-N floatplane fighters based at Tulagi, VF-5 pilots struck Japanese facilities on Guadalcanal, and VF-6 Wildcats flew air cover. A series of air battles followed, one of which resulted in the loss of nine Wildcats in exchange for five victories. It was the beginning of a long hard slog.

An early problem in Pacific fighting was the tendency of the Wildcat's 0.50in (12.7mm) Browning guns to jam for no apparent reason. In early flight testing and carrier operations, the problem had gone unnoticed but in the harsh conditions of tropical combat more than one 'Zero' pilot escaped with his life because the Brownings failed to fire. US Navy ordnancemen suggested dividing the ammunition trays to keep ammunition belts from shifting. The Navy tested this modest change, and it was adopted.

Major John L. Smith's VMF-223, the 'Rainbow' squadron, was launched from the escort carrier USS *Long Island* (CVE-1) on 20 August 1942 and landed at Henderson Field. The next day the squadron strafed Japanese troops near the Tenaru river. On 24 August 1942, accompanied by five Bell P-400 Airacobras, Smith's aircraft intercepted an enemy flight of fifteen bombers and twelve fighters. VMF-223 pilots shot down ten bombers and six fighters, Captain Marion Carl scoring three of the kills. Carl became the first Marine ace of the war and Smith became the third Wildcat pilot to be awarded a Medal of Honor. The men who flew from Henderson Field (a 'bowl of blast dust or a quagmire of mud' in an official history) held their own in the Wildcat versus 'Zero' contest.

At Guadalcanal, Japanese bombers would approach 27 at a time in Vee formations and Wildcat pilots refined their technique of trying to avoid 'Zeros' and get at the bombers. Wildcats would dive on the bombers and destroy some before the 'Zeros' pounced on them. These hit-and-run tactics forced the Japanese pilots to over-use precious fuel. Once dogfighting began, the Americans learned the importance of teamwork, finding that reliance on one's wingman was crucial and that no 'lone wolf' survived for long.

Fighting Tactics

At Midway Lieutenant Commander John S. Thach of VF-3 in *Yorktown* devised a criss-cross dogfighting tactic which compensated for the Wildcat's sometimes inferior manoeuvrability vis-a-vis the 'Zero', and the 'Thach Weave' became part of naval aviation lore.

A number of F4F-3P photo aircraft were assigned to Marine squadron VMO-251 at Espiritu Santo in the New Hebrides during 1943. Wildcat fighters, including two F4F-3Ps, also saw action with the US Navy in North Africa in late 1942. The Wildcat was in the thick of all the significant actions in the Pacific until superseded by Hellcats and Corsairs a year later.

Although the General Motors-built FM-2 Wildcats did not really come into full service until Hellcats and Corsairs had eclipsed the older fighter, FM-2s served in composite squadrons and provided air cover for Marine amphibious forces. Some 1,400 FM-2s from the Linden plant had been fitted with three Mk 5 zero-length launcher stubs for 5in HVARs (high-velocity aircraft rockets) used in air support during the final fighting in the Philippines and on Okinawa. On 5 August 1945 an FM-2 of VC-98 flying from the USS *Lunga Point* (CVE-94) off the coast of Japan claimed the final Wildcat victory of the war, a twin-engined reconnaissance bomber.

In the Atlantic and Mediterranean, US Navy Wildcats first tasted action in April 1942 when fighters from *Wasp* flew combat air patrols for the carrier while she was ferrying RAF Spitfires to Malta. During Operation 'Torch', the Allied invasion of North Africa in November 1942, Wildcats from *Ranger*, USS *Sangamon* (ACV-26), USS *Suwanee* (ACV-27) and USS *Santee* (ACV-29) covered the armada of warships carrying men and material into the fight. Landings on French Morocco were initially opposed by Vichy French forces which claimed six Wildcats in the first battle with French fighters on 8 November 1942. Later, F4F-4s participated in air strikes in October 1943 against German shipping at Bodo, Norway.

FM-1 and FM-2 Wildcats continued to play a crucial role aboard escort carriers even after Hellcats and Corsairs were in service elsewhere. A VC-13 Wildcat from the USS *Core* (CVE-13) was shot down by the German submarine *U-487* on 13 July 1943. In other actions Wildcats from escort carriers scored aerial victories in both the Atlantic and Pacific.

Performance figures for the Wildcat show a fighter that could hold its own in many respects against the best the enemy had but never really possessed that extra edge needed to excel. The F4F-3 had a maximum speed of 325mph (523km/h), while the FM-2, apparently the fastest variant, reached 332mph (534km/h). The rate of climb attributed to

General Motors FM-2 Wildcat on an early acceptance flight near the Eastern plant at Linden, New Jersey. The taller vertical tail seen on the FM-2 was originally tested on Grumman's XF4F-8. (USN)

different versions varied widely, but some could achieve a respectable 3,300ft (1,021m) per minute. Service ceiling was around 35,000ft (10,670m) and range 770 miles (1,239km) on internal fuel, rising to 900 miles (1,448km) with drop-tanks. Like many fighters, the Wildcat grew slightly in weight with each progressive version, and suffered a corresponding loss in performance.

Dimensions of the Wildcat included: wing span 38ft (11.6m), length 28ft 9in (8.5m) on some versions and up to 28ft 11in (8.6m) on the FM-2, height of 11ft 11in (3.6m), and wing area 260sq ft (24.15m^2).

The F4F-4 version had an empty weight of 5,578lb (2,612kg) and a maximum take-off weight of 7,952lb (3,607kg); so the Wildcat was never a heavyweight, even in its later versions.

Wildcat Units

US Navy squadrons which flew the F4F Wildcat during the war years included VF-2, VF-3, VF-4, VF-5, VF-6, VF-7, VF-8, VF-9, VF-22, VF-41, VF-42, VF-71, and VF-72. Operating alongside TBM Avengers from escort carrier decks were FM-2 Wildcats of composite squadrons VC-3, VC-4, VC-5, VC-8, VC-10, VC-14, VC-20, VC-21, VC-27, VC-33, VC-58, VC-59, VC-65, VC-66, VC-75, VC-76, VC-78, VC-80, VC-81, VC-83, VC-85, VC-93, VC-96, VC-98 and VC-99. Also operating from small carrier decks were armed observation squadrons VGF-28 and VGF-29

and armed scouting squadrons VGS-30 and VGS-31.

The Marine squadrons, which did some of the most difficult fighting in the Wildcat, included VMF-111, VMF-112, VMF-121, VMF-122, VMF-211, VMF-212, VMF-223, and VMF-224. F4F-3P photo-reconnaissance aircraft were flown by observation squadron VMO-251 which saw action at Espiritu Santo in the New Hebrides during 1943.

Total production of the Wildcat fighter was 7,825, including 1,988 F4Fs built by Grumman between September 1937 and May 1943, and 5,837 FMs built by General Motors between August 1942 and August 1945.

More than a few Wildcats, especially the FM-2 model, survived the war to appear on the US civil register for several years afterwards. At least one was fitted with spraying gear for agricultural duties. Lex Dupont of Wilmington, Delaware, has appeared at air shows throughout the United States in a pristine FM-2 Wildcat (BuNo 47030, registered N315E) which has been known to evoke a tear or two of nostalgia from Wildcat veterans. Ex-Grumman test pilot Dick Foote is a frequent open-day entertainer in another Wildcat, which takes unique advantage of the distinctive, portly shape of the Grumman fighter's fuselage: Foote's craft has had its rotund interior modified to hold four passengers! For those who prefer to see this near-great of the war years in a more realistic guise, the Naval Aviation Museum at Pensacola, Florida, has two beautiful FM-2 Wildcats in wartime markings.

A fine example of a preserved Wildcat, this General Motors FM-2 (BuNo 86940) bears the civil registration N6290C and is seen during a visit to Gastonia, North Carolina, on 5 October 1968. (via Rowland P. Gill)

P-47
Thunderbolt

The cocky, competitive young man plying his trade in the narrow steel seat of a fighter is, by nature, aggressive, hard-charging, bent on success. He fights to win. He is driven. He wants to take on a worthy opponent, fight well, and prevail. Even during the lean pre-war years when funding for combat aircraft was sparse, readiness mattered to but a few visionaries, and American fighters were resoundingly second-rate, it was an accepted truth that the American taxpayer owed the American fighter pilot the finest flying machine money could buy. To provide less would be to betray the peculiar qualities so essential in that pilot – brashness, at times even a little recklessness, and above all supreme confidence in himself and his aircraft. Manufacturers' literature of the late 1930s promised the public, those who paid attention, that this was happening. It was not.

As global war came storming down on the American consciousness, aircraft designers saw a way to improve fighters and shore up their promise with an element of truth. The answer was the liquid-cooled, in-line engine which made it possible to streamline a fighter, reduce drag, and increase speed. European builders were getting good performance with in-line-engined fighters such as the Hurricane, Spitfire, Dewoitine D.520, and Messerschmitt Bf 109. Lockheed, Curtiss, and North American followed this trend and its final embodiment was the P-51 Mustang.

But Alexander Kartveli, who led the engineering effort at Republic Aviation Corporation at Farmingdale, Long Island, ignored their wisdom and went against the grain. Kartveli stayed with the radial engine. A round, blunt radial confronting the airstream would produce drag, admittedly, but a fighter

that was big enough, and powerful enough, was going to give that pilot the means to fight and win whether it looked good or not.

Kartveli was in his prime, in his late 40s, a serious man in a double-breasted suit with the chiselled, handsome features of cartoon police detective Dick Tracy. Working first under Major Alexander P. de Seversky (until Seversky left the firm in October 1939 and it changed his name for Republic), and later with an unusual degree of independence, Kartveli kept perfecting the big, heavy, radial-engined fighter. His P-35 and XP-41 had not lived up to some of the promises in the brochure, but Kartveli was getting much closer with the Republic P-43 Lancer.

With the P-43 (company designation AP-4), Kartveli tried to coax more speed without altering his basic idea of what a fighter should be. He had made an attempt to put a streamlined cowling around a radial with the XP-41, but with the Lancer he remained faithful to the flat-faced radial. He wanted increased power, a cleaner airframe, and fully retractable landing gear.

Power came from a 1,200hp Pratt & Whitney R-1830-35 Twin Wasp radial. Kartveli solved his landing gear problem with an undercarriage that retracted inwards instead of aft. Despite its blunt nose, the P-43 Lancer became, in fact, a rather appealing aircraft which looked as though it was speeding through the air even when it had not moved an inch.

Test P-43s

On 12 May 1939, thirteen service test examples of the turbo-supercharged YP-43 Lancer were ordered. The fighter was specified to reach 351mph (565km/

h) and was armed with two synchronized 0.50in (12.7mm) machine-guns in the cowling and two 0.30in (7.65mm) guns in the wings. Delivery of the YP-43 began in September 1940 and was completed in April 1941.

The P-43 Lancer – closely resembling a much more important fighter of Kartveli's that was to follow – began flying in 1939. Curiously, there appears to be no surviving record of the date, location, or pilot of the P-43's first flight. This item of information, long considered routine for so many aircraft, does not exist in the former Republic firm's records or in Pentagon documents. An article in the Dayton *Daily News* for 8 November 1940, 'Latest Fighting Plane Soon to Receive Final Tests Here', described the pending transfer of the first P-43 from Farmingdale to Wright Field, but gave no maiden flight date.

In any event, the P-43 demonstrated modest improvement, at least, over the P-35s and P-36s then in service. The P-43 was to become the first air-cooled-engined fighter with a turbo-supercharger to equip Air Corps squadrons.

Republic (meaning Kartveli) were also working on a similar pursuit ship to be powered by the 1,400hp Pratt & Whitney R-2180-1 radial and this was expected to reach 386mph (621km/h) – which was closer to the maximum speed being reached by liquid-cooled fighters. Eighty of these aircraft were

ordered on 13 September 1939 as the P-44 Rocket (company designation AP-4J), properly called the P-44-1. Still looking for more power in a radial design, Kartveli also fashioned a version powered by the 2,000hp Pratt & Whitney R-2800-7 to increase the speed of the aircraft to 406mph (653km/h). On 12 July 1940 the US Army Air Corps announced plans to purchase 225 of these aircraft and on 9 September 1940 made a commitment for 602 more. These machines were designated P-44-2 (company designation AP-4L). One source says that the P-44 series was to be named the 'Warrior' since another Republic design, as noted later, also bore the 'Rocket' appellation.

An interesting sidelight is that Kartveli's engineers proposed a biplane version of the P-44 in which the upper wing, attached to the forward fuselage, would serve as an expendable additional fuel tank. The wing could be jettisoned in combat. If the pilot had to ditch, it would keep the aircraft afloat.

Two further developments in this design progression were ordered in prototype form as the XP-47 (company designation AP-10) and the XP-47A.

Neither of these should be confused with the very different XP-47B Thunderbolt which came later. Only a full-scale, wooden mock-up of the XP-47A was completed, inside a cluttered warehouse at Farmingdale to which only a few personnel were granted access. Although powered by the liquid-cooled engine, which was anything but a Kartveli trademark, the XP-47A lacked the sleek and graceful lines that usually went with in-line-engined fighters. Indeed, the XP-47A mock-up looked more like a bloated version of the Curtiss XP-46.

Whatever consideration may have been given to the XP-47A design, it did not go very far and by mid-1940 Kartveli was hard at work on the future Thunderbolt fighter – the first of which was to be designated XP-47B. The Thunderbolt, like virtually every American fighter that later saw action in the conflict, had its design fixed long *before* Pearl Harbor belatedly brought the United States into the war.

All Republic's work on other designs did not prevent the first production P-43 Lancers from appearing in May 1941. These were identical to the YP-43 service-test ships. The P-44-1, P-44-2, XP-47 and XP-47A were all cancelled without ever reaching the prototype stage. Funding from the initial purchase of 80 P-44s was diverted to the same number of P-43A Lancers, which began to enter service in September 1941. These were followed by 125 P-43A-1s ordered on 28 June 1941 with Lend-Lease funds for China.

With the P-43A-1, the original R-1830 engine for the Lancer was replaced by an R-2800-57 Wasp. An

When the war started, the Republic P-43 Lancer was the ultimate in pursuit ships developed by the Seversky firm, which changed its name to Republic in 1939. The P-43 served in small numbers in USAAF units, but was quickly overshadowed by its successor, the mighty Thunderbolt. (via M. J.Kasiuba)

additional pair of 0.50in (12.7mm) machine-guns was added.

Although performance of the P-43 Lancer was respectable enough for a decidedly pre-war pursuit ship, the P-43 was kept in production for the primary purpose of keeping the Farmingdale line in operation, a decision which was intended to help, and did help, when the P-47 Thunderbolt came along.

To summarize P-43 Lancer production: 13 YP-43s were followed by a 1943 order for 54 production P-43s. When the P-44 failed to materialize, 80 P-43s were ordered, followed by 125 P-43A-1s. Further designations were allotted to these same aircraft when converted with cameras for the reconnaissance role: 150 P-43Bs were converted P-43 and P-43A aircraft; two P-43Cs were converted P-43As. Designations P-43D and P-43E went to P-43s and P-43A-1s, respectively, fitted with cameras. A total of 108 aircraft in the P-43 series was delivered to China.

Chinese Drill

Experience in China proved frustrating for those attempting to use this solid but unspectacular fighter under difficult operational conditions. On 4 September 1942 Republic's George Doughty wrote back to company official C. Hart Miller that China's air arm was having plenty of problems. 'The greatest difficulties (are) leaking gas tanks and faulty brakes,' Doughty wrote. 'The gas tank problem is a serious one as there is no available sealing compound in China. The majority of leaks occur at the vertical seams in the wheel wells.'

Doughty wrote that while in Kunming he had helped to dismantle a P-43 which had made a wheels-up landing in a rice paddy. 'The ships are used practically every day for tactical purposes, so we have to be careful not to tear down a ship so that it cannot be put into immediate service if necessary.' As Doughty soon reported, in spite of the very great Chinese need for fighters, the P-43s were deemed too vulnerable to gunfire for use as fighters, but served well as high-altitude photo-reconnaissance aircraft.

Eight P-43s reached the Royal Australian Air Force and were used by No 1 PRU.

Although most of Kartveli's work seemed to follow a logical order – improving steadily on a basic, radial-engined design – there was one radical departure in the form of his proposed AP-12 Rocket, a pursuit ship which existed only on the drawing-boards. The AP-12 was an extremely sleek, flush-canopy design with a buried Allison liquid-cooled engine driving contra-rotating propellers and six guns, four in the wings, two in the nose. It had some

elements in common with the also unbuilt Republic XP-69 which came later – but meanwhile the Thunderbolt was taking shape. The AP-12 never acquired a military designation.

It is time, then, to turn to Kartveli's triumph.

As recently as 1990 a USAF history stated: 'The Thunderbolt first took shape in a sketch made by Kartveli on the back of an envelope. That was at an Army fighter-plane requirements meeting in 1940.' The legend is heartwarming, but overlooks the step-by-step 'building block' process whereby the Thunderbolt came into being only after the progression of pursuit ships already described.

The final result of Kartveli's radial-engined fighter work, the Republic P-47 Thunderbolt (continuing the company designation AP-10) was a very big, very tough ship by any standard. It remains an impressive sight even today. It also became the subject of much wrongminded historical information and misunderstanding.

There were many things the P-47 was not. It was not difficult to fly. It was not even difficult to land, although the pilot had to be careful not to flare and to bring the machine straight down for a solid, thumping reunion with the ground. Nor was it true, as myth had it, that the P-47 was effective only at high altitude – as strafing missions late in the war were to prove.

Above all, in the list of misconceptions to be set straight, the Thunderbolt was not nicknamed 'Jug' because it was a juggernaut – although it was one, and with eight 0.50in guns was also one of the most heavily armed fighters of the war. The plain fact is that the nickname 'Jug' came because the P-47's fuselage resembled an illicit container for home-made whiskey.

The XP-47 and XP-47A designations, as noted, went to aircraft that were never built. These were lightweight aircraft which Kartveli, departing from his norm, fashioned around the 1,150hp Allison V-1710 in-line engine – that rare departure of his from the portly P-43 Lancer and P-44 Rocket. The XP-47 and XP-47A do not seem to have enjoyed much support from the Army Air Corps, and a full-scale mock-up of the latter languished, receiving very little attention, even while the design was being seriously proposed.

On 5 June 1940 an Army board meeting at Wright Field reviewed the limitations of existing Air Corps fighters in the light of reports from the air war in Europe and issued a specification for a 'super fighter' which would break the long-challenged 400mph (644km/h) barrier, with heavy armament and a ceiling of 40,000ft (12,384m). Kartveli responded a week later with his concept for an eight-gun,

Because the P-47 and P-47A designations were assigned to a different aircraft which was never built, the prototype in the Thunderbolt series was the XP-47B, seen here resplendent in natural metal at Republic's Farmingdale, Long Island, facility. XP-47B was the biggest single-seat fighter of its era and had a remarkably roomy cockpit. (Republic)

11,500lb (3,560kg) fighter retaining a turbo-super-charger and powered by the 2,000hp Pratt & Whitney XR-2800. On 6 September 1940 the Air Corps ordered one example – the XP-47B, aeroplane number one in the long series which was to bear the name 'Thunderbolt'.

XP-47B Design

The XP-47B Thunderbolt marked a return to Kartveli's tradition of big, sturdy aircraft. Its size and sheer brute strength were appropriate for the 2,535hp Pratt & Whitney R-2800 Double Wasp air-cooled radial which powered all production versions.

In natural metal, the prototype XP-47B (40-3051) made its first flight on 6 May 1941, piloted by Lowery Brabham. At the Republic plant in Farmingdale, the runway was not yet paved and spring rains had layered the strip with mud so, as planned, Brabham proceeded to land at nearby Mitchel Field. Brabham felt mild concern when oil residue burning in the supercharger ducts caused smoke to swirl around him in the canopy, but he landed easily and cheerfully, speaking of the new fighter in superlatives.

This XP-47B was the only aircraft in the series (save the XP-47E, see later) to have a car-style door designed to swing open on the side. Airflow made it almost impossible to open this door during an in-flight emergency, so it was abandoned on production machines in favour of a more practical sliding canopy. The XP-47B did not actually have a name until C. Hart Miller, Republic's director for military contracts and a test pilot, offered the opinion that it might be nice to call it the 'Thunderbolt'.

The new aircraft was far more than an enlarged version of the Lancer or Rocket. The power of the R-2800 engine was too much for the three-bladed propeller of the P-43 Lancer, so the Thunderbolt mounted a massive 12ft four-bladed controllable-pitch propeller. Its supercharging system was the key to success and was placed in the fuselage aft of the pilot, with exhaust gases piped back to the turbine and expelled at the rear, ducted air being returned to the engine under pressure. Despite teething problems, the system worked well and the Thunderbolt was a real performer, especially at high altitude.

So confident were Army Air Corps planners about the new fighter that in September 1940 they issued a $56 million contract to Republic for P-47B and P-47C aircraft before the first one had even flown. This was the largest single order placed by the Air Corps for fighters. The first production P-47B (41-5895) of May 1941 was number one among 171 P-47Bs with flush canopies and an upper fuselage that peaked in a sharp spine, resulting in the term 'razorback'. This configuration was retained with the lengthened P-47C model (602 built) and with early P-47Ds.

In due course, the bulky Thunderbolt was to become the most numerous American fighter ever manufactured, with 15,683 being turned out by Republic and Curtiss. Initially, only Thunderbolts built at Republic's second outlet in Evansville, Indiana, were to be known as P-47D, but in time the designation was applied to Farmingdale, New York, fighters as well; while identical airframes built by Curtiss in Buffalo were called P-47G. The first order for P-47D models was placed on 13 October 1941.

The 'razorback' configuration did not last as long

as the P-47D designation. Republic engineers fitted one Thunderbolt with a bubble canopy taken directly from an RAF Hawker Typhoon. This 'one-off' variation of a P-47D-5 (42-8702) was tested from July 1943, eventually received the out-of-sequence designation P-47K, and set the stage for the installation of a bubble canopy on all Thunderbolts from the P-47D-25-RE onwards. To go with the new canopy design, the fighter's rear decking was cut down and radio equipment relocated, giving the fuselage a slimmer and more streamlined form. In due course, a dorsal fillet on later 'D' models and subsequent Thunderbolts compensated for resulting minor problems of longitudinal stability. In 1944, to improve the 'D' model's performance in combat, early Thunderbolts were retrofitted with the 13ft paddle-bladed Curtiss Electric propeller which was installed during production from the P-47D-20 onwards.

Test Models

The sole XP-47E (41-6065) was taken from the P-47B line and completed as an unarmed test-bed for a pressurized cabin. It was part of a test programme seeking a high-altitude escort fighter, the intake for the pressurization unit being located in the port wing root. For reasons unknown, the XP-47E also had the discredited car-type door instead of a sliding canopy.

The sole XP-47F, also from the 'B' model line, was used to test laminar-flow wings, but crashed on 14 October 1943, killing Captain McAdams.

While P-47 Thunderbolts were tested in battle from Europe to New Guinea, new test-beds emerged to try improvements to the design. Two XP-47Hs

(42-23297 and 42-23298) flew with the 2,500hp Chrysler XI-2220-11 in-line engine, the only Thunderbolts with liquid-cooled power. The XP-47J (43-46952) was a test-bed for the familiar R-2800 with a new cooling fan system and other modifications; first flown on 26 November 1943, it was tested extensively and on 5 August 1944 reached the remarkable speed in level flight of 504mph (811km/h). The sole XP-47L (42-76614) also evaluated the bubble canopy which improved visibility in the Thunderbolt and later the P-51 Mustang as well.

The P-47M Thunderbolt (133 built) was an interim improvement on the 'D' model. The slightly increased speed of the P-47M, employed in Europe, enabled it to combat German V-1 flying bombs and Me 262 jet fighters more effectively than other Thunderbolts.

The P-47N was the ultimate Thunderbolt design with a longer-span wing and clipped wingtips. The P-47N was produced expressly for operations in the Pacific theatre where range was important and 'wet' wings permitted a fuel capacity of 1,266(US)gal, increasing range to 2,350 miles (3,760km). 1,667 P-47Ns came from Farmingdale, 149 from Evansville. The P-47N had the R-2800-77 engine, enlarged ailerons and square-tipped wings for rapid roll, and zero-length rocket-launchers.

When P-47C Thunderbolts joined the USAAF's 4th Fighter Group at Debden, England, in January 1943, pilots accustomed to the Spitfire considered the 'Jug' over-heavy, unresponsive and unmanoeuvrable. 'A discomforting transition,' said Major Donald Blakeslee who shot down a Focke-Wulf Fw190 on 15 April 1943 in the first kill by a Thunderbolt. In another unit, Lieutenant Robert V. Brulle was

The classic 'razorback' configuration was seen in the early P-47 Thunderbolts and remained much in evidence throughout the war. P-47D-23-RA 42-277731 of the USAAF's 1st Air Commando Group is seen at Kiangwan aerodrome in Shanghai on 6 December 1945, months after the end of hostilities. Nickname 'The Flying Abortion' appears on nose. (Peter M. Bowers via Norman Taylor)

Previously unpublished look at 42-754217, a Republic P-47D Thunderbolt ('UN-K') of Colonel Hubert (Hub) Zemke's famous 56th Fighter Group at Halesworth. Barely discernible is paint trim around the cowling used as an identifying feature to distinguish the P-47 from the German Focke-Wulf Fw 190. (via Bill Crimmins)

RAF Thunderbolts saw combat only in South-East Asia, but some were used for conversion training in Egypt. Thunderbolt I HD176 (a P-47B) belongs to No 73 Operational Training Unit at Fayid, Egypt, in 1945. Emblem on nose is an ace of spades with a grinning skull in the centre. Flying with the canopy open was a good way to get a real 'feel' for the big fighter. (via Bruce Robertson)

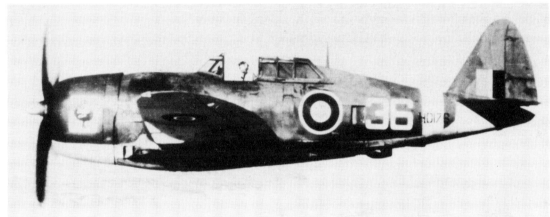

Thunderbolt 43-25730 is a 'razorback' P-47D, seen in natural metal apparently at a training location in the USA (Vultee BT-13 'Vibrator' 42-89124 in background). It was not unusual for a Thunderbolt to operate from a rough field like this. Most wartime fighters did not need broad expanses of concrete. (via Larry Davis)

Republic P-47D-27-RA
Thunderbolt 42-26885, another
'razorback', bearing the nickname
'The Pied Piper' on the nose
cowling, seen in the South-West

Pacific. (Peter M. Bowers via
Norman Taylor)

RAF Thunderbolt II (P-47D
'razorback') fighter-bombers of
No 135 Squadron seen on the
Arakan front in Burma in
November 1944 after moving

forward from their base at
Chittagong, India (now
Bangladesh). RAF Thunderbolts
operated in the China-Burma-
India theatre, but this was the

location of most of the 830
Thunderbolts delivered to the
British under Lend-lease. (via
Robert F. Dorr)

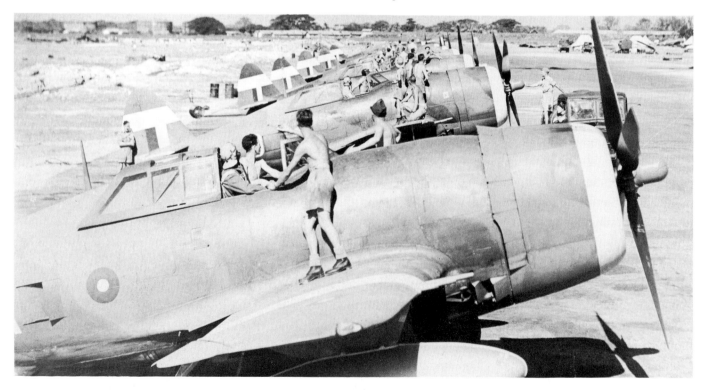

A late-model P-47D Thunderbolt in the Pacific theatre. Nickname of the aircraft, on the nose starts 'The Little . . .' and the serial number appears to be 44-327099. Hard volcanic rock beneath the 'Jug' suggests that the location could be Iwo Jima. (via Larry Davis)

'Big Stud', alias P-47D Thunderbolt 45-49365, was the first 'Jug' flown on the air show circuit by air ace Colonel Robert Baseler, who had the aircraft painted in the markings of the 325th Fighter Group he had led in Italy. Baseler later applied the same nickname to P-47N 44-88593 used in publicity activities to promote the Air Force. (via David W. Menard)

Powered by a 2,800hp R-2800-57 radial engine in a lightened airframe, the XP-47J Thunderbolt (43-46952) was the fastest aircraft in the series and reportedly attained a speed of 505mph (812.71km/h) on 5 August 1944. For part of its career, the 'J' model had the cartoon character Superman painted on its nose. (USAF)

View from hangar top shows natural-metal P-47D Thunderbolts of the USAAF's 404th Fighter Group at air base Y-86 in Fritzlar, Germany, on the eve of VE-Day. Once the Allies were on the ground in continental Europe, the 'Jug' was used mainly for strafing and bombing, and had an important role in supporting the drive towards Berlin. (Kemal Saied)

44-32794 was a P-47D flown by Kemal Saied of the 404th Fighter Group. As they advanced across Europe, Thunderbolt pilots found themselves operating at times from crude grass airstrips. Maintenance and support people had to struggle to keep the aircraft flying. (Kemal Saied)

From any angle the 'Jug' appeared massive. This rather plain view of a P-47 Thunderbolt with bubble canopy (and with a small dog relaxing next to its port landing gear) illustrates the size of this enormous fighter. (via M. J. Kasiuba)

pleased to discover that the P-47 was the first aircraft he had flown where seat and controls could be adjusted for a pilot of small stature.

The 56th Fighter Group at Halesworth, England, under Colonel Hubert Zemke, was the best-known Thunderbolt outfit and produced its share of the war's aces. Colonel Roderick MacDowell of the 78th

Fighter Group said of the P-47:

'The Germans had the advantage of fighting over home ground. Though our machine-guns worked at long range, their cannon did too. The odds were evened by us having the P-47 with superior performance above 20,000ft (6,096m) and incredible dive acceleration which enabled us to catch up with any

Side-by-side, a bubble-canopy and 'razorback' Thunderbolt, both of the 404th Fighter Group, take off from airield A-92 at St Trond, Belgium, during fighting on the continent. In the background are damaged B-17 and B-24 bombers which landed at A-92 after being unable to return to their home bases in Britain. (Kemal Saied)

German who used the standard technique of breaking off an engagement by going into a half-roll and diving.'

Once Luftwaffe pilots learned that diving to escape a P-47 was tantamount to suicide, they developed a corkscrew climb manoeuvre to break an engagement, unaware that Curtiss paddle-bladed propellers enhanced the Thunderbolt's climb rate, leaving Bf 109s and Fw 190s highly vulnerable. Lieutenant Colonel Francis S. Gabreski with 28 kills and Major Robert S. Johnson with 27, the top-scoring American aces in Europe, both flew P-47s. A number of well-known pilots who later graduated to the P-51 Mustang scored their first kills in the P-47. Thunderbolts are credited with 3,916 enemy aircraft.

Combat Figures

Those who kept track of such numbers determined that the P-47 Thunderbolt accounted for 86,000 railway wagons, 9,000 locomotives, 6,000 tanks and armoured vehicles, and 68,000 lorries. The air-to-ground prowess of the Thunderbolt was important from the Normandy invasion onwards, as 'Jug' pilots ranged over German forces, picking off high-value targets at tree-top level. One P-47 pilot, Colonel Robert V. Brulle, used the title 'Angels Zero' for his memoirs – denoting a particularly difficult war, fought in fields and hedgerows, where every kind of ground fire threatened the 'Jug' pilot as he risked wrapping himself around a tree or telegraph pole.

Colonel Brulle combined one of these hazardous ground-level missions with a duel against the formidable Focke-Wulf. His description symbolizes all the fighting done by all P-47 pilots:

'We were in the air when . . . a large group of German fighters were coming directly at our airstrip (on the continent after the Normandy invasion). We met the German aircraft head-on. There were about 50 Me 109 and Fw 190 fighters. We were busy getting our aircraft cleaned up [jettisoning bombs],

turning on our gun sights and guns, and switching the gas to main tank.

'I picked up an Fw 190 and was already on his tail before I had my gun sight on. He dove down to the deck and was really skimming the ground. I tried to get right behind him but his prop wash almost caused me to hit the ground. I could not depress my nose enough to bring my guns to bear on the aircraft, and it was hard, because of my eagerness, to hold fire even though my bullets were going over him. Once he pulled back on the throttle and I almost overshot him, but slowed down enough to prevent it. For a few moments we were in formation together, and I can still remember the pilot was crouched over his controls. We finally came to some trees and as he pulled over them I got in a good burst and he blew up.

'I flew right through his explosion and had my windshield covered with his oil, making it hard to see through for a few minutes. Another Fw 190 pulled in front of me and I started after him. However, before I could get into position I saw cannon shells flying over my canopy. Going into a steep turn, I saw an Me 109 firing at me. I was fascinated by the slow flashes of the cannon firing through the propeller hub and the faster flashes of the machine-guns on the cowling and wing. I kept it in a steep turn for about 180 degrees when the Me 109 suddenly broke off combat. I then got on the tail of another Fw 190 and was able to get a few bursts at him. There were frantic calls on the radio from other guys with aircraft on their tails. I used up my ammunition shooting at an Fw 190 and had to break off combat.

'I observed an Me 109 heading back towards Germany pursued by two P-51s about 1,000 yards back. As the Me 109 started to go below my wing, I rolled over so I could keep my eye on him. He saw me and thinking I was going to dive on him, veered away. This allowed one of the P-51s to turn inside him and get close enough to set up a deflection shot and get him. I always felt I should have gotten an assist for shooting down that enemy aircraft.'

It must be said of the Thunderbolt that, despite its many qualities, it never quite grew the 'legs' it would have needed to escort American bombers all the way to Berlin. Time and again, changes were made to try to improve fuel capacity and range. Both internal fuel and external drop-tanks were repeatedly re-designed and improved. The Thunderbolt was a superlative fighter but for the ultimate mission of escorting bombers all the way to targets deep within the Third Reich, it had to step aside and give centre stage to the P-51 Mustang.

Pacific Fighting

In the Pacific, white-tailed razorback P-47Ds of the 348th Fighter Group under Lieutenant Colonel Neel Kearby matched the best the Japanese had. On 11 October 1943 Kearby shot down six Japanese fighters in a gruelling engagement at the limits of fuel and endurance, earning the Medal of Honor; his

Three factory-fresh Republic P-47N Thunderbolts (44-88576 in foreground) on an early flight over Farmingdale. The 'N' model was in many respects the ultimate Thunderbolt and was designed for the long distances confronting Allied airmen in the Pacific theatre. (Republic)

Thunderbolt II KL887 is a P-47D (American serial 44-90335). This bubble canopy-equipped RAF 'Jug' is seen in the scrapyard after the conflict. (via Robert F. Dorr)

aircraft was P-47D-2-RA 42-8145, nicknamed 'Firey Ginger'. Five months later, when he had 22 victories to his credit and was top ace in the Pacific, Kearby was shot down and killed. P-47C and P-47D fighters fought throughout the Pacific. P-47Ns operated from Iwo Jima and escorted B-29s over Japan.

Fighting in the Pacific often meant vast distances, difficult navigation, and abominable conditions at friendly airfields. It was difficult to take on a 'Zero' or lug a bomb to its target when pilots were burning up with tropical fever or running to the latrine every five minutes. At least the Thunderbolt provided a comfortable seat and a spacious, roomy cockpit. Although not as long-ranged as it needed to be in Europe, the Thunderbolt offered other qualities that were essential in the Pacific, among them sheer toughness and the strength to survive under fire.

P-47 Thunderbolts served with no fewer than 42 American fighter groups in combat Best known in the Pacific was Kearby's 348th. No detailed roster has ever emerged of the relatively few units which flew Thunderbolts in the China-Burma-India region and in the Pacific (where the final P-47N model reached combat over the Japanese islands). A listing of P-47 groups in Europe and the Mediterranean is possible, due in part to research by American historians like Ernest R. McDowell. This roster includes the following fighter groups (with their squadrons in parentheses):

In the 8th Air Force: 4th (334, 335, 336); 56th (61, 62, 63); 67th (359, 360, 361); 78th (82, 83, 84); 353rd (350, 351, 352); 356th (359, 360, 361); 361st (374, 375, 376).

In the 9th Air Force: 36th (22, 23, 53); 48th (492, 493, 494); 50th (10, 81, 313); 354th (353, 354, 356); 358th (365, 366, 367); 362nd (377, 378, 379); 365th (386, 387, 388); 366th (389, 390, 391); 367th (392, 393, 394); 368th (395, 396, 397); 371st (404, 405, 406); 373rd (410, 411, 412); 404th (506, 507, 508); 405th (509, 510, 511); 406th (512, 513, 514).

In the 12th and 15th Air Forces: 27th (522, 523, 524); 57th (64, 65, 66); 86th (525, 526, 527); 324th (314, 315, 316); 325th (317, 318, 319); 332nd (99, 100, 301, 302); 350th (346, 347, 354).

In the RAF the 240 Thunderbolt Is (P-47B) and 590 Thunderbolt IIs (P-47D) served in sixteen squadrons and were used exclusively by South-East Asian Command, operating mainly in Burma. A Brazilian fighter squadron operated P-47Ds in Europe with considerable success, a Mexican squadron in the Pacific with little. Lend-Lease Thunderbolts also fought in small numbers for the Soviet Union, where they were among the most advanced Russian fighters of the war.

In all versions, the P-47 was instrumental in the Allied victory. Among the most numerous of American warplanes ever built, it would surely have become the most numerous had the war dragged on: VJ-Day saw orders for 5,934 further Thunderbolts cancelled abruptly, leaving the total built at 15,683.

The P-47 Thunderbolt became a common sight in post-war Europe. Many served in units which acquired new jets and flew side-by-side with them. In 1948 the 'Jug' was redesignated F-47. Thunderbolts took on the new red, white, and blue emblem of the newly independent US Air Force and served

Thunderbolts were used only briefly in the post-war years. P-47D 45-49283 made it to the New Jersey Air National Guard, and operated from the airfield near Fort Dix which is known today as McGuire Field. (via Clyde Gerdes)

Thanks to a few dedicated history buffs who never lost their appreciation for the distinctive whine of the Thunderbolt's engine, a few P-47s have been preserved. P-47D Thunderbolt 42-26422, civil registration N47DB, of the Confederate Air Force is seen on a 6 July 1974 visit to Olathe, Kansas. (Clyde Gerdes)

well past 1950 in Air National Guard units. The P-47 was also used, mostly in the post-war era, by Bolivia, Brazil, Britain, Chile, China, Colombia, the Dominican Republic, Ecuador, France, Honduras, Iran, Italy, Mexico, Nicaragua, Peru, Turkey, Venezuela and Yugoslavia.

Not everything about the Thunderbolt was perfect. Its take-off run was unduly long. It could never turn inside the agile Fw 190 at any altitude. Its tendency to make excessive use of gravity in establishing contact with the ground has already been noted. The Thunderbolt's cockpit design, however, was exceedingly comfortable and it was as stable as any fighter could be. It was the ideal firing platform.

At one time in the early 1960s no surviving

Thunderbolt was in flyable condition. That situation has been rectified with the 'warbird' movement of the 1990s, and a number of P-47s can now be seen flying at air shows. A magnificent 'razorback' Thunderbolt flown at air shows by Don Lykins is a P-47G (serial 42-25234, registered NX3395G) painted in camouflage and markings to represent the mount of wartime ace Major Walker (Bud) Mahurin. During the actual conflict, there were very few two-seat Thunderbolts, but this air show fighter has an added seat which makes it possible for a passenger to ride along in one of America's greatest combat aircraft. The US Air Force Museum in Dayton, Ohio, has two Thunderbolts, both P-47Ds, one of which flew for a time in Peru.

Another Confederate Air Force 'warbird' is Republic P-47D Thunderbolt 44-90471, registered as N47DA and seen at an air show in June 1972. (via Clyde Gerdes)

F4U Corsair

The Vought F4U Corsair is perceived by some as a moderately interesting fighter which came along because the US Navy needed a back-up to the superb Grumman F6F Hellcat.

In fact, design work on the Corsair began before the Hellcat was even a flicker in anyone's mind. The Corsair earned, and is entitled to, the adjective 'superb' itself. Its designer, its builders, and many who flew the Corsair in battle never saw it as anything but the leading naval fighter of its era. In some ways, with gull wings and innovative construction, the Corsair was technically way ahead of the Hellcat, so both its track record and its advanced design meant that no 'second fiddle' ranking of the Corsair was ever justified.

More often, the Corsair is remembered as late in coming, reaching service only after pilots and engineers had grappled with infuriating flaws.

In contrast to the later, quicker Hellcat, the Corsair was slow in reaching its full potential. But the tardiness of the gull-winged Vought thoroughbred is often exaggerated. There were teething troubles galore, as indeed there were with a number of fighter types, yet the Corsair entered the war at Guadalcanal, in February 1943 – early enough for its pilots, plane captains, and maintenance men to experience some of the most gruelling operating conditions of the war.

It would be a grave mistake to dwell upon the Corsair's teething troubles and overlook some pointed facts:

The businesslike, gull-winged Vought F4U Corsair was capable of operating from carrier decks but did most of its wartime fighting from land. These Goodyear FG-1D Corsairs (BuNo 76635 in foreground) are lined up on the volcanic flatland of Iwo Jima – the island won at terrible cost in Marine lives in order to bring US aircraft within range of the Japanese home islands. (via M. J. Kasiuba)

When introduced in the Solomons in early 1943, the Corsair immediately took command of the sky. Japanese fighters had previously faced serious challenge only when outnumbered, and outclassed American pilots coaxed more from their ageing Wildcats than anyone had a right to expect. The Corsair gave these pilots speed, power, and killing potential. And once the Corsair began to appear, it appeared in numbers. It was nothing less than a turn of the tide.

The Corsair was in production longer than any other American fighter. It was the last propeller-driven fighter built in the United States. F4U Corsair pilots flew 64,051 combat sorties, 54,470 from land and 9,581 from carriers. For a loss of 189 Corsairs in air-to-air combat, they claimed the destruction of 2,140 Japanese aircraft, a spectacular 11-to-1 kill ratio, which has stood up in the face of 'revisionist' versions of history.

Chance Milton Vought learned how to fly from the Wright Brothers in 1910. In 1926, as one of the first American builders of aircraft, Vought supervised the painting of an imaginative nickname on the rudder of the O2U-1 observation biplane he had sold to the US Navy. 'Vought Corsair', it said. On 1 January 1928 Lieutenant Christian F. Schilt of the US Marine Corps, under fire in Chipopte, Nicaragua, won the highest American award for bravery, the Medal of Honor, for strapping eighteen wounded troops to the wings of his O2U-1 Corsair and flying them out to safety. When the wartime F4U came along, its name should have been Corsair II . . .

Vought himself died in 1930, but his name was to grace carrier-borne warplanes for the remainder of the century. The Vought company's offices moved from Long Island City, New York, to Stratford, Connecticut, where a shotgun marriage with a very different builder made it Vought-Sikorsky – until January 1943 when the Chance Vought appellation was restored.

Design Effort

Design work on the F4U Corsair began in 1938 (together with work on the forgettable Grumman XF5F-1 Skyrocket and Bell XFL-1 Airabonita) in a Navy effort to bring carrier-based performance up to that of land-based fighters.

The first order for the Vought XF4U-1 was placed on 30 June 1938. A full-scale plywood mock-up of the XF4U-1, not noticeably different from the actual aircraft which followed, was ready for inspection at Stratford as early as February 1939.

The XF4U-1 was the first Navy warplane built around the 1,850hp Pratt & Whitney XR-2800-4 Double Wasp radial, the same heavyweight that powered the Army's P-47 Thunderbolt. The Vought fighter had a propeller of 13ft 4in (4.13m) diameter, larger than the Thunderbolt's, but with three blades. Rex Beisel, chief engineer on the design project – and a veteran of service with the Curtiss and Spartan companies – searched for a way to give the big propeller ground clearance without making the landing gear too stalky or heavy. Beisel's solution was to gull the wings downwards, the inverted-gull configuration having the added benefit of reducing drag at the juncture of wing and fuselage.

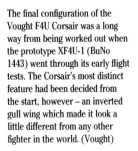

The final configuration of the Vought F4U Corsair was a long way from being worked out when the prototype XF4U-1 (BuNo 1443) went through its early flight tests. The Corsair's most distinct feature had been decided from the start, however – an inverted gull wing which made it look a little different from any other fighter in the world. (Vought)

Finished with a smooth spot-welded skin and armed with twin 0.50in (12.7mm) machine-guns each in nose and wings, the natural-metal prototype Corsair had exactly the kind of practical undercarriage Beisel had sought, with wheels retracting backwards and swivelling 90deg flat into the wing. The inverted-gull wing folded for carrier stowage, not to the rear as on the Hellcat but upwards as on most other shipboard aircraft.

The F4U Corsair design resulted from hard work by Beisel's team. Igor Sikorsky, contrary to some published accounts, was not involved in any way in the Corsair project, although the manufacturing firm was known as Vought-Sikorsky for a time. Beisel needed no help in creating a fighter which looked unorthodox when first seen because of its ingenious wing shape. The passage of time made the Corsair familiar and, to many, much loved.

The Corsair was heavier than the Japanese 'Zero' which became its principal adversary. It was as manoeuvrable but with better speed, range, and staying power. Cockpit visibility was to remain a minor problem through much of the Corsair's life despite repeated changes in cockpit configuration, with only the final Goodyear F2G-1 variant acquiring the bubble canopy standard on Army fighters.

At Stratford on 29 May 1940, test pilot Lyman A. Bullard made the maiden flight of the new fighter. It was to be manufactured at Stratford throughout the war and, during the post-war era, in Dallas following yet another company move.

Flight tests made it evident that the Navy had a high-performing aeroplane, but on its fifth flight the only prototype was caught with almost empty fuel tanks amid gathering rain squalls. Test pilot Boone T. Guyton made a courageous effort to save the valuable XF4U-1 by landing on the posh Norwich golf course, but wet grass caused the Corsair to slide and it slammed into trees, coming to a halt almost fully demolished but with just enough space under the inverted fuselage for Guyton to get out. This proved an unexpected demonstration of the Corsair's toughness, for the aircraft was able to be repaired and reflown, but months were lost in the development programme.

When the silver prototype did get aloft once more, on 1 October 1940, it reached a speed of 405mph (652km/h) – faster, then, than any other US fighter. Indirectly this event helped elsewhere, for it contributed to the Army's decision not to rely solely on liquid-cooled engines for fighters and to proceed with the similarly powered P-47 Thunderbolt.

On 30 June 1941 an order was placed for 584 F4U-1s. Pearl Harbor came within six months and the need for this shipboard fighter became much greater. Plans were established for Goodyear and Brewster to produce versions of the aircraft which became the FG-1 and F3A-1 respectively.

On 25 June 1942 the initial production F4U-1 (BuNo 02153) flew with the 2,000hp Pratt & Whitney R-2800-8 (an improved version of the Double Wasp two-stage 18-cylinder radial), lengthened fuselage, and cockpit moved back to make room for additional fuel. The engine consumed about 195gal of fuel during normal rated cruise, which was somewhat high. To increase the range of the new fighter, its

Vought F4U-4C Corsair carrying a load of eight 12in high-velocity aircraft rockets. Some in the US Navy viewed the Corsair as a kind of back-up insurance in case the Grumman F6F Hellcat proved less than completely successful. In time, though, the Corsair amassed its own record of achievements, including considerable success against Japanese fighters. (Vought)

237(US)gal internal tank was supplemented by a 160(US)gal drop-tank carried on the centre-line.

Navy Delivery

Delivery to the Navy occurred on 31 July 1942, one day after the first flight of the rival Hellcat with a similar engine. The F4U-1 was fitted with six 0.50in (12.7mm) Browning M-2 machine-guns, 2,350 rounds of ammunition, 155lb (70.30kg) of armour, and the now-requisite self-sealing fuel tanks. Vought delivered 1,550 F4U-1 aircraft.

The F4U-1A became the next version, with more power and water injection. The main recognizable difference was the changeover from the Corsair's original 'bird cage' canopy to a totally new raised canopy which gave better visibility, had fewer frames, and was a prototype for the standard canopy shape in future aircraft in the series.

The F4U-1B, or Corsair I for the Royal Navy, was identical to production F4U-1/F4U-1A aeroplanes except that it had wingtips clipped by 8in (0.203m) for below-deck stowage in smaller British carriers. This, incidentally, produced an aircraft which was more racer-like in appearance.

The F4U-1C was a batch of 200 armed with four 20mm M2 (Hispano) cannon. Arguments over whether machine-guns or cannon were more effective have persisted until recent times when the latter emerged the clear winner. With cannon a single hit on an enemy aircraft could be crippling, but many pilots preferred 0.50in (12.7mm) machine-guns because they carried more rounds of ammunition.

The F4U-1D (and comparable Goodyear FG-1D) introduced changes which included fittings for drop-tanks, bombs and rockets. It marked the first time the factory built-in a fighter-bomber capability for the Corsair, while earlier F4U-1As and others were later modified in the field. (Other solutions included locally developed bomb racks, one of them tested in the field by Vought adviser Colonel Charles Lindbergh, and a Brewster-designed adapter rack which held a centre-line 1,000lb (454kg) bomb.) The -1D model also incorporated the increased-performance R-2800-8W engine with water injection, which could be used for a maximum of five minutes in a combat-emergency situation.

Vought produced 4,102 F4U-1Bs, -1Cs and -1Ds, including 95 Corsair I and 510 Corsair II fighters (differing only in cockpit design) for the Royal Navy and 370 for the Royal New Zealand Air Force.

The Corsair had been conceived from the outset to serve aboard the US Navy's growing fleet of aircraft-carriers, fast becoming the capital ships of the Pacific war. Carrier qualification tests began on 25 September 1942 aboard the USS *Sangamon* (CVE-26) with F4U-1 number seven (BuNo 02159), piloted by Commander Sam Porter. The tests showed that the Corsair was a bit too fast and visibility poor on the final approach.

With the Hellcat coming along, the US Navy was reluctant to commit the Corsair to full-fledged carrier operations until its teething troubles could be resolved. When carrier operations were delayed, the Marine Corps, which operated most of its fighters from land, became the first user of the Corsair in combat in the Pacific.

The Marines had been badly mauled while flying the F4F Wildcat and were relieved to have the Corsair to give them a solid chance against Japanese fighters. Operations began on 15 February 1943, the first squadron in combat in the tropical torture chamber called Guadalcanal being VMF-124 'Checkerboards'. By August 1943 a Marine technical expert in the field reported significant progress towards equipping all eight Marine fighter squadrons in the Pacific with Corsairs.

Although minor technical problems impeded the Corsair's upbringing (notable, perhaps, only because the F6F Hellcat was so lacking in them), Goodyear began delivery of FG-1 Corsairs in April 1943. It is often reported that this version from the Akron, Ohio, manufacturer, otherwise identical to the F4U, lacked folding wings. In fact, FG-1, FG-1A, and FG-1D aeroplanes did have folding wings for carrier storage.

The troubled Brewster firm began turning out its F3A-1 (and similar F3A-1A) Corsairs in July 1943. Brewster completed 735 aircraft before management problems led to the Navy closing down its Johnsonville, Pennsylvania, facility in July 1944.

Production Corsairs now had a maximum speed of 417mph (671km/h). Navy and Marine squadrons wanted Corsairs faster than they could be delivered.

New Corsairs

The F4U-2 designation went to a night fighter version which came into being based on an 8 November 1941 proposal. The Naval Aircraft Factory converted twelve F4U-1 Corsairs to the nocturnal warfare configuration by installing a radome on the starboard wingtip. Other modifications came into being in the field, so that there were a total of 24 F4U-2s, 22 with the 'birdcage' cockpit of the F4U-1 and two with the raised cockpit of the F4U-2.

On this night fighter, the outboard gun on the starboard wing only (not both outboard guns, as often reported) was deleted. On 31 October 1943 over New Georgia, an F4U-2 accomplished the US Navy's first successful radar-guided interception. Three squadrons of Corsair night fighters served in the Second World War: VF(N)-75, VF(N)-101 and VMF-532.

The Navy applied the F4U-3 designation to three high-altitude machines planned in March 1943 and intended to be powered by a turbo-supercharged R-2800-16 with a belly air intake. The project stalled and only one example was completed, not flying until after the war.

Five XF4U-4 test aircraft were followed by the F4U-4, first appearing in October 1944. The production F4U-4 is often considered the definitive wartime version of the gull-winged Vought fighter, although

XF4U-5 Corsair (BuNo 97364) with blunt gun barrels for its four 20mm cannon. The Corsair enjoyed the distinction of being the Second World War fighter that stayed in production longest; it was still coming out of the Vought Dallas factory during the 1950–53 Korean conflict. (via Roger Besecker)

relatively few aeroplanes of this mark actually reached the combat zone, and only as late as March 1945.

The F4U-4 had a redesigned nose shape and a 2,100hp Pratt & Whitney R-2800-18W driving a four-bladed propeller. The engine's supercharger featured water injection, which raised maximum speed to 448mph (721km/h). Versions of the 'dash four' model included: the F4U-4B built for the US Navy and Marine Corps, and, as the Corsair IV, for the Royal Navy with four 20mm cannon (which saw combat exclusively in Korea); the F4U-4E night fighter with air interception radar; the similarly

equipped one-off F4U-4N night fighter (BuNo 97361); and the F4U-4P photo-reconnaissance machine (nine built); as well as the Goodyear FG-4. Goodyear completed only two FG-4 Corsairs which were never actually released to the Navy and were eventually scrapped by the manufacturer. At one time 3,149 F4U-4s had been on order, including 287 F4U-4Bs, but the figure was reduced to 2,356 with contract cancellations on VJ-Day.

To summarize versions of the Corsair built by Goodyear, these were the FG-1, FG-1D, and FG-4. Late in the war the Akron, Ohio, firm (better known for its rubber products) was approached by the Navy

Corsairs over the South Pacific. The date is 2 November 1944 but the location is no longer on record. By late in the war, air opposition was no longer a serious problem, but Corsairs continued to be flown intensively, carrying out air-to-ground combat missions. (USN)

Production of the Corsair was also carried out in Akron, Ohio, by the Goodyear Corporation – better known as a maker of tyres – which turned out production FG fighters and F2Gs with a bubble canopy. This Goodyear FG-1D is a weathered post-war survivor. (via Roger Besecker)

Vought F4U-1D Corsair from Marine fighter squadron VMF-312, in the wrong place at the wrong time. The location is Okinawa, the date April 1945, and the Corsair has gone over on its back, either on take-off or landing. Clearly this aircraft was a total write-off. (via Jim Sullivan)

to build a higher-performance version of the Corsair. This bubble-canopy aircraft was turned out in two versions, the F2G-1 land-based version with manually folding wings, and the F2G-2, a carrier version with hydraulically folding wings and arrester hook. The F2G-1D sub-variant featured an auxiliary rudder which improved handling.

Powered by the 3,000hp Pratt & Whitney R4360-4 Wasp Major engine, described elsewhere in this volume as one of the largest powerplants ever put into a fighter, the F2G could climb to 30,000ft (9,288m) in just four minutes. Eighteen F2Gs were completed and flown by Goodyear before the contracts were cut back at the end of the war.

Post-war Corsairs included the F4U-5, which continued the series from July 1946. An F4U-5N night fighter followed. Perhaps a new height of complexity in aircraft designations was reached with the F4U-5NL, which was a winterized (L), night fighter (N) adaptation of the fifth variant (5) of Vought's (U) fourth (4) fighter (F) design. After this came the XF4U-6 close support aircraft (later redesignated AU-1) used solely by the Marine Corps, and the F4U-7 delivered to France. During the Korean War an F4U Corsair shot down a MiG-15 jet fighter – no small accomplishment.

The Corsair not only continued to fight in the 1950–53 Korean conflict but even remained in production, the final F4U-7 being delivered on 24 December 1952. In all, 12,571 were built. No other fighter even came close to the Corsair's record of longevity on the production line.

Corsair Described

With its low gull wing, the F4U Corsair may have looked somewhat unconventional. But it was, in fact, a straightforward design of all-metal construction. Not easy to taxi or to land and take off, because of its poor pilot visibility over the long nose, the Corsair was exceedingly graceful once aloft and is worth mentioning among those warplanes significant for their aesthetic qualities.

A production Corsair's inverted gull wing had a span of 41ft (12.49m). Its rounded fuselage was 33ft

A Marine F4U-1D Corsair of VMF-124/213 (a composite unit made up from two squadrons) lands aboard the USS *Essex* (CV-9) on 27 February 1945 while a TBM Avenger passes overhead. Note the bulky centre-line fuel tank attached at two points. (via Jim Sullivan)

F4U-1D Corsairs of VMF-221, VMF-451 and VF-84 warming up for a mission to Tokyo from the deck of the USS *Bunker Hill* (CV-17) on 16 February 1945. All three squadrons aboard the carrier wore the upward-pointing arrow as their geometrical symbol. By this point in the war, carrier task forces were operating close to the Japanese home islands. (via Jim Sullivan)

4in (10.16m) in length. The Navy fighter stood 16ft 1in (4.90m) in height, and wing area was a relatively modest 314sq ft (29.17m^2). On a typical mission the aircraft weighed 8,982lb (4,074kg) empty, and about 14,000lb (6,350kg) fully loaded.

From the time of its first flight, there was never any doubt that the Corsair was a quantum leap over pre-war fighters in terms of speed and endurance. Maximum speed on a typical combat mission was 417mph (671km/h) at 19,900ft (6,065m), although far greater speeds were reached diving in clean condition. The Corsair was credited with an initial climb rate of 2,890ft (881m) per minute. Service ceiling was 36,900ft (11,247m). Early Corsairs were credited with a range of 1,015 miles (1,633km) in clean condition, a figure which rose to around 1,300 miles (2,092km) in later aircraft. With drop-tanks, the range of the Corsair went up to 1,596 miles (2,569km) when cruising at 179mph (288km/h).

Flying the F4U

It is perhaps unfortunate that not many naval aviators were in a position to compare the Corsair and Hellcat. Most fighter squadrons converted from the F4F Wildcat to one of the two more advanced fighters, but very few pilots actually flew both.

Those who flew the F4U Corsair no doubt felt that they had, in their hands, the finest naval fighter of its era. Although the Hellcat was developed more quickly (after starting later), it had been recognized all along that the less orthodox Corsair was more powerful, could range further, and could carry a heavier weapons load.

The pilot of the F4U Corsair sat high and tightly strapped in a narrow metal seat which had life-raft and emergency supplies stowed underneath. The all-

aluminium fuselage and inverted gull wing were stronger than they looked and the Corsair was stressed for high manoeuvrability: the right pilot with the right touch could literally fling it around the sky. The Corsair pilot certainly lacked good forward visibility when taxiing on the ground (a problem which some solved by having a ground crewman sit, legs hanging over the wing leading edge, giving hand signals). Much exaggerated, however, are accounts of visibility problems while landing and taking off, especially on and from carrier decks. These accounts overlook the fact that an aircraft can move: the Corsair pilot needing to check his alignment on runway or carrier deck needed only to dip a wing in order to have an excellent view.

Once the air-to-ground potential of the Corsair had been exploited to the full, a newspaper article of the era dubbed the aeroplane the 'Super Stuka'. In air-to-air combat, the F4U owed no apology to the Hellcat or the 'Zero' and its record of aerial kills speaks for itself.

An early plan to equip the Corsair with 20 small anti-aircraft bombs was discarded (the idea had been that the bomblets would be dropped on opposing fighters from above), but with both machine-guns and cannon the Corsair proved to be an exceedingly stable gun platform.

Commander William F. (Toby) Tobin, Jr, one of the very few Hellcat pilots who did make the switch (as quoted by researcher Barrett Tillman) offered some insights into belatedly strapping into a Corsair. Tobin joined squadron VBF-75A in the final months of the war after considerable experience in the Hellcat. 'I didn't care much for the Corsair the first ten or fifteen hours,' Tobin admitted. Only 5ft 6in (1.70m) in height himself, he cited the inherent problem of visibility for a pilot who was not built like a basketball player. When a shift was made from FG-1D to F4U-4, the latter with improved canopy, things got better. 'Once I could see out of it, I loved it.' In the immediate post-war weeks, Tobin proclaimed F4U-4 BuNo 97420 'the best damn machine the Atlantic Fleet ever had'.

Because the Corsair began the war as a land-based Marine fighter it was with Marine squadrons that the Corsair won much of its glory. Almost all had previously operated the F4F Wildcat. These included:

VMF-111 'Devildogs', which made use of one of several early modifications to the F4U-1A Corsair to enable the fighter to become a fighter-bomber with a centre-line bomb, flying the very first Corsair fighter-bomber strike from Mille atoll on 18 March 1944.

VMF-112 'Wolf Pack', which was briefly headed by Major Gregory (Pappy) Boyington (Marine ace of aces with 28 victories), credited with 140 enemy aircraft, and eventually went aboard the carrier USS *Bennington* (CV-20) and fought over Japan.

VMF-113, which fought in the Marshalls.

VMF-114, which fought at Peleliu.

VMF-115 'Joe's Jokers', later nicknamed 'Able Eagles', which was headed for a time by Medal of Honor holder Major Joseph J. Foss. The squadron was assisted by a visit by Colonel Charles A. Lindbergh who was instrumental in converting the

A Vought F4U-1D Corsair of VF-84 launches from the USS *Bunker Hill* (CV-17) within range of the Japanese home islands on 16 January 1945. Note lowered flaps partitioned at the trailing edge of the Corsair's distinctive inverted-gull wing. (via Jim Sullivan)

Corsair to a fighter-bomber. Later on, the squadron fought in the Philippines. Its pilots experimented with wedging a second person, an army observer, into the cramped single seat of the F4U-1A to point out Japanese targets on the ground.

VMF-121 'Wolfraiders', which achieved 208 air combat victories.

VMF-122 'Werewolves', in which Boyington also served, which scored 35 air-to-air kills, and fought at Peleliu.

VMF-123 'Eight Ball', which tallied up 56 aerial victories and flew from the carrier *Bennington*.

VMF-124 'Checkerboards', headed by Major

These Marine Corps F4U-1A Corsair fighters, wings folded for deck stowage, were aboard the escort carrier USS *Kalinin Bay* on 21 January 1944. Several days later, squadron VMF-422 launched these F4U-1As to an island base and lost many aircraft and pilots in a severe storm. (via Jim Sullivan)

William Gise, which was the first squadron to take Corsairs into combat, starting on Guadalcanal in February 1943. The squadron downed 78 enemy aircraft. Later in the war this squadron also flew from *Essex*.

VMF-211, originally a Wildcat unit which suffered ground losses at Pearl Harbor, which was best known for close support on Bougainville. Later in the war this squadron ended up in China with some of the few F4U-4 versions to become operational during the conflict.

VMF-212 'Lancers', which produced Medal of Honor winner Major H. W. Bauer, and fought from Vella Lavella (where strikes were mounted against Rabaul) through to Okinawa.

VMF-214 'Black Sheep', which was 28-kill Boyington's best-known squadron. The squadron operated from Vella Lavella in support of troops on Bougainville and against Rabaul, and later was at Eniwetok flying strikes on Wotje, Maloelap, Mille, and Jalult in the Marshalls where late Japanese resistance continued well into 1944.

VMF-213, which fought in New Caledonia.

VMF-215 'Fighting Corsairs', commanded initially by Major Robert Owens, which struggled through the mud at Munda, New Georgia, and lost a fair number of its birdcage-cockpit Corsairs to accidents under primitive operating conditions. The squadron went on to achieve 137 aerial victories.

VMF-216, which landed some of the first F4U-1A Corsairs to arrive on Bougainville in December 1943 when that island was retaken from the Japanese. One of the squadron's fighters got into a gruelling battle with Japanese fighters over New Britain on 12

January 1944 and was so badly damaged that its vertical and horizontal tail were virtually non-existent, yet the F4U-1A managed to survive and land safely. The squadron belatedly operated from the carrier USS *Wasp* (CV-10).

VMF-217, which fought at Peleliu and operated from *Wasp* after the restriction on carrier operations by the Corsair was lifted. VMF-216 and VMF-217 later flew from *Wasp* against targets on the Japanese mainland, hitting Yokosuka and Tateyama airfields during the invasion of Iwo Jima.

VMF-221 'Wake Island Avengers', also called 'Fighting Falcons', which regrouped at Guadalcanal following the Wake loss and returned to Japan aboard the USS *Bunker Hill* (CV-17). In the late carrier operations, the squadron produced two aces almost overnight, Captain W. M. Snider with 6½ kills and First Lieutenant J. McManus with 6.

VMF-222 'Flying Deuces', which achieved 53 aerial victories. The 'Deuces' at Green Island in February 1944 created locally one of the first devices to carry a 500lb (227kg) bomb under the Corsair's centre-line.

VMF-224, which fought through to the end of the war.

VMF-311 'Hells Belles', which flew the cannon-armed F4U-1C version and went into action late in the war, making its combat debut on Okinawa.

VMF-313, which fought at Leyte.

VMF-321 'Hell's Angels', which flew briefly from a carrier deck and at Guam.

VMF-322, which was one of the first squadrons to land on Okinawa, the final prize of the island-hopping campaign, in April 1945.

VMF-323, which fought at Okinawa and was one of a number of squadrons late in the war to introduce 5in HVAR (high velocity aircraft rockets) for air-to-ground combat.

VMF-422, which is remembered most for a bizarre 25 January 1944 incident in which bad weather literally wiped out a squadron of Corsairs. Flying from Hawkins Field on Tarawa atoll – won at enormous cost in the island-hopping campaign which brought the Allies closer to Japan – 23 Corsairs took off on the 700-mile (1,127km) trip to Funafuti with a stop planned at Nanomea 463 miles (745km) from Tarawa. After a series of problems with blinding rain squalls, all but one of the Corsairs had to be ditched at sea in a series of incidents which cost 22 aircraft and six lives.

VMF-441 'Black Jacks', which was the second of the two Marine squadrons to operate the cannon-armed F4U-1C Corsair. The squadron went into action at Yontan Field, Okinawa, in April 1945.

VMF-451 'Warlords', which flew the F4U-1D in action at Okinawa in April 1945. In heavy fighting off

Okinawa, this Marine squadron aboard *Bunker Hill* produced air ace Major A. G. Donahue with a score of 5.

VMF-511, which operated F4U-1Ds from the escort carrier USS *Block Island*.

VMF-512, which flew from the USS *Gilbert Islands*, a Navy carrier which had all-Marine squadrons on board, during the final island-hopping battle on Okinawa.

VMF-532, as previously noted, which was the only Marine night fighter squadron to fly Corsairs during the war.

The USS *Essex* (CV-9) boasted the first operational Marine Corps squadrons to fly Corsairs from the deck of a fast carrier. VMF-123 and VMF-124 flew their first combat air strikes on 3 January 1945 against Okinawa, as part of Task Force 38.

Navy Squadrons

The US Navy's best-known Corsair squadron was VF-17, the 'Skull and Crossbones', commanded by Lieutenant Commander John T. (Tommy) Blackburn.

Ironically, VF-17 began its career by being removed from *Bunker Hill* to land-based duty because the Corsair did so poorly on its first carrier suitability flights. The US Navy did not want the Corsair on carriers until its spirited landing characteristics could

be tamed. A related factor was a nagging shortage of Corsair parts which went beyond the routine problem of stocking spares for a new aircraft type.

Despite this awkward beginning which resulted in its first combat being mounted from land bases, Blackburn's VF-17 produced no fewer than fifteen air aces, among them Lieutenant Ira C. (Ike) Kepford who flew an F4U-1A and had downed 16 Japanese aircraft by early 1944. In the Solomons, VF-17 downed 156 enemy aircraft in 76 days! 146½ more aerial victories followed.

Numerous other Navy squadrons operated the Corsair throughout the conflict. Of many in the Pacific war, VF- and VBF-83 downed the most Japanese aircraft, producing no fewer than eleven aces and scoring 228 kills from the deck of *Essex* between March and August 1945 as the war pressed towards its conclusion.

Today, the Corsair is a rare bird. Considering how many were built, the type survives only in disappointingly small numbers. Furthermore, the very few Corsair 'warbirds' which appear at air shows are nearly all post-war models. So a great deal of credit should go to an intrepid British flier who has restored a rare F4U-1 Corsair with 'birdcage' cockpit and flies it regularly at open days on the continent. For the purist, the US Naval Aviation Museum in Pensacola maintains in non-flying condition no fewer than three Corsairs, an F4U-4 and two FG-1Ds.

Another view of Goodyear FG-1D Corsair (BuNo 17883) which became a 'warbird', appearing at air shows long after VJ-Day. On 7 June 1974 during a show at Olathe, Kansas, the Corsair was damaged at the end of its display, making an emergency wheels-up landing in a cornfield. It was repaired. (Clyde Gerdes)

The 'Also Rans'

The upheaval and suffering of a global conflict gave the Allies fighter aircraft never to be forgotten, among them the Spitfire, Mustang and Hellcat. But the war also produced a series of fighters that failed to make the grade for one reason or another, or which were overtaken by events. Many of them contributed significantly to our knowledge and understanding. Most, like the 'also rans' of horse racing which fail to win a place, achieved little glory and earned little space in the history books.

Throughout the war the idea came up again and again of a powerful, long-range, twin-engined fighter which could intercept an enemy far from friendly shores or escort bombers on deep penetration missions. The Grumman XF5F-1 Skyrocket, a twin-engined shipboard fighter for the Navy, has already been mentioned. In November 1939 a revised version, the company G-46, was offered to the Army Air Corps. Enough interest was shown for the Army to contract for a single prototype. The order was placed on 3 August 1939, at the same time as the Lockheed XP-49 touched upon earlier. It was one of the few occasions when only one example of an aircraft type was placed on order, and this was to prove a short-sighted economy.

By January 1941 Grumman were able to advise the US Navy that 'this contractor is constructing an airplane for the US Army Air Corps which is similar in general design to the XF5F-1 but incorporates most of the latest combat features and also tricycle landing gear. With these features already incorporated, it is believed that this model airplane more truly represents the type of fighter now desired by the (Navy). Flight tests of the airplane are scheduled to begin two weeks from this date'.

The Grumman XP-50, as the company G-46 became known, was said to be capable of a maximum speed of 427mph (687km/h) and a service ceiling of 40,000ft (12,192m), both very respectable figures. In retrospect, it is believed that these figures were greatly exaggerated and that the XP-50 actually attained 360mph (579km/h) and 35,000ft (10,668m) – even so, quite a respectable performance.

It looks like a Lightning, but the XP-49, first flown on 11 November 1942, was intended as a major improvement over its P-38 predecessor and would have been a flying arsenal, armed with two 20mm cannon and four 0.50in (12.7mm) machine-guns. The XP-49 was underpowered and never won a production contract, but like so many one-off experimental aircraft, it contributed substantially to fighter development. (Lockheed)

The XP-50 had a non-folding wing, large fuselage of beautiful streamline form, and, as promised, tricycle gear. Dimensions of the new fighter included: wing span 42ft (12.80m), length 38ft 11in (11.86m), height 11ft 5.5in (3.49m), and wing area 303.5sq ft (28.19m^2). Power was provided by two supercharged 1,200hp Wright R-1820-67/69 Cyclone 9-cylinder radial engines driving three-bladed Curtiss constant-speed propellers. The Cyclone was, of course, the key to many wartime fighters, not surprisingly the F4F Wildcat for one.

The very busy Bob Hall took the sole XP-50 (39-2517) aloft for its first flight on 18 February 1941. Ever since then many written accounts have stated that the XP-50 crashed on its first flight. It may never be known how this misconception became so deep-rooted. Grumman, who maintain by far the best history office of any US manufacturer, possess no surviving report of this maiden flight and neither Hall nor designer Dick Hutton are still alive to be asked. So far as can be determined, the premier voyage of this graceful 'twin' was eventless.

XP-50 Myths

Nevertheless, the XP-50 gave birth to widely published inaccuracies. One report says that the airframe was eventually written off after suffering serious damage. In March 1941 the XP-50 was damaged when its right mainwheel undercarriage leg collapsed during a skid on an icy runway, but the fighter was flying again by May.

The XP-50 might not have been able to travel very far on a combat mission, the usual figure for its range of 585 miles (941km) being optimistic at best, but there can be no doubt the aircraft was heavily armed. Planned armament was two fixed 0.50in (12.7mm) machine-guns and two fixed 20mm cannon in the fuselage nose. A study for the installation of a 37mm cannon was planned. The aircraft was said to be able to carry two 100lb (45kg) bombs beneath its wings. However, no documents exist to confirm that the weaponry was ever installed.

The capabilities of the XP-50 were never to be realized because of what happened not on its first flight but on its fifteenth, by which time some 20 hours' flying time had been accumulated. On 14 May 1941 Hall had the XP-50 in a steep climb at almost full power when one engine's turbo-supercharger failed violently. Hall heard a loud crack and the rending of metal. The aircraft could still be flown with one engine and Hall managed to lower one main landing gear, but the nose wheel would not come down even when Hall applied additional pressure from an emergency air bottle. Hall's words:

'What had happened, one of the turbo-superchargers had blown up. The flying blades cut the hydraulic lines to the landing gear and to the nose wheel. And they also cut the emergency cable which would enable me to unlock and lower the nose wheel without any hydraulics. So I flew around, talking to the ground and trying to get the landing gear down and the nose wheel down, and by that time the oil in the hydraulic lines was all gone and

With Bob Hall at the controls, the sole Grumman XP-50 runs up its twin R-1820-67/69 engines on an unpaved airfield near the Grumman plant at Bethpage, New York. The XP-50 was lost so early in its test programme that it never really had a chance to be properly evaluated. (via M. J. Kasiuba)

The Grumman XP-50 is not often depicted in flight and, in fact, did not fly for very long before test pilot Bob Hall had to abandon the aircraft and bale out over Long Island Sound. The fighter looks as if it would have been potent, but would have had short range. (via M. J. Kasiuba)

This close-up of the Grumman XP-50 is believed to be previously unpublished. Although contributing little to the war, the XP-50 did influence the post-war F7F Tigercat which fought with US Marines in Korea. (Grumman)

The Grumman XF5F-1 Skyrocket, closely related to the XP-50, was the mount of the fictitious 'Blackhawk' cartoon hero of the 1940s but was never a part of the Fleet, perhaps because Grumman was very busy manufacturing excellent single-engined fighters. (Grumman)

the main wheels were down and the nose wheel was still up. It was quite impossible for me to land the airplane without a nose wheel because it would have gone end over end and I wasn't about to ride that, so I left it over Long Island Sound and came down in a parachute and was picked up about forty minutes later.'

Hall is modest in describing the contortions he went through in mid-air. Rather than simply jump and risk being hit by the XP-50's twin tail, he climbed very deliberately from the cockpit, slid along the turtle-back of the fuselage, and dropped off from between the vertical tails. He apparently watched the aircraft crash in the water north of Eaton's Neck.

A small boy on City Island beach who watched the final frenzy of the XP-50 saw a piece of the aircraft splash into the water close by. He fished out one of the superchargers, which had been assembled with bolts made of the wrong metal. The two halves of the wheel had pulled apart and the blades (buckets) had separated, the fragments slashing the hydraulic lines.

Here, on the eve of global war, was the ultimate absurdity – producing only one example of a prototype rather than several. Grumman were very busy with Navy contracts and had never solidly connected with the Air Corps with any of their designs, but even after the crash, production chief Leon A. (Jake) Swirbul was asked whether Grumman could construct another XP-50. (The firm was soon to negotiate with the Air Corps for yet another twin-engined fighter, the XP-65). Swirbul replied that Grumman were so busy that they would not undertake to build another XP-50 unless the Air Corps were ready to order a thousand P-50s. Thus ended Grumman's brief fling with producing anything important that did not go to the Navy.

The Army's next designation, P-51, became well enough known to occupy no small amount of space

elsewhere in this volume. The Bell XP-52 was to have been a twin-boom pusher fighter (not unlike the massive Vultee XP-54 described later), powered by a 1,200hp Continental XIV-1430-5 liquid-cooled engine. The Curtiss XP-53, a more conventional aircraft planned as a P-40 replacement, was to have been powered by a derivative of the same engine; with a different powerplant, it emerged as the XP-60 described later in this section. Apart from this reincarnation, neither the XP-52 nor the XP-53 progressed anywhere near the point of actually being built and flown, but the three designations to follow were allotted to pusher fighters which did at least get into the air and make a technical contribution.

Vultee XP-54

Of the three pusher fighters built in response to US Army 'Request for Data R40-C' dated 20 February 1940 and flown experimentally (Vultee XP-54, Curtiss XP-55, Northrop XP-56), Vultee's aeroplane was by far the largest and might well have proved the ideal mixture of high speed and heavy firepower.

The XP-54 (company model 84) was, very simply, the largest single-engined fighter to wear US Army Air Corps insignia. Its dimensions indicate its size: wing span 53ft 10in (16.41m), length 54ft 9in (16.69m), height 13ft (3.96m), wing area 456sq ft (42.36m^2) – a DC-3 transport was only 10ft longer. At maximum take-off weight, the XP-54 tipped the scales at 19,335lb (8,770kg), or rather more than half again the weight of a fully loaded Mustang on a combat mission.

Ordered in 1941 together with the superficially related XP-55 and XP-56, the twin-boom, single-seat, tricycle-gear Vultee fighter was designed around the 1,850hp Pratt & Whitney XR-1800-A4G engine and was to have contra-rotating propellers.

The Vultee XP-54 was a twin-boom pusher fighter and was the largest single-seat fighter of its era with a wing span of 53ft 10in (16.41m) and a maximum take-off weight of 19,335lb (8,770kg). Unfortunately, it had no clearly defined advantages over fighters in production at the time. (Convair)

The Curtiss CW-24B was a full-scale flying test-bed for the planned XP-55 pursuit ship for the US Army Air Forces. It was evaluated at a little-known site in the Californian desert, named in reverse after the Corum brothers who settled the region. In later years Muroc became less remote and in due course became Edwards Air Force Base. (USAF)

The Curtiss CW-24B went through several minor modifications while being tested. The final version shown in both illustrations had enlarged elevator and wingtip extensions protruding beyond the vertical tails. (USAF)

With this power, the aircraft was expected to reach a speed of 446mph (717km/h). Neither Germany nor Japan had anything quite like it, although a smaller aircraft of almost identical configuration, the SAAB J 21, was being developed in Sweden.

The intended powerplant of the big XP-54 was cancelled prematurely and the aircraft had to be completed instead with a 2,300hp Lycoming XH-2470-1 24-cylinder liquid-cooled engine driving a single four-bladed propeller. Two XP-54 prototypes were built (41-1210 and 41-1211), the first flying on 15 January 1943. The camouflaged first prototype made 86 flights in California before being ferried on 28 October 1943 to Wright Field, Ohio, where further testing apparently occurred only on a limited basis.

The second XP-54, which remained in natural metal, reportedly made only one flight. The potential of the XP-54 was apparent, especially as it was yet another Army fighter designed to carry a heavy armament: plans called for two 37mm cannon and two 0.50in (12.7mm) machine-guns. In addition, the XP-54 was fitted with a nose section that could be tilted upwards to lob its low-velocity cannon shells at their target, while its machine-guns remained in

depressed position. This feature remained of interest long after the XP-54 was no longer flying, and was studied by armament experts at Eglin Field, Florida, possibly as late as 1944.

Another gadget in the ingenious XP-54 harkened to the future ejection systems which would be needed for jet aircraft (in fact, its Swedish cousin, the SAAB J 21, was history's first warplane with an ejection seat). In an emergency bale-out from the XP-54, the pilot's seat slid downwards and a hinged panel protected him from being hurled back into the pusher propellers. A similar arrangement was to be employed operationally on jet warplanes long after VJ-Day.

Actual performance figures of the XP-54 with its second-choice powerplant include a maximum speed of 403mph (649km/h), initial climb rate of 2,300ft (701m) per minute, service ceiling of 37,000ft (11,278m) and an unimpressive range of 500 miles (805km). As with so many of the experimental aircraft of the war era, these figures may reflect hope rather than documentation. An even bigger version with the same configuration, the Vultee XP-68 Tornado, progressed far in the design stage but was never built or flown.

Curtiss XP-55

Second in the trio of pusher fighters assembled in response to the 1940 requirement, the Curtiss XP-55 Ascender was essentially a flying wing with a small fuselage and a canard (with only the horizontal portion of the tail forward of the wing). Troubled, delayed, and certainly not top priority at Curtiss's St Louis, Missouri plant, the XP-55 was long in coming but in due course led to a test programme which involved four airframes.

Curtiss built a full-scale flying test-bed, the company model CW-24B, powered by an 850hp Menasco C65-5 engine. In 1942, under conditions of great secrecy, the fabric-covered CW-24B went to a new US Army test site, the remote and hush-hush airstrip at Muroc Dry Lake, California. Early flight tests with this 'proof of concept' vehicle were only partly resolved by moving its vertical fins further out from their initial mid-position on the swept-back wing.

The full-size XP-55 fighter was ordered in 1942, based on the proven 1,475hp Allison V-1710-F23R engine being used for the first time as a pusher. As with its Vultee counterpart, the Curtiss XP-55 had been planned for contra-rotating propellers but flew instead with a single three-bladed propeller.

After the CW-24B programme, the first of three XP-55 experimental aircraft (42-78845 to 42-78847) was delivered on 13 July 1943 and underwent early flights at Scott Field, Illinois, just across the Mississippi from the Curtiss plant. These early flights showed a need for an elevator re-design, which was accomplished. But before it could be rebuilt in response to the problem, the first machine was lost during spin tests at St Louis on 15 November 1943. The pilot parachuted to safety.

The second XP-55 was flown at St Louis on 9 January 1944. The third followed on 25 April 1944 and, soon after, went to Eglin Field, Florida, for tests of its four nose-mounted 0.50in (12.7mm) machine-guns. The XP-55 had the advantage of being constructed largely from non-strategic materials and for a time a jet version, the company model CW-24C, was studied. But lingering problems, including generally poor stability, remained unsolved when the third XP-55 was returned to Wright Field, Ohio, for further tests continuing into 1945. The third machine is the only example known to have flown with drop-tanks beneath its wings.

On 27 May 1945, at a Wright Field air show and bond rally attracting a crowd of more than 100,000, Captain William C. Glascow took off in this third XP-55 to give a public flying display. It must have been quite a sight, for Glascow flew across the field leading five other fighters in formation. The pilot made one roll before the crowd, began another, and suddenly dived into the ground inverted. Portions of the wreckage killed a nearby motorist and Glascow, thrown from the wreckage, sustained mortal injuries.

Practical testing of the XP-55 seems already to have been at an end at this juncture and the crash merely provided a sombre finish to what had been an exceedingly ambitious flight programme and one which contributed substantially to aviation knowledge. The second XP-55 has survived and is in the hands of, although not yet displayed by, the National Air and Space Museum in Washington, DC.

Figures of XP-55 performance show a maximum speed of 390mph (627km/h), service ceiling of 34,600ft (10,546m), and range of 490 miles (789km). Dimensions included wing span 44ft 6in (13.56m), length 29ft 7in (9.01m), height 10ft (3.04m), wing area 235sq ft (21.83m²). The aircraft was very much

Based upon the CW-24B demonstrator, three examples of the XP-55 Ascender fighter were built and tested. Although it remained trouble-plagued and failed to win a production order, the XP-55 was flown extensively and contributed much to fighter development. (USAF)

At Muroc Dry Lake, short-lived
Northrop XP-56 'Bullet' number
one (41-786) with pilot John
Myers. After Myers' first flight, to
correct troublesome yaw
tendencies, a glove-like vertical
stabilizer was fitted where the
upper rear antenna fairing is seen
here. (Northrop)

a lightweight and had a maximum take-off weight of just 7,330lb (3,325kg).

Northrop XP-56

The Northrop XP-56, sometimes called the 'Bullet' or 'Black Bullet', completes the triumvirate of experimental pusher fighters built to the US Army's 1940 requirement, each with rear-mounted engines planned, at least, to drive contra-rotating propellers (as the XP-56 actually did). All were based on the idea that the pusher configuration offered lower aerodynamic drag (while leaving the nose in clean shape for armament) and, hence, better performance. More than the others, Northrop's design was truly a flying wing, not the first created under Jack K. Northrop's tutelage and most decidedly not the last.

Gaining from experience with the company's earlier N-9M flying wing and first flown by John Myers at Muroc Dry Lake on 6 September 1943, the XP-56 remained a well-kept secret until the war's end.

The Army had ordered two XP-56 fighters, serials 41-786 and 42-38353, at the bargain price of $411,000. The 2,400hp air-cooled Pratt & Whitney R-2800-29 Double Wasp powered the aircraft, which flew well despite its revolutionary configuration but would not have been able to manoeuvre very

convincingly in a dogfight. The unpressurized cockpit was positioned immediately ahead of the engine and the intended nose armament consisted of two 20mm cannon and four 0.50in (12.7mm) machine-guns, although these were never installed and gunnery tests were never conducted. It has been said in jest that the pilot had no time to worry about out-manoeuvring a foe or firing the guns: he was too busy worrying about how to bale out in an emergency with a six-bladed Curtiss Electric contra-rotating propeller at his back!

In fact, the problem had been thought of, and engineers even knew that ejection seats lay in the near future. Meanwhile, the problem of emergency egress was alleviated with an explosive cord wrapped around the engine gearbox. On paper at least, if the pilot was forced to jump, the cord could first be detonated, blowing away the propellers and the rear portion of the aircraft, and so, permitting a safe escape. It is impossible not to wonder if Crosby, apparently the only man other than Myers to fly the XP-56 (and later killed flying another Northrop aircraft), genuinely felt confidence in this rather unique method of insuring survival of the fittest.

After the all-silver XP-56 41-786 was wrecked in a mishap, which injured Myers (who lives in Los Angeles today), the camouflaged 42-38353 first flew on 23 March 1944 at Hawthorne, California, with

The camouflaged second Northrop XP-56 (42-38353) in a rare in-flight view taken over California. Test pilot Harry Crosby is at the controls. The second XP-56 has been saved and now belongs to the National Air and Space Museum. (Northrop)

In August 1944 at Hawthorne, California, watched by carefully vetted Northrop workers, Harry Crosby runs up the second XP-56. Blown-air outlet at rear wingtip steered this unorthodox pusher flying wing. (Northrop)

pilot Harry Crosby at the controls. This second machine had a greatly enlarged dorsal vertical stabilizer (not actually a rudder, since steering was done by blown-air jets at the wingtips, as the next paragraph explains) to improve yaw tendencies. Crosby found the XP-56 underpowered and, because it was nose-heavy, difficult to handle during the prolonged take-off run.

As ingenious as the pilot escape system were the XP-56's rudder bellows used for steering. During routine flying, air travelled through a horizontal passage at each wingtip. When a turn was necessary, the pilot moved rudder pedals which operated a valve that diverted the airflow to the bellows. Thus the power of the airstream itself was used to assist in operating split-flap rudders at the wingtips. This feature appeared only on the second XP-56.

By 1944 the few people privy to the secret already knew that jet-propelled warplanes offered more promise than a pusher – particularly this one, which looked as if someone had forgotten the fuselage and stepped on the blueprint for the wings. Northrop engineers had a number of suggestions to improve performance deficiencies, but at this late point in the war it no longer seemed economical to pursue them.

If figures generated at the time can be believed, the XP-56 'Black Bullet' would have been a commendably fast fighter. Performance figures included: top speed 465mph (748km/h), service ceiling 33,800ft (10,302m), and range 660 miles (1,062km). In the heat of California's Mojave Desert, another superlative figure would have been the already mentioned long take-off run, but no measurement for this seems to have been recorded.

The XP-56 weighed about 8,700lb (2,946kg) empty and had a maximum take-off weight of 12,143lb (5,507kg). Dimensions included wing span 43ft 7in (13.28m), length 27ft 7in (8.40m), height 11ft (3.35m), and wing area 307sq ft (28.52m^2). It is intriguing to note that the XP-56's compact size might have made it an ideal candidate for stowage aboard an aircraft-carrier, had there been any reason.

As this volume went to press, a group of California aviation enthusiasts had almost completed the restoration of the surviving XP-56.

Tucker XP-57

In the arcane world of 'also ran' fighters, few are as obscure as the unbuilt Tucker XP-57. The entrepreneur (first name unknown) Tucker is best remembered as a builder of motor cars who sought to revolutionize ownership of efficient cars amid post-war prosperity. The XP-57 was not just the only

fighter but the only aircraft designed by the Tucker firm in Detroit and marks one of several efforts (the Bell XP-77 is another) to discard unnecessary weight and equipment and to develop an exceedingly simple, lightweight fighter.

Inspired, apparently, by pre-war racers which set numerous speed records, the XP-57 was to have made extensive use of wood in its construction, with a modicum of aluminium-covered steel tubing, making it attractive for its paucity of strategic materials. Proposed in 1940, it seems to have been doomed from the start by its manufacturer's financial and management difficulties.

A single-seat fighter with a 720hp Miller L-510-1 liquid-cooled engine driving a simple two-bladed propeller, the XP-57 would have had its engine buried behind the pilot and driven by an extension shaft passing between the pilot's legs. The XP-57 was said to be capable of 308mph (495km/h) with a service ceiling of 20,000ft (6,096m) and range of 960 miles (1,545km), although these figures must be viewed with some scepticism. So far as can be determined, no accurate likeness of the proposed XP-57 exists today. Like so many builders of the wartime era, Tucker went out of business in the immediate post-war years, apparently without making any effort to preserve historical records.

In the first chapter dealing with the immortal Lightning, the much larger Lockheed XP-58 Chain Lightning was mentioned. Another attempt to produce a very large, twin-engined fighter for long-range work – strongly supported by Colonel Elliott Roosevelt, the President's son – the XP-58 stemmed from a 27 April 1943 Army contract to create a bigger, better-performing version of the P-38 and similar XP-49. The XP-58 was designed by Lockheed's engineering wizard, Clarence (Kelly) Johnson.

On D-Day, 6 June 1944, the first of two of these behemoths (41-2670 and 41-2671) took to the air. Tests were conducted at Muroc and later at Wright Field, although the second prototype was never completed. The XP-58 was powered by two 2,100hp Allison V-3420-11 turbo-supercharged, liquid-cooled 24-cylinder engines driving huge four-bladed propellers. Flying continued until the end of the war, but the Army had long since resisted the concept of a 'convoy fighter' to escort long-range bombers to their targets, having found the P-51D Mustang with drop-tanks more than adequate.

The size of the XP-58 is illustrated by its dimensions: wing span 70ft (21.34m), length 49ft 5in (15.06m), height 12ft (3.66m), and wing area 600sq ft (55.74m^2). Even when empty, the twin-boomed, mid-wing craft weighed no less than 20,000lb

In motion at the Lockheed facility at Burbank, the giant XP-58 Chain Lightning reveals its awesome size and (from the front at least) its graceful shape. A vigorous test programme was carried out with the XP-58 before the idea of a large 'convoy fighter' was dropped. (Lockheed)

The huge Lockheed XP-58 Lightning on an early test flight over California. Two aircraft were built and the first belatedly made its first flight on D-Day, 6 June 1944. (Lockheed)

▷ A little-seen view of the XP-58, apparently at Wright Field, Ohio. While superficially it resembled Lockheed's P-38 Lightning, the XP-58 was fully one-third larger. (USAF)

(9,072kg) and when fully loaded its weight became 39,200lb (17,781kg). The XP-58 was said to be capable of a speed of 436mph (701km/h), service ceiling of 40,000ft (12,192m), and range of 3,000 miles (4,828km).

Hughes D-2

The 'convoy fighter' concept also led to an aircraft developed solely on a private basis by Howard Hughes, and tested in a California locale more remote even than Muroc, where it remained so secret that no photo of it has ever been published. Even USAAF chief General Henry H. (Hap) Arnold was refused permission by Hughes' company to visit the facility at Harper Dry Lake where the Hughes D-2 was hangared.

The Hughes D-2 was viewed as a flying 'destroyer' able to shoot down enemy aircraft with the sheer force of its firepower. The D-2 was to have had four 0.50in (12.7mm) machine-guns in the nose and four more in a remotely controlled turret at the rear of an elliptical fuselage body located between twin booms in the manner of the Lockheed XP-58.

When Arnold asked Hughes to bring the D-2 to Bolling Field in Washington, DC, to be inspected by the top brass, the entrepreneur – although hoping

for a production order – not only refused but declined to say whether the sole example had actually flown. Apparently it never did, although even that fact remains uncertain.

Eventually Hughes did roll out the sole D-2 for viewing by Colonel Roosevelt, who favoured it over the XP-58 and was in fact quite enthusiastic. However, in due course Roosevelt shifted his own interests and viewed the aircraft as a photo platform for the anticipated 1946 invasion of Japan. Before any decision could be made on its use and before the aircraft could be shown to the outside world, the Hughes D-2 was destroyed in a mysterious hangar fire, said to have been caused by a lightning strike in a thunderstorm.

Although the world never saw the Hughes D-2 or learned what it might have done, a similar aircraft emerged in the post-war period as the Hughes XF-11 (company DX-5), two prototypes of which were built as photo-reconnaissance machines and tested extensively. Flight tests of the sleek, twin-boom, high-wing XF-11 are outside the scope of this book, but it might be mentioned that the first aeroplane was the one in which Howard Hughes survived a spectacular crash on 7 July 1946. Known in his final years for his isolation and eccentricities, Hughes was as much an aviation pioneer as many

of the other figures whose work in aircraft development is described here.

The US Army Air Corps assigned the XP-59 designation to the Bell Airacomet, the first American jet-propelled fighter. Because the advent of the jet is part of the war's finale, the XP-59 is described in the concluding chapter.

The Curtiss XP-60 came earlier and might have been one of the successful propeller-driven fighters of the war had not so many other aircraft been more readily suitable for mass production.

In fact, fighters holding the XP-60 designation, starting from the foundation laid by the unbuilt XP-53 design, became a family of aircraft, quite different from each other, each representing another stab at a P-40 replacement. Curtiss's apparent trial-and-error approach produced four airframes which ended up holding nine designations: XP-60, XP-60A, YP-60A, P-60A, XP-60B, XP-60C, XP-60D, XP-60E and YP-60E. Few records or photos have survived of this diverse assortment of Curtiss fighters, but at the time each occupied designers and engineers on an urgent basis.

Powered by a 1,300hp Packard V-1650-1 licence-built Merlin liquid-cooled engine, the XP-60 (42-79245) was a low-wing, single-seat fighter which made its first flight on 18 September 1941. It was the one aircraft in the series that bore the greatest external resemblance to the familiar P-40. Three YP-60A fighters were similarly powered, but the Air Corps had no interest in diverting Merlin engines from the up-and-coming P-51 Mustang. The XP-60A and XP-60B designations were allocated to versions having other engines which apparently were studied but not built.

The XP-60C was originally to have been powered by the mighty Chrysler XIV-2220 employed by the XP-47H. Before this modification of an existing aircraft could be completed, the powerplant was changed to an R-2800-53 radial with Curtiss-Wright contra-rotating propellers. With this engine, the XP-60C flew on 27 January 1943, by which time the USAAF had already decided that this series of fighters would not receive a production order.

The prototype in the series was rebuilt as the XP-60D with a V-1650-3 of the kind that powered the P-51B Mustang. This 'D' model had enlarged tail surfaces and other minor changes.

The XP-60E was another model powered by the R-2800 engine and first flew on 26 May, 1943, while the similarly powered YP-60E introduced a bubble canopy. The YP-60E may have been close to the

Although the Curtiss XP-60 was originally designed for the Rolls-Royce Merlin engine, the XP-60C (42-79425) ended up with the Pratt & Whitney R-2800 radial. In neither guise was the P-60 able to prove itself more desirable than the Thunderbolt and Mustang already in mass production. (USAF)

best-looking American fighter of the war, but its time had passed. To an engineer, the full story of these four aircraft attracting nine designations might make a fascinating study. To the US Army, the XP-60 series ended up having no operational mission.

Curtiss XP-62

Curtiss still had one final aircraft to complete in the long series which included the XP-42, XP-46, XP-53 and XP-60. Possibly the largest single-engined fighter of the war, the Curtiss XP-62 was powered by the huge 2,300hp Wright R-3350-17 radial with contra-rotating, three-bladed propellers. Armament was to have been a powerhouse of up to eight 20mm cannon. At one time the Army was committed to a purchase of 100 P-62As, but the R-3350 engine was sorely needed for the B-29 Superfortress. The sole

XP-62 made its first flight on 21 July 1943. The single example was used as a test-bed for cabin pressurization and contra-rotating propellers.

North American P-64

Fliers at Luke Field in Glendale, Arizona, in the immediate pre-war months saw on their flight line a snub-nosed North American aeroplane which looked like a trainer, was called a pursuit ship, and may have been of little use in either role. The North American P-64 (company model NA-68) had close family connection with the AT-6 Texan advanced trainer which gave many a pilot his wings but, unlike the AT-6, had but one seat.

In its civil guise, the aircraft had been ordered by Siam (Thailand) on 30 December 1939, and was itself an outgrowth of an earlier fighter which had

Viewed from above, the Curtiss P-60C fighter showed itself to be a very solid machine. Its paint job may not have been the best: heavy foot traffic appears to have severely weathered the camouflage on the port inboard wing. (USAF)

been delivered in modest numbers to Peru. In October 1940, the civil NA-68s were embargoed along with many other aircraft intended for foreign users. Taken into the US Army as the P-64, the first of six examples (41-19082 to 41-19087) made its first flight on 1 September 1940 piloted by Louis Wait.

The North American P-64 had a wing span of 37ft 3in (11.53m), length of 27ft (8.35m), height of 9ft (2.78m), and wing area of 228sq ft (21.18m^2). The aircraft was powered by an 870hp Wright R-1820-77 air-cooled radial driving a three-bladed propeller.

Performance figures credit the P-64 with a maximum speed of 270mph (435km/h), service ceiling of 14,000ft (4,267m) and range of 860 miles (1,384km). The aircraft weighed 4,660lb (2,114kg) empty and

5,990lb (2,717kg) fully loaded. Armament of two 0.30in (7.62mm) machine-guns on the nose cowling was installed but plans to include a 550lb (250kg) bombload and two wing 20mm cannon apparently did not materialize.

It appears that all P-64s remained at Luke and served as base 'hacks' or to enable pilots to log flying time. At least one of the half-dozen examples survived the war and was airworthy in the United States as recently as the late 1970s.

This, then, is a summary of a few of the 'also ran' fighter aircraft in American livery during the war years. Although none of them entered operational service, nearly all contributed to engineering knowledge and sometimes to the development of power-plants, weapons and tactics.

The designation of the North American P-64 may well have been assigned out of sequence, since the small pursuit ship was in service before Pearl Harbor. This side view at Luke Field was taken on 16 September 1941. (USAF)

Never published before, this snapshot by a wartime pilot is unique in showing two North American P-64s side-by-side at Luke Army Airfield, Arizona, early in the war. (via Robert F. Dorr)

The P-64 was in many respects a trainer with a single seat, and would never have stood a chance in air-to-air combat with top-line fighters of its era. This view, also at Luke Field, shows its family resemblance to the AT-6 Texan trainer. (USAF)

P-51 Mustang

I n 1939 Britain, despite the pre-war expansion programmes, urgently needed more fighters. Sir Henry Self of the British Purchasing Commission, who had been posted to New York to see how American industry could help his country's war needs, was seeing terms like 'urgent' and 'high priority' in despatches which came to him from home. Among Self's contacts was the aircraft manufacturer North American of Inglewood, California, which was doing a superb job building trainers but had no track record in the design and construction of warplanes.

Self's 1939 discussions with the firm's President and General Manager, James B. (Dutch) Kindelberger, marked the start of events which were to lead to the design of the North American P-51 Mustang.

Interestingly, Kindelberger had visited the Heinkel and Messerschmitt aircraft factories in 1938 and had taken notes on how the Germans were developing fighters with liquid-cooled engines.

For nearly half a century afterwards accolades bestowed upon the spirited filly from Inglewood affirmed that the Mustang was a '120-day wonder', dreamed up, designed, rolled out, and test-flown in the incredibly brief span of four months. A few detailed histories relate that this high-speed miracle occurred, in part, because Self secured co-operation from a more experienced maker of fighters, the Curtiss firm in Buffalo. To those who wanted to find out, it was known that North American's design team had access to Curtiss documents on the P-40, which at an earlier time had been Britain's choice.

Classic portrayal of the Mustang at war. One by one, stretching as far as the eye can see, P-51D Mustangs of the 457th Fighter Squadron, 506th Fighter Group, roll down the dusty path from their parking areas to the runway at Iwo Jima for a mission against the Japanese home islands. (via Jeffrey Ethell)

North American engineers who worked on the P-51 Mustang had access to a body of knowledge from another manufacturer, Curtiss. The Curtiss XP-42, actually a converted P-36 airframe (serial 38-4), was one of the 'also ran' fighter designs of the immediate pre-war era. (USAF)

Still, the legend persisted that North American's Vice President, J. Leeland Atwood, and a masterful team (led by Edgar Schmued and Raymond Rice) designed the Mustang from scratch and created it at lightning speed. In fact, Atwood spent months working with the British and with the Curtiss firm. Curtiss designer Don Berlin had created a sleek fighter called the XP-46 and Atwood gained access to it. Because it would have been uneconomical to halt P-40 production to introduce the only marginally better-performing XP-46, wind-tunnel data on Berlin's fighter were sold to North American in April 1940 for $56,000. It requires no graduate diploma in aeronautical engineering to see that the XP-46 and P-51 look very similar, but the sale of data and the full magnitude of the Curtiss/Don Berlin contribution

to the Mustang remained largely an insider's secret until researcher Jeffrey Ethell told all in his book *Mustang: A Documentary History* (Jane's, London, 1981).

What insiders knew, and Ethell disclosed, was that no plan ever existed to complete the prototype Mustang in 120 days. Nor was North American's design team working in isolation. None of this, however, should detract from the simple truth that the first aircraft was completed very rapidly and was, in almost every respect, a superb fighter design.

Some 78,000 engineering hours and 127 days went into the first aircraft, which was rolled out at Mines Field in Los Angeles on 9 September 1940. So hastily had the new fighter been assembled that it had no engine (until a couple of weeks later) and

Until the 1970s, when fresh research into the Mustang story was carried out by Jeffrey Ethell, it was not generally known that the Mustang's designers had access to material on the Curtiss XP-46, another of the experimental fighters of pre-war times. In fact, the XP-46 influenced the P-51 Mustang and the resemblance is apparent. (USAF)

Little-known view of XP-51 Mustang 41-38 taken late in its flying career, long after camouflage had been added to the once-silver aircraft (and given time to become weathered); post-1943 national insignia had also been added. The basic design was similar to the A-36 Apache dive-bomber, an early Mustang variant. (via Roger Besecker)

The XP-51B Mustang on the ground, carrying the four 20mm cannon also associated with the A-36 Apache. Unlike the XP-51, this machine has a four-bladed propeller. North American's emblem appears high on the vertical tail. (via Roger F. Besecker)

rolled on wheels borrowed from an AT-6 trainer. This first machine, known by its company designation NA-73X and bearing the civil registration NX19998, made its first flight on 26 October 1940 at Mines Field, with Vance Breese as pilot.

By this time France had fallen beneath the German onslaught and the need for better-performing fighters became critical. Outwardly there was little about the all-silver NA-73X to mark it as a quantum leap forward. A low-wing, flush-canopy, in-line-engined aircraft, the NA-73X introduced no real design innovations and looked more or less the same

as any other fighter in its class, Spitfire and Messerschmitt Bf 109 included. But the NA-73X did offer great promise, mostly because it used good ideas and used them well. Among these was a low, square-cut wing whose laminar-flow aerofoil reduced drag, and a radiator intake streamlined into the lower fuselage behind the pilot.

Although the progenitor of this fighter series had been designed for a greater fuel load than many of its contemporaries, the extra weight proved to be no impediment. Breese was delighted when the NA-73X attained a speed of 382mph (615km/h),

The second aircraft in this motley line-up is a P-51C, 42-103435, which was built with the flush canopy associated with early versions. This one survived the war but is part of a batch being destroyed by technicians using explosives during the dramatic reduction of the armed forces just after VJ-Day. (US Army)

making it as fast as early Spitfires which carried half as much fuel.

The life of NX19998 was to be cut short, however. On its ninth flight, on 20 November 1940, pilot Paul Balfour made an error in switching fuel-feed and the engine went dead at a critical moment. There was no time to attempt a re-start before aircraft and ground came together, the NA-73X piling up in an upside-down wreck. Unhurt, Balfour was more annoyed than worried as he clambered out of the inverted fighter. A major delay had just been introduced into the Mustang development programme, although the NA-73X did in fact resume flying on 11 January 1941 and continued to operate as part of the initial development programme until being retired on 15 July 1941.

The NA-73 was ordered into production for the RAF on 20 September 1940 under terms which specified that two examples would be delivered for testing to the US Army, designated XP-51. The first of these (41-038, also assigned British serial AG348) flew on 20 May 1941 at Inglewood, piloted by Robert Chilton.

P-51 Programme

Early plans for the new North American fighter called for the delivery to Britain of 620 production machines, designated Mustang Mk I by the RAF. Power was provided by a 1,150hp Allison V-1710-39 liquid-cooled engine driving a three-bladed propeller. After being rolled out on 16 April 1941, the

first Mustang I for the RAF (AG345), retaining the company designation NA-73, made its maiden flight on 23 April 1941 at Inglewood, piloted by Louis Wait. The first aircraft to be delivered (AG346) reached Liverpool on 24 October 1941.

This first Mustang to reach England was a test aircraft for the many that were to follow. Assembled at RAF Burtonwood, AG346 received a British radio and other minor changes in internal equipment. Although service ceiling at this time was limited to 30,000ft (9,288m), British pilots were pleased with the fighter, noting only that camouflage paint slowed its maximum speed by some 8mph (13km/h).

Looking back, it is not clear why Britain needed so many Mustangs so early, when the incomparable Spitfire was already well on its way to becoming more numerous than any American fighter of the war. At the time the decision was made, however, the outcome of the Battle of Britain was by no means assured and from June 1940 onwards Britain was on her own having to fight both Germany and Italy.

Early aircraft developed for the US Army (which was still a long way from accepting the Mustang as its own standard fighter) included 150 P-51s appearing in July 1942 and armed with four 20mm cannon. Fifty-five of these aircraft were equipped with paired K-24 cameras in the rear fuselage and were designated F-6A to denote their photo-reconnaisance role.

An offshoot of early Mustang development efforts was the A-36 Apache dive-bomber (also called the Invader). The A-36 was powered by a 1,325hp

Allison V-1710-87, one of numerous versions of this engine which was to be employed in numerous aircraft variants to come.

Production of the A-36 was undertaken in part to keep the Inglewood production line purring. Together with Kindelberger and Schmued, designer Stanley Worth had a strong hand in transforming a sleek fighter into an American equivalent of the Junkers Ju 87 'Stuka'. The Mustang design had been evolved with anything but the dive-bombing role in mind, yet the airframe lent itself well to the installation of dive brakes and bomb shackles for two 500lb (228kg) bombs fitted under each wing beneath the trays for six 0.50in (12.7mm) machine-guns. The A-36 Apache's dive brakes were of the lattice type which opened both above and below the mainplane, giving well-stabilized control during a dive. Despite early hydraulic problems, the A-36 became a splendid dive-bomber and saw much combat in the Mediterranean and Far East in 1943–44.

The P-51A designation went to the first aircraft in the US Army's stable to be built in at least modest numbers. Power was provided by a 1,200hp Allison V-1710-81 with an improved supercharger and introducing a larger Curtiss 10ft 9in (3.32m) three-bladed propeller. Four 0.50in (12.7mm) machine-guns were installed in the wings, with none in the nose. New 150(US)gal drop-tanks, coupled with the greater

efficiency of the -81 version of the engine, raised the ferry range of the aircraft to 2,700 miles (4,345km), giving pilots and planners their first taste of the long range which was eventually to bring the Mustang to Berlin. P-51A 43-6003 flew for the first time on 3 February 1942, piloted by Robert Chilton.

A batch of 310 of these aircraft (43-6003 to 43-6312) was ordered. Fifty were delivered to the RAF. These were designated Mustang Mk II (company model NA-83) and the first British example (AL958) made its first flight at Inglewood on 13 February 1942, piloted by Chilton. The early hydraulic difficulties were by now history and the P-51A, in both American and British livery, performed well.

The 'A' model, or Mustang II, was the final version of the fighter powered by the Allison engine. In all, 1,570 Allison-engined Mustangs came from the builder, of which 764 went to Britain.

The main problem with the Allison engine was its poor performance at altitude and the decision to switch to the superb British Rolls-Royce Merlin was a choice that illustrated the Mustang's great potential. As early as 1942 Ronald W. Harker, a test pilot with Rolls-Royce, flew an early Mustang and told his superiors that the fighter would perform even better with a Merlin 61. Lieutenant Colonel Thomas (Tommy) Hitchcock, Air Attaché at the US Embassy in London, was also reporting to Washington on the

This P-51A Mustang (or possibly an A-36 Apache) wears a disruptive camouflage pattern and appears to have a locally created position for a second crew member, apparently for filming purposes. The location is clearly an airfield in the southern USA, but details of the camouflage and its tests are elusive. (USAF)

With the bubble canopy, the Mustang reached real maturity. 43-12102 appears on serial number lists as a P-51B, although the bubble canopy is decidedly a P-51D feature. Camouflage on a bubble canopy-equipped aircraft is also unusual. (via M. J. Kasiuba)

The distinctive bubble canopy shape is also evident on this P-51D, which wears its serial on the rear fuselage. (via Larry Davis)

merits of the Merlin which, according to Rolls-Royce engineers, could give the Mustang a maximum speed of 432mph (695km/h). An American version of the Merlin was built by Packard as the V-1650 and this engine became the basis for the next production version of the North American fighter.

The first of two XP-51B fighters (41-37352 and 41-37421), retaining the basic airframe but powered by a 1,450hp Packard V-1650-3 Merlin, first flew for 45 minutes on 30 November 1942, piloted by Chilton. It was found that a chemical reaction between different metals in the cooling system and the glycol coolant was clogging the radiator. A new radiator design and intake were fitted to the second aircraft (41-37421) which proved free of the problem and performed well.

The P-51B went into production with the US Army ordering 400 and Britain over a thousand, of which just 25 (FB100 to FB124) were in due course delivered to the RAF as the Mustang Mk III. North American, who had previously never built a fighter, were now getting more business than they could handle. The company's Dallas, Texas, plant was chosen as a second outlet for the Mustang to produce aircraft identical to the P-51B which, in their Lone Star State identity, were designated P-51C (company NA-103).

The first P-51B (43-12093), or company NA-102, flew on 5 May 1943 with Chilton again as pilot. The first P-51C (42-102979) took to the air in August 1943 at Dallas. Some 1,350 aircraft of the 'C' model were built by the Dallas factory. 944 P-51B/Cs became Mustang Mk IIIs with the RAF.

The Mustang design was now close to a level of maturity that would back its claim to being the finest fighter of the Second World War. Steady improvement of every facet of the aeroplane's design, from radiator to supercharger, from armament to electrical systems, had produced a better and better fighter. There remained one final change to create the definitive Mustang: the bubble canopy. As happened with the Thunderbolt, the flush canopy was discarded and the bubble adopted instead, itself the result of research which had developed the plastic bomb-aimer's nose on US Army bombers. The 'razorback' aft fuselage was cut down level with the fuselage forward section and the bubble installed. A dorsal fin was added to correct some minor stability problems which had come with the Merlin engine.

Two P-51Bs (43-12101 and 43-12102) were taken from the assembly line and converted into 'proof of concept' vehicles for the P-51D, although they retained camouflage and lacked the dorsal fin. In the first of these, referred to at the time as an XP-51D, Chilton made the first flight of a bubble-canopy Mustang at Inglewood on 17 November 1943. Two prototype P-51Ds (company NA-106) from Inglewood (42-106539 and 42-106540) also came from the P-51B line.

With its armament, the P-51D solved what had been a nagging problem. Because the four 0.50in (12.7mm) machine-guns of earlier Mustangs had been mounted on their sides and tended to jam, the six guns in the P-51D were installed upright. The P-51D also carried more rounds per gun than previous models. Each inboard gun had 400 rounds, the four outboard guns 270. This was still not a lot, and pilots had to keep in mind that they were equipped with, at most, enough machine-gun bullets to fire for a few seconds. Lengthy bursts applied only to Hollywood.

The first large P-51D production order, known by the company designation NA-109, was for some 2,500 aircraft. The company designation NA-110 went to 100 similar aircraft delivered to Australia for assembly by Commonwealth. The manufacturer's models NA-111, NA-122 and NA-124 covered

The bubble-canopy Mustang brought US wartime fighter designs to a height of maturity. Aircraft 44-64164 looks like the well-known P-51D which eventually ruled European skies, but is in fact the fifth of 555 lightweight P-51F models on an early flight over southern California. The 'H' model did not get into combat. (North American)

'L'il' Jan', alias 44-14235, a typical product of North American's Inglewood, California, factory, belongs to the 343rd Fighter Squadron, 55th Fighter Group, and is banking gently over English countryside. Some aeroplanes from this group later had a silhouette of a mustang painted on the vertical tail. (via Jeffrey Ethell)

This Mustang belongs to the 2nd Aerial Camera Group. The setting appears to be a civil airfield in the USA. P-51D 44-15338 was manufactured at Inglewood and may have been completed as an F-6D camera ship, although the rear-fuselage camera installation cannot be seen from the starboard side. The Mustang appears with a lightning bolt on the fuselage and an exclamation mark on the tail. (via Jeffrey Ethell)

further contracts for P-51D production, which altogether totalled 6,502 machines built at Inglewood and 1,454 built at Dallas. These numbers include photo-reconnaissance aircraft which became known as the F-6D. The P-51E designation was not assigned.

Although the Mustang was clearly a thoroughbred from the start, almost from its inception engineers and pilots spoke of creating a lighter-weight version. A fair amount of both funding and design work went into this effort, although the real impetus, as with the original design, came from the British.

Little recognition has been bestowed, however, on the resulting XP-51F, XP-51G, and XP-51J lightweight fighters – even though they had so many internal differences that they resembled other Mustangs only in a superficial way. These 'F', 'G', and 'J' model Mustangs, a total of seven airframes all known by the company designation NA-105, came into existence because NAA designer Edgar Schmued travelled to England and inspected Supermarine factories, as well as captured Messerschmitts and Focke-Wulfs.

The lightweight Mustang test aircraft were then built to a British specification. The simple logic was that less weight, with all other factors including engine horsepower remaining the same, would

mean a faster fighter, as well as improved performance in other areas.

The first flight of the XP-51F was made by Bob Chilton on 14 February 1944. Three were built (43-43332 to 43-43334), one posing for photos for record purposes on 10 April, although the pictures apparently were not released until later. The XP-51F was powered by a 1,380hp Packard-built V-1650-3 Merlin driving a three-bladed Aeroproducts propeller, and was described by Chilton as the best-performing fighter in the Mustang series. Coated with pounds of Simonize (a motor car polish), the XP-51F attained 493mph (793km/h), but the magic 500mph (805km/h) figure proved frustratingly beyond reach.

Since the intention was to test the redesigned, lightweight airframe with several powerplants, the XP-51G followed, powered by another Merlin, an imported 1,430hp Rolls-Royce RM-145M.

The first flight of the XP-51G appears to be a matter of some dispute. Most sources say that the maiden flight was made 10 August 1944 by Edward Virgin, who later directed North American operations in Washington, DC, and told the author in the 1950s of flying the fighter. A document from the manufacturer, however, credits Chilton with the first flight on 12 August, while Paul Coggan (see later) states that pilot Joe Barton may have achieved this honour on 9 August.

Two XP-51Gs were built (43-43335 and 43-43336). The second aircraft went to Boscombe Down and flew with the RAF as FR410. Apparently British priorities had changed and the fate of FR410 is unclear after the end of test flying in February 1945. The first XP-51G was fitted with a five-bladed Dowty Rotol propeller, which was used only once on a 20-minute flight and deemed a failure. Contrary to what most sources have told the world, all other flying was carried out with more conventional Aeroproducts Unimatic A-542-B1 four-bladed propellers.

Remarkably, this first, very rare XP-51G fighter has survived. The book *Mustang Survivors* by Paul A. Coggan (Bourne Hill, Aston, 1987) tells of the efforts by John Morgan of La Canada, California, to restore and fly 43-43335. Morgan's task is not easy, for the

XP-51G has parts not interchangeable with heavier, mass-produced Mustangs, as well as a different centre of gravity.

A gap seems to have intervened before North American completed the final model in this lightweight trio of Mustangs. Two XP-51Js (44-76027 and 44-76028) bring to seven the total of these lightweight fighters. The XP-51J made its maiden flight on 23 April 1945, piloted by Joe Barton who flew the bulk of the American tests with all three lightweights. Barton, incidentally, rarely receives mention at all in accounts of Mustang testing, let alone credit for the major role he played. Power was provided by the previously discarded 1,460hp Allison V-1710-119 engine with water injection.

After the war, Bob Chilton was asked why no inflight photos of the XP-51F, XP-51G, and XP-51J seemed to have survived. Chilton said that, to his knowledge, none was ever taken; pilots and others

To meet a British specification for a lightweight version of the Mustang, North American produced seven airframes in the XP-51F, XP-51G and XP-51J series before settling on the P-51H, which became the final production version. XP-51G 43-43335 is seen with a five-bladed Dowty propeller, which proved unsuccessful. (North American)

The XP-51J was the last of three experimental lightweight Mustangs which were tested with various engines and which contributed to the eventual production P-51H. 'J' model 44-76027 is seen with the manufacturer's emblem (the word logo did not exist then) on 26 April 1945. (via Jeffrey Ethell)

were too busy with testing programmes to fit in photo sessions. In later years North American's Gene Boswell searched for some photographic record of these experimental lightweight Mustangs in the air, but his search was in vain.

While the lightweight Mustangs were not superior in every aspect of mission performance – it is apparent, for example, that they were not as easy to maintain and that they were ill-equipped to operate from rough airfields – it seems clear that the XP-51F, 'G', and 'J' outperformed other Mustangs. Equally clear is the fact that, belatedly, they led to a production aircraft which incorporated all the thinking that had matured on how to build a lightweight Mustang.

The P-51H Mustang (company NA-126), powered by a 1,380hp V-1650-9A Merlin with water injection, looked very good to Army planners, who placed an early order for a block of 2,400, of which 370 had been produced by VJ-Day.

The first flight of a P-51 (44-64160) was made by Chilton at Inglewood on 3 February 1945. Although the 'H' model also faced early directional stability problems, which were resolved with minor changes, the P-51H might have become a formidable part of the American arsenal had a final invasion of Japan proved necessary. The P-51H was faster in level flight and in a dive than other Mustangs. In fact, with a speed approaching the landmark of 500mph (805km/h) under certain circumstances, it was possibly the fastest propeller-driven fighter to attain

operational service. But the P-51H never saw combat in the Second World War, or for that matter in Korea, although it served valiantly with Air Force and Air National Guard squadrons in the post-war years.

The designation P-51K was bestowed on 1,335 Mustangs which were produced at Dallas and were identical to the P-51D except for having a different propeller. Included in this total are photo-reconnaissance versions, designated F-6K. The P-51L was a further proposal for a lightweight version of the Mustang which showed promise but was never built.

Long after the war was over, and again not really part of this story, North American built a new fighter aircraft which looked like a pair of Mustangs joined together by a single wing. In fact, the first XP-82 Twin Mustang (44-83886), flown on 16 June 1945 by Joe Barton and Edward Virgin, was in many respects a new aircraft. Numerous versions served in the post-war years, including air-to-air combat in Korea.

Mustang in Combat

It is thought that the combat debut of the Mustang took place with the North American fighter wearing British colours during the ill-starred raid on Dieppe on 19 August 1942, when an American in the RAF, Pilot Officer Hollis Hills, shot down a Focke-Wulf Fw 190. Hills' No 2 Squadron also lost a Mustang, apparently the first to go down in battle, that day.

While Hills went on to achieve five aerial victories and become the first Mustang ace on 11 June 1943, the operational debut of the Mustang in American livery seems to have occurred on 9 April 1943, when a 154th Observation Squadron aircraft piloted by Lieutenant Alfred Schwab carried out a successful reconnaissance mission. On 23 April 1943 a Mustang from the same squadron was shot down in error by Allied gun batteries, making it the first American Mustang to be lost in the war.

Also in April 1943, flush-canopy or 'razorback' A-36 Apaches went with the 27th Fighter-Bomber Group to Rasel Ma, French Morocco, where the Allies were engaged in the all-important North Africa campaign. On 6 June 1943 A-36 dive-bombers accompanied a strike on the Italian island of Pantelleria. The 86th Fighter-Bomber Group picked up the attack version of the Mustang soon afterwards.

Half way around the world, the 311th Fighter-Bomber Group went into combat in the autumn of 1943, using the A-36 to cover Allied operations along the Ledo Road in Burma. The 311th also had a few Allison-powered P-51A aircraft. One of those keepers of numbers, whose arithmetic must always be taken with a grain of salt, noted that A-36s flew 23,373 combat sorties (how does the Air Force know the figure was not 23,372 or 23,374?) and dropped 16,000,000 pounds of bombs in the China-Burma-India region. Although supposedly not an air-to-air combatant, the A-36 also shot down 84 Japanese aircraft.

In due course, the 311th traded its Allison-powered dive-bombers and fighters for Merlin-powered P-51Bs. The 23rd Fighter Group, which was able to trace its lineage directly to General Claire Chennault's 'Flying Tigers' and continued to wear a shark's mouth on each of its aircraft, received Merlin-powered P-51B Mustangs in early 1944.

As the bombing campaign over the European continent grew, the US 8th Air Force in England looked at the disturbing growth of losses of men and aircraft and assigned greater priority to a need it had earlier identified, the need for a long-range fighter – one which could escort heavy bombers and duel with the Germans' superb Messerschmitt and Focke-Wulf fighters. The 8th sent Colonel Cass Hough, head of its technical section, to test-fly the P-51B. He reported back on the Mustang's many qualities and its enormous potential, but also said that directional stability problems needed to be corrected. After the P-51D with teardrop canopy and dorsal fin came along, and in spite of the fact that the Thunderbolt packed eight guns to the Mustang's six, no one worried about problems any more.

The Merlin-powered Mustang had significantly better fuel consumption than other Allied fighters. The final change that had to be taken was to install an 85(US)gal fuel tank behind the pilot. As so often happens, a benefit in one area of performance led to a problem in another. The added fuel tank exacerbated the directional stability problem to the extent that for the first hour or two on a mission the pilot would have to concentrate very hard on keeping flying the way the nose was pointing. By then, the extra tank would be empty and the pilot could switch to the usual 184(US)gal tanks in the wings, his directional stability problem solved. With two 75(US)gal drop-tanks under the wings, the Mustang needed a long, nerve-racking take-off run and could only just stagger into the sky, but when the entire fuel load was added up (419(US)gal) this fighter had now become a long-legged demon. Test pilot Colonel Mark Bradley flew one from Inglewood down to Albuquerque, spent some time loitering around in the air over New Mexico's largest city, and then, without landing, returned to the factory. The significance of this little jaunt over the south-west was that Bradley had just done the equivalent of England to Berlin and back!

The arrival of Mustangs with 8th Air Force units

In flight, 44-84767 reveals the typically clean lines of the North American Mustang. Built at Dallas, the aircraft has yet to join a squadron. Pilot enjoyed superb visibility and easy handling qualities. (via Roger Besecker)

in Britain gave the Allies a tremendous boost in their aerial campaign against Hitler's 'Fortress Europe'. Whatever Lightning or 'Jug' pilots might have said then, or might say today with a half-century of hindsight, the Mustang's combination of speed and manoeuvrability was superior to other US fighters and it had the 'legs' to go deep into enemy territory.

The 354th Fighter Group at Boxted under Colonel Kenneth Martin was the first unit in the ETO (European Theatre of Operations) to take the Mustang on charge, the first arrivals being P-51Bs. In the Mustang's first combat mission, an 11 December 1943 bomber escort to Emden, not much happened. A few days later Lieutenant Charles Gumm shot down a twin-engined Messerschmitt Bf 110 for the Mustang's first aerial victory of the war. On 11

The quintessential study of the Mustang at war. 'WZ' code letters were used by both the 31st and 78th Fighter Groups. This P-51D is understood to belong to the former's 309th Fighter Squadron and to be operating over Italy in 1944. (via Jeffrey Ethell)

January 1944 Major James H. Howard of the 354th repeatedly risked his life to defend heavy bombers from Luftwaffe fighter attack.

Separated from his flight, Howard was alone near a B-17 bomber formation which came under attack from six to eight twin-engined German fighters. There were at least dozens of Luftwaffe fighters not far away. Howard unhesitatingly went into harm's way and shot down, in quick succession, a twin-engined aircraft, a Focke-Wulf Fw 190, and a Messerschmitt Bf 109. Moments later, he shook another Bf 109 off the tail of an American aircraft. Howard continued fighting aggressive and persistent German pilots for the next half-hour. His aircraft during the engagement was 43-6315, nicknamed 'Ding Hao'. A softspoken person who wrote up a report of the incident without mention of his own heroism, Howard became the only Mustang pilot in the Second World War to receive the highest American award for valour, the Medal of Honor.

In the Mediterranean theatre Mustang maintenance crews, crew chiefs, and pilots struggled against moisture and mud, even when relatively sunny skies prevailed. The 332nd Fighter Group, which converted from the Thunderbolt to the P-51D Mustang in June 1944 at Lesina, Italy, was the only

Taxiing out, very clean in appearance and lacking the colourful markings which typified Mustangs in Europe, these P-51Ds of the Pacific's 7th Fighter Command are beginning a mission to escort B-29 Superfortress bombers, operating from hard-won Iwo Jima. (via Jeffrey Ethell)

Seen from a B-29 en route to Japan, these Iwo Jima-based P-51D Mustangs make a beautiful sight in July 1945. 44-72864 (foreground) is a typical Inglewood product. (via Jeffrey Ethell)

US fighter unit in the entire segregated Army to have pilots who were called negroes, then, and are known as blacks today. Lee A. Archer was the group's top-scoring ace with five aerial successes and six ground victories. He and his wingmen fought discrimination and fought Hitler. On one occasion Archer and Wendell O. Pruitt went rushing into a formation of Messerschmitts which outnumbered them six to one. Each American scored two kills and came through the fight unharmed.

By the summer of 1944 rapidly arriving P-51Ds were in command of the air. By D-Day, 6 June 1944, the German air arm was on the defensive, as much a dangerous foe as a cornered wildcat, but never again to hold air superiority in any engagement.

Although the highest-scoring American aces in Europe flew P-47 Thunderbolts, the Mustang was the aircraft of many air aces whose mastery over the Luftwaffe made their names familiar to a generation of aviation followers: Lieutenant Colonel John C. Meyer with 24 air and 13 ground victories; Major George E. Preddy, Jr, with a tongue-twisting score of 26.83 enemy aircraft shot down plus 5 destroyed on the ground (the decimal figure was caused by more than one pilot sharing credit for the same kill); and Captain Don S. Gentile with 21.83 air and 6 ground kills. These were perhaps the best known. Gentile wrecked an aircraft while 'beating up' his own airfield, an incident which caused him to be sent packing. As with all such historical quirks, it is impossible to avoid wondering how Gentile might have fared had he been able to complete a normal tour of duty.

The Mustang was rather a late-comer to the war, but it eventually became an almost universal sight. It is unlikely that any comprehensive list will ever identify every unit with which North American's famous fighter served. The best-known groups (many of which used earlier fighters at an earlier stage in the war and finished with Mustangs) were:

In the Mediterranean theatre: the 31st, 52nd, 325th and 332nd Fighter Groups.

In the European theatre: the 4th, 20th, 55th, 78th, 339th, 352nd, 353rd, 354th, 355th, 356th, '357th, 359th, 361st, 364th and 479th Fighter Groups.

In the CBI (China-Burma-India) theatre and in the Pacific: the 1st Air Commando Group, 3rd Air Commando Group, the 21st, 23rd, 51st, 311th and 348th Fighter Groups.

In addition, the 27th and 86th Fighter-Bomber Groups in the Mediterranean and the 311th Fighter-Bomber Group in India employed the A-36 Apache. Numerous American units employed F-6A through F-6G photo-reconnaissance versions of the Mustang.

In the Royal Air Force, Nos 2, 4, 16, 19, 26, 63, 64, 65, 112, 249, 250, 260, 303, 306, 309, 315, 400, 414, 430, 441 and 442 Squadrons were operators of the Mustang, among many others. Australia, New Zealand, and South Africa also flew the Mustang in combat.

The Mustang looked as if it were doing 450mph, just sitting still. The practice of putting the serial number on the rear fuselage (here obscured by the starboard elevator) was noted in the China-Burma-India theatre. (via Larry Davis)

F6F Hellcat

The Grumman F6F Hellcat is seldom mentioned when experts try to name the half-dozen or so most important warplanes of all time. The Hellcat, simply, has never been given the credit it deserves. Although not as fast as a Mustang, not as manoeuvrable as a 'Zero', lacking the lightweight peppiness of a Yakovlev and, as noted earlier, by no means as advanced as the Vought F4U Corsair which began its life on the drawing-board at an earlier date, this sturdy and functional product of the 'Grumman Iron Works' was the US fighter that turned the tide of the Pacific air war.

The Hellcat was one of those few aircraft designed right from the start, needing minimal changes during flight test and development and moving quickly from drawing-board to combat. It is often described as the only mass-produced fighter to have been designed

after the global conflict began. Here is how one naval aviator describes the creation of the Hellcat:

'A questionnaire was sent to all Navy and Marine Corps pilots in mid-1942 asking them what they would like in the way of design, manoeuvrability, horsepower, range, firepower, and the ability to operate off an aircraft-carrier. The naval aviation people went to Grumman and presented them with what they learned, thus was born the F6F Hellcat. The pilots really liked this bird for carrier ability.'

In truth, the Hellcat was not spawned after Pearl Harbor. Nor was it, as is often said, a direct response to Japan's 'Zero'. The questionnaire was very real, and it meant something to hard-pressed Navy people aboard carriers at sea that their opinion was being sought, but the occasion was the improvement of the basic Hellcat design, not its beginning. It was true then, and is still true today, that this manufacturer

Hellcat pilots went to war from packed carrier decks where any mistake was an invitation to disaster. Nothing is wrong here beyond smoking tyres under full braking strain as this F6F piloted by Lieutenant H. J. Mueller lands without its tail hook deployed. The carrier is the USS *Yorktown* (CV-10) during strikes on the Bonin Islands on 24 July 1944. (USN)

The clean lines of the Grumman F6F Hellcat were evident with the XF6F-1, first flown on 26 June 1942 by the manufacturer's test pilot, Robert L. Hall. Although the initial Wright R-2600-16 power-plant was replaced by the Pratt & Whitney R-2800-10, the Hellcat was essentially 'right from the start', and proved to be an aircraft remarkably devoid of design flaws. (Grumman)

tried harder than most to solicit feedback from the men who use its equipment.

The Hellcat really owes its origin to Grumman company models G-33 and G-33A of February 1938. These were proposals to install a 1,500hp Pratt & Whitney R-1830 radial engine in a derivative of the XF4F-2 Wildcat, as well as to improve the aero-dynamic shape of the earlier fighter. Grumman's design team, headed by William Schwendler and Richard (Dick) Hutton, found after some examination that these proposals were not right for the future. Indeed, they concluded that nothing less was needed than a completely new airframe design.

The engineers quickly discarded the Wildcat-based studies and moved on, in March 1938, to company model G-35, a wholly new fighter with a 1,600hp Wright R-2600 radial. Like their neighbour Alexander Kartveli at Republic, who was just ten miles away, Schwendler and Hutton were looking at a rich variety of possible fighter configurations but remained 'sold' on radial rather than in-line power.

This pre-war effort came to a halt when the US Navy ordered the Brewster XF2A-1 Buffalo in preference to the XF4F-2 Wildcat, forcing Grumman to concentrate their efforts on improving the Wildcat before moving on to a newer aircraft. Nevertheless, work on a new fighter was resumed in September 1940, more than a year before Pearl Harbor.

Much literature has described the Vought F4U Corsair as 'back-up' insurance against the Hellcat when, if anything, the reverse was true: Grumman forged ahead with their model G-50 to assure the Navy a high-performance fighter if the Corsair were delayed. The Corsair did in fact run foul of development problems and because considerable effort went into the Hellcat, it was able to fly combat missions from carriers earlier.

New Fighter

Although early plans to retain some features of the Wildcat were discarded, the new G-50 (which became the F6F Hellcat) was similar enough to make it easy for Grumman to swing into a mass-production mode.

On 12 January 1941 the Navy inspected a G-50 full-scale mock-up and recommended some changes, including increases in length and wing span. The new fighter was going to be a heavyweight for its size, but it was also to have enormous structural strength, to enable it to survive against Japanese fighters armed with cannon. Design work proceeded smoothly at Grumman's Bethpage, Long Island facility and on 30 June 1941 the Navy awarded Grumman a contract for two prototype XF6F-1 fighters (02981 and 02982).

In an unusual parade of friends and foe, a Grumman F6F-5 Hellcat maintains a stateside formation with a Supermarine Spitfire V and a captured Mitsubishi J2M Raiden ('Thunderbolt'), code-named 'Jack' by the Allies. The Spitfire (some 600 of which were flown by the USAAF under reverse Lend-Lease) is among the half-dozen all-time greats. Hellcat comes close. 'Jack' was decidedly an 'also ran'. (National Archives)

A low-wing monoplane with wing-mounted, rear-ward-retracting landing gear, the Hellcat had its cockpit above the main fuel tank which placed the canopy high on the fuselage. Downthrust of 3deg for the engine and propeller improved forward visibility, and the Hellcat never had the reputation of being difficult to land that went with its stablemate, the Corsair. While minor details were altered as improvements were made, the configuration of the Hellcat was changed very little through all its production versions.

One reason for Grumman's success was that the Hellcat was functional and straightforward, a real contrast to the Vought Corsair, which had far more radical features – and corresponding problems. Grumman's approach was to keep it simple, build it rugged, and turn it out in mind-boggling numbers.

Maiden Flight

An all-silver aircraft wearing national insignia but no Navy markings, the XF6F-1 made its first flight on 26 June 1942, flown by test pilot Robert L. (Bob) Hall. This first aircraft was powered by a 1,600hp Wright R-2600-16 radial with a Curtiss Electric three-bladed propeller. It was armed with six 0.50in (12.7mm) Browning M2 machine-guns with 400 rounds of ammunition each.

The Hellcat was the right aeroplane with the wrong engine. The second prototype was to have flown briefly with a turbo-supercharged R-2600 under the designation XF6F-2, but this never happened. Schwendler, Hutton, and other Grumman fighter experts knew that with a different engine they would have a real winner.

So the second prototype Hellcat (02982) was completed as the XF6F-3, with a 1,800hp Pratt &

Whitney R-2800-10 two-stage radial, again driving a Curtiss Electric three-bladed propeller. Grumman's busy Robert Hall made the first flight of the XF6F-3 on 30 July 1942. Shortly afterwards the prototype Hellcat was modified to XF6F-3 configuration. For reasons which have never been clear, the Navy at some juncture exchanged the bureau numbers of the two prototypes, so that aeroplane 02982 became 02981 and vice versa. This confusing step in the history of Navy bureau numbers (no other example of such a change is known to have occurred) led to further confusion when one of the XF6F-3s was damaged in a belly landing on 17 August 1942, with Bob Hall as pilot. The damaged aircraft was the first XF6F-3 (02981, ex-02982) while the other machine (the only XF6F-1, which had become the second XF6F-3) continued flying. A minor tail flutter problem was solved by slightly lengthening the Hellcat's fuselage, and production F6F-3 fighters soon followed.

On 3 October 1942, a hurried five months after the first flight of the XF6F-3, the first production F6F-3 (04775) took to the air. This initial production version of the Hellcat differed from the two test specimens in having a Hamilton Standard fully feathering propeller without spinner hub, and minor changes to the engine cowling and exhaust ports.

The production F6F-3 began to pour from the Grumman plant before a few final details were worked out. The first 910 aircraft were built with the dorsal radio antenna mast canted forward, while aircraft from 911 onwards had a perpendicular mast. A landing light under the port wing was deleted after F6F-3 number 272. Minor cowling changes were introduced after the 1,265th aeroplane. The simplicity principle continued to apply: minor improvements here and there, but no high-risk radical

The inhospitable atmosphere in the South Pacific is evident in this view of F6F-3 Hellcats on Munda airstrip, New Georgia, in September 1943. Aircraft in foreground bears nickname 'June'. Although it has been stated that these machines belonged to Marine squadron VMF-222, the late Richard Hill, noted naval historian, was convinced that this was Navy land-based squadron VF-38. There is little in the way of individualized markings to prove the point. (via Jim Sullivan)

No fewer than nineteen deck hands are busily occupied in this view aboard the USS *Puget Sound* (CVE-113) in 1945 as carrier-based Marines push an F6F-5 Hellcat on the flight deck under orders from the plane director (foreground). Both Navy and Marine fliers operated the Hellcat from busy decks, including those on very small escort carriers like this one. (via Lou Drendel)

The first stage of the wing folding (or unfolding) process gives an illusion of swept-back wings to this F6F-5 Hellcat which has just landed aboard the USS *Hornet* (CV-12) after a raid over the Marianas in June 1944. (USN)

changes. None of the F6F-3s had any provision for external load except the 150(US)gal jettisonable fuel tank, so the -3 was very much an air-to-air fighter.

In all, 4,402 aircraft in the F6F-3 series were built, reaching a peak of 500 per month. Later in the war, in March 1945, Grumman actually manufactured 605 Hellcats in a single month. These figures reflect an incredible situation, wherein Hellcats were shoulder-to-shoulder, nose-to-nose, and chock-a-block all over every square inch of the Bethpage facility, even though a ferry pilot was picking up and delivering a new Hellcat every few minutes.

It was one of those miracles of the American industrial machine which never ceased to amaze the world, in an era where American industry was unchallenged as the world leader. There were also

problems, among them inadequate plant space at Bethpage. In spring 1942, Grumman bought up thousands of steel girders from New York city's dismantled Second Avenue 'el' (elevated railway) and World's Fair pavilion to help in the construction of a new Bethpage plant. Work proceeded so rapidly that assembly jigs often came ahead of roofing, with Hellcats progressing along the line before the factory was finished.

F6F-3 sub-variants included the F6F-3E and F6F-3N night fighter versions, of which eighteen and 205 were manufactured respectively. Both the -3E and the -3N had a radar antenna on the starboard wing: the F6F-3E carried an AN/APS-4 unit in a pod attached to the wing, while the F6F-3N carried a Dalmo-Victor Westinghouse AN/APS-6 radar in a

During stateside carrier work-ups on 24 August 1943, prior to heading to the war in the South Pacific, a Grumman F6F-3 Hellcat of squadron VF-1 aboard the USS *Barnes* (CVE-20) gets the go-ahead sign. The same manufacturer's TBF Avenger torpedo-bomber is barely visible in the background. (via Jim Sullivan)

An F6F-3 of VF-19 takes off from the USS *Lexington* (CV-16) on 10 October 1944. Placement of the aircraft side number (4) behind the cockpit is very unusual; the normal location was on either or both nose and tail. (via Jim Sullivan)

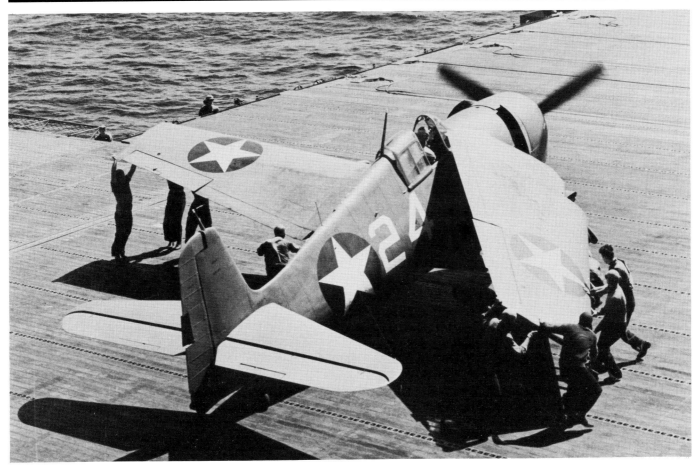

faired, wing-mounted radome. In both night fighter Hellcats, the radio transmitter/receiver was situated in the fuselage, with the radar screen centred in the instrument panel. Other changes included red cockpit lighting and the removal of the curved Plexiglass fairing ahead of the bulletproof windshield, which experience had shown became easily scratched and less and less transparent. The night fighters retained the R-2800-10W engine.

Other F6F-3 versions included F6F-3K drones developed after the war and F6F-3P photo-reconnaissance aircraft modified in service by installation of a long focal length camera in the lower port fuselage, aft of the wing. F6F-3P photo ships retained the armament carried by fighters, namely six 0.50in (12.7mm) machine-guns.

Hellcat Figures

The production F6F-3 had dimensions which were typical of the Hellcat series. These included: wing span 42ft 10in (13.26m), length 33ft 7in (10.38m), height 13ft 1in (3.99m) and wing area 334sq ft (31.03m²). This made the Hellcat not merely a sturdy ship but a big one, compared with the 'Zero' and many other fighters, although it was still dwarfed by

the Thunderbolt being manufactured in the same, crowded neighbourhood.

The F6F-3 weighed 9,101lb (4,128kg) empty, 12,441lb (5,643kg) loaded, and up to a maximum of 15,487lb (7,025kg). There were modest increases in weight figures in the subsequent -5 model.

Performance figures credit the F6F-3 Hellcat with a maximum speed of 386mph (621km/h), initial climb rate of 3,410ft (1,039m) per minute, service ceiling of 37,300ft (11,369m) and range of 1,040 miles (1,674km). Again, the Hellcat produces no numbers which stand out when compared with the fastest, the highest-flying, or the longest-legged – but everything about the Hellcat was respectable.

Development continued with the XF6F-4. The second aeroplane built (02981, which had begun life as 02982) was re-engined with a 2,000hp Pratt & Whitney R-2800-27 single-stage radial driving a three-bladed Hamilton Standard propeller. This version was armed with four 20mm cannon with 200 rounds of ammunition per gun. First flight in the new -4 identity was made on 3 October 1942. An early decision was made not to produce the cannon-armed version. The XF6F-4 remained in this configuration for some time, however, and was still undergoing evaluation – and apparently being compared with captured enemy fighters – at the Naval Air Test Center, Patuxent River, Maryland, as late as 11 February 1944. In fact, the XF6F-4 retained its cannon armament until struck off charge at Quonset Point, Rhode Island, on 31 October 1946.

The designation F6F-4 was applied to a planned version of the Hellcat, studied in July 1943, to operate from escort carriers. At the time, the FM-2 Wildcat was considered the optimum fighter for operation from these small ships. Studies showed that the F6F-04, made into a lightweight by the removal of two 0.50in (12.7mm) machine-guns and other equipment, would have offered advantages over the Wildcat, but in the end other priorities beckoned and the F6F-4 was not produced.

The F6F-5 made its first flight on 5 April 1944. All F6F-5 variants were powered by R-2800-10Ws with water injection. An improved windshield resulted from Navy complaints that dust was accumulating between the curved windshield and the bullet-proof transparent plate in earlier machines. Consideration was also given to fitting the Hellcat with a bubble canopy, but the idea was rejected because it would have created a drastic reduction in production rate.

The F6F-5 became the final production version of the Hellcat. Provision for water injection to increase combat power was added in late 1943 as production -10W engines for it became available. Wing stub racks were added for bombs, or for additional fuel

tanks to supplement the single centre-line belly fuel tank that had become a standard operational feature. Also with the F6F-5, from April 1944 onwards, came necessary strengthening of the rear fuselage and horizontal stabilizer, along with other improvements – including engine cowling changes to reduce drag and aileron spring tabs to reduce roll stick force in combat manoeuvres. With structural changes, dive speed and pull-out restrictions on the Hellcat were removed.

F6F-5 Night Fighters

The F6F-5E designation went to a small number of night fighters fitted with AN/ASP-4 radar beneath the starboard wing.

The F6F-5N night fighter, very little changed from the F6F-3N, carried the AN/APS-6, or slightly modified Dalmo-Victor Philco AN/APS-6A radar, in a faired nacelle on the starboard wing. Late production F6F-5Ns had the inboard 0.50in (12.7mm) machine-guns replaced by a 20mm cannon, the idea being that pilots during night actions did not have time to pump prolonged bursts of fire into an enemy and needed to improve the probability of scoring a kill during a brief encounter. Two F6F-5N Hellcats (70729 and 79139) were equipped with an airborne searchlight pod on the port wing leading edge and were evaluated for night anti-submarine operations

The Grumman F6F-3E Hellcat night fighter version, of which only eighteen were built, was unique in having AN/ASP-4 radar housed in a detachable pod beneath the starboard wing. Other night fighter Hellcats, the F6F-3N and F6F-5N, had radar contained in a permanent fairing on the starboard wing leading edge. (National Archives)

F6F-3 Hellcats on the flight line at NAS Banana River, Florida, 19 April 1944. These Hellcats are being used in an advanced training role and have had landing gear wheel covers removed. This was done to reduce the time needed to repair or replace strut covers damaged frequently by hard landings. (via Jim Sullivan)

during and after the war. 1,432 aircraft of the F6F-5N model were produced by Grumman.

The F6F-5P photo-reconnaissance aircraft, like its predecessor the -3P, retained armament and fighting capability. No record seems to exist of how many -5 models were completed as -5Ps.

F6F-5K was the designation applied to most Hellcat drones. After the war, -3K model drones gathered particles from an atomic cloud during Operation 'Crossroads', the nuclear detonations at Bikini Atoll. F6F-5Ks were used as remotely controlled robot bombs during the Korean War.

The XF6F-6 designation went to a pair of production F6F-5 Hellcat fighters (70188 and 70913) which were modified to handle the R-2800-18W engine with a four-bladed propeller, the only four-blade version. The XF6F-6 first flew on 6 July 1944 with Paul Gallo as pilot. This Hellcat was substantially faster than its predecessors and reportedly attained a top speed of 440mph (708km/h), although the figure most often quoted is a still respectable 417mph (671km/h) at 21,900ft (6,780m). The F6F-6 was scheduled to go into production in September 1944 but was delayed because -18W engines were sorely needed for the Vought F4U-4 Corsair. Had the

war continued, the F6F-6 would certainly have been manufactured in large numbers.

A number of other Grumman fighter designs, closely related to the Hellcat, never received Navy designations and were never built. The company model G-54 was a Hellcat-like fighter with laminar-flow wings conceived in 1942. G-59 and G-60 manufacturer's designations went to studies aimed at seeing whether the colossal 3,000hp Pratt & Whitney R-4360 28-cylinder engine could reasonably be installed in a Hellcat. G-61 was a Grumman study for a mixed-power Hellcat with a General Electric I-20 turbojet in the rear fuselage to augment the R-2800 radial. G-69 was a projected fighter-bomber version of the Hellcat powered by a 2,100hp R-2800-22 engine.

Hellcat at War

The first Hellcat squadron was VF-9, which began working up at Oceana, Virginia, in January 1943. Oceana has long been the Navy's prime fighter training base on the east coast, and it was here that additional Hellcat squadrons were formed. The F6F first saw combat on 31 August 1943 with the Pacific

Previously unpublished view of factory-fresh F6F-5N Hellcat night fighters being ferried from Grumman's Bethpage, Long Island, plant to the west coast for shipment to the Pacific war. These aircraft are being delivered by VRF-1, possibly the only squadron to have had a 'fighter-transport' designation. (Will Carroll)

Previously unpublished view of a new-built F6F-5 Hellcat pausing at a small, possibly civil airstrip in the USA while being ferried to the west coast to go to war. Ferry pilots of squadron VRF-1 got to know hundreds of airfields, as well as hotels and eateries, carrying out their unique mission of delivering these warplanes. (Will Carroll)

F6F-5N Hellcat night fighter newly built at Bethpage being ferried by VRF-1 to an operational squadron. Absence of windows behind the pilot's enclosure was a distinguishing characteristic of late-model aircraft in the F6F-5 series. (Will Carroll)

Fleet. Navy warplanes from several carriers went into action near Marcus Island and Lieutenant Richard Loesch of VF-6 scored the first aerial victory to be credited to a Hellcat.

In the island-hopping campaign which raged across the Pacific, Hellcats achieved success after success in the Solomons, Gilberts, and Marshalls, including the bloody Marine invasion of Tarawa in the Marshall Islands. With its contemporary the Vought F4U Corsair still operating from land, the carrier-based Hellcat established decisive superiority over Japan's 'Zero'. Ensign Robert W. Duncan of VF-5 scored a 'first' on 5 October 1943 when he became the first Hellcat pilot to shoot down two 'Zeros', an achievement that was often repeated.

The Hellcat was not perfect. Visibility could have been better. The aircraft had a tendency to weather-cock on the ground unless the tail wheel was locked. Its main landing gear provided so little clearance that at some angles of attack the propeller would hit the ground (or carrier deck), with catastrophic results. Still, Hellcats went to war, pilots adjusted to flying them, and the result proved more than worthwhile. In the first big air battle near Kwajalein on 4 December 1943, 91 Hellcats tangled with 50 'Zeros' and shot down 28 with the loss of just two of their own aircraft.

Even before F6F-3E, -3N, -5E, and -5N night fighters were available, some form of night fighting capability was sorely needed, given the level of

Ensign Ardon R. Ives has plenty on his mind as he scrambles out of a late-model F6F-5 Hellcat on the flight deck of the USS *Lexington* (CV-16) on 25 February 1945. The aircraft had landed with a major fuel leak which apparently was ignited by a spark. Ives escaped safely. (USN)

The classic shape of an early Hellcat, with early-war national insignia and the windows behind the cockpit found on most versions. (USN)

Japanese activity during the nocturnal hours. One tactic was the hunter/killer team, using from one to three Hellcats in formation with a TBF-1C Avenger or SBD Dauntless with air-search radar. Teams trained and practised together, working rigorously to develop technique. In a night air action on 26 November 1943, Medal of Honor holder Lieutenant Commander 'Butch' O'Hare, at the controls of a TBF, shot down a Japanese 'Betty' bomber but lost his life when his Avenger was downed, while Hellcats destroyed a number of the enemy.

The real beginning of Hellcat night fighting came in February 1944 when F6F-3Ns from VF(N)-76 began to fly combat missions from the decks of *Essex*-class carriers. VF(N)-77 and -78 soon followed and the three squadrons racked up an impressive record of nearly two dozen night kills. It became the practice for four Hellcat night fighters to operate with each VF (fighter squadron) aboard a carrier. Several additional night fighter squadrons also participated in the fighting and at least five Hellcat pilots became aces during night engagements.

F6F-3N night fighters belonging to Marine Corps squadron VMF(N)-534 began combat operations from Guam in August 1944. The following month VMF(N)-541, also equipped with F6F-3Ns, arrived on Peleliu. Initially, the Marines produced no results in their effort to take the night back from the Japanese, but in later months the story changed.

Pacific Fighting

F6F Hellcats joined the increasing tempo of the island-hopping counter-offensive as 1944 unfolded. On 17–18 February 1943, during carrier strikes on Truk, Hellcats from ten squadrons destroyed 127 Japanese aircraft in the air and 86 on the ground. On 29–30 March 1943 Hellcats from no fewer than eleven aircraft-carriers shot down 150 Japanese aircraft in and around Palau.

Hellcats are not usually remembered for fighting in Europe, but they did see some action against Hitler's forces. During the Allied landings in southern France in 1944, at least two squadrons from the escort carriers USS *Tulagi* (CVE-72) and USS *Kasaan Bay* (CVE-69) provided air cover, strafed and bombed, and shot down three Heinkel He 111 bombers. After that, both vessels and Hellcats were reassigned to the Pacific.

The Hellcat was flown by every Navy ace in the Pacific. Captain David McCampbell became the Navy's all-time ace of aces, with 34 kills. As skipper of Carrier Air Group 15 aboard the USS *Essex* (CV-9), McCampbell actually shot down nine aircraft in a single mission on 24 October 1944, which ended with him being so low on fuel that he could not taxi his aeroplane after recovering on a carrier – and for which he was awarded the Medal of Honor. McCampbell found the F6F Hellcat to be easy to fly,

F6F-5 Hellcat from the USS *Bon Homme Richard* (CV-31) in flight over a stateside location. (USN)

Blurred combat photo in the Pacific on 1 November 1944 shows a US Navy F6F Hellcat fighter (top) firing at, and scoring a hit on, a Japanese Mitsubishi A6M 'Zero', code-named 'Zeke' by the Allies. At the outbreak of war, no US Navy fighter was a match for the 'Zero'. The Hellcat changed that. (USN)

a satisfying performer, and a stable gun platform. He was pleased when the arrival of the F6F-5 model provided a limited air-to-ground capability.

Other leading Navy aces were Lieutenant Commanders Cecil Harris with 24 kills, Gene Valencia with 23, Alex Vraciu and Pat Fleming with 19 each. The Hellcat reportedly produced more aces than any other aircraft, including more who became aces in a single engagement, no fewer than seven men attaining this achievement during the 'Marianas Turkey Shoot'.

Hellcats fought across the Pacific and were in action at Saipan, Iwo Jima, and Okinawa. During the fighting at Okinawa, three Marine squadrons, VMF(N)-533, -542, and -543, accounted for 68 Japanese aircraft shot down during night battles. Improved Japanese fighters such as the Nakajima Ki-84 'Frank' and Kawanishi N1K1 'George' could challenge the Hellcat more effectively than the 'Zero' did, but they were too few, too late; the Americans now had not only a better warplane but overwhelming numerical superiority.

In late 1944 the Marines' VMF(N)-541 moved to Tacloban, on Leyte in the Philippines, where it claimed 22 aerial kills and five Japanese aircraft destroyed on the ground in a six-week period ending on 11 January 1945. At that time a number of Marine day fighter squadrons were training with air-to-ground rockets in preparation for action in Europe against V-1 flying-bomb launching sites, but these Marines were deployed to the Pacific when Allied soldiers overran the installations without their help.

Other Marine squadrons that flew the Hellcat in combat from the decks of escort carriers included VMF-351, -511, -512, -513 and -514. A Marine photo squadron, VMD-354, flew F6F-5P Hellcats at Guam late in the war.

With Japan resorting to suicide tactics in its 'Kamikaze' attacks during the fighting for the Philippines, the US Navy established VBF (fighter-bomber) squadrons in addition to its traditional VFs, giving each aircraft-carrier an added fighter capability. Both F6F Hellcats and F4U Corsairs equipped these squadrons, which had only limited success countering the 'Kamikazes'.

Early plans for licence production of the Hellcat by Canadian Vickers never bore fruit. The only foreign user of the Hellcat during the Second World War was Britain, which had once planned to name the aircraft the 'Gannet'. 1,177 Hellcats reached the Fleet Air Arm: 252 F6F-3s became Hellcat Mk Is in Royal Navy service and began arriving in May 1943; 849 F6F-5s and 76 F6F-5Ns became Hellcat Mk IIs. Some of the latter mark were modified by Blackburn Aircraft for a limited air-to-ground capability, while others had cameras installed for the photo-reconnaissance role.

On 3 April 1944 British Hellcat pilots of Nos 800 and 804 Squadrons covered strikes against the German battleship *Tirpitz*, anchored in Kaafjord, Norway. While operating from the escort carrier HMS *Emperor*, Hellcats also covered a convoy to Gibraltar in June 1944 and, like their American counterparts, covered Allied landings in southern France in August 1944.

The British Hellcats operated throughout the Dutch East Indies, Malaya, Burma, and in the final assault on Japan. On 29 August 1944, first blood was drawn when British Hellcats aboard HMS *Indomitable* covered air strikes in the East Indies. By late 1945 all but two of the Fleet Air Arm's fifteen Hellcat squadrons had been disbanded or re-equipped, but one handsome Hellcat II was used by the commander at RNAS Lossiemouth as his personal mount as late as April 1953.

Wartime Fleet Air Arm squadrons were Nos 800, 804, 808, 881, 885, 888, 889, 891, 892, 896, 898, 1839, 1840, 1844 and 1847.

Other Users

After the war countries which operated the Hellcat included Argentina, France, Paraguay and Uruguay. But in American service the Hellcat disappeared from the scene almost as quickly as it had come – designed, developed, tested, made operational, thrown into combat, withdrawn and retired all within the span of half-a-dozen years. 12,275 Hellcats were manufactured by Grumman between June 1942 and November 1945, by far the largest number of fighters ever to be produced at a single factory, and in a remarkably short span of time (the Corsair, produced in similar numbers, came from more than one factory and remained in production until 1953).

Today, a Hellcat is a rare sight indeed at an air show or open house, with only eight examples actually flying around the world. One of the best restorations belongs to 'warbird' rebuilder Bob Pond, who appears around the United States in his mint-looking F6F-5. The US Naval Aviation Museum in Pensacola, Florida, has a pristine F6F-5 (BuNo 94203) painted in accurate Second World War markings.

An F6F Hellcat with 1943 markings seen in a decrepit condition, with a 1950s-era Martin P5M Marlin in the background. It did not become one of the two dozen preserved Hellcats on display in various locations in the USA, so its disposition is unknown. (via M. J. Kasiuba)

More 'Might Have Beens'

Those who remember the war years invariably think of the great and near-great fighters which fought in key battles, produced air aces, and helped to hasten the Allied victory. The industrial plants of the vast American heartland turned out thousands of fighters. In fact, the total figure for the war years was just a few dozen less than 100,000, but only about half were Thunderbolts, Mustangs, Corsairs and Hellcats.

It was a big war, and there was plenty of room in it for fighters which were not the fastest or the best. Some, like the P-63 Kingcobra and the P-70 night fighter, made a solid contribution even though they garnered little glory. Others, a long string of them, showed potential and enhanced knowledge, but never came off the production line. These were more of the 'also rans', the 'might have been' fighters of an era when invention and innovation flourished.

Larry Bell's Buffalo, New York, firm kept disgorging fighter after fighter from its factory doors. None of them began to measure up to the Mustang or the Spitfire, but there existed a strong need for fighters which could do the job, even though others might do it better. For one thing, there was a big and ravenous Lend-Lease customer ready to devour anything and everything American industry could produce. And the Russians wanted numbers. Even if an aircraft was not the best, it would work for the Russians if there were very many of them.

Bell's P-63 Kingcobra was an entirely new aircraft which capitalized on the layout of the P-39 Airacobra and made use on a production basis of the laminar-flow wing and taller tail tested on the XP-39E. On 27 June 1941 the US Army placed an order for two XP-63 prototypes (41-19511 and 41-19512) to be powered by the 1,325hp Allison V-1710-47 liquid-cooled engine located behind the pilot and driven by an extension shaft. As with nearly all the fighters which fought against the Axis, the design was far advanced before the Japanese attacked Pearl Harbor. In the climate of the time, the P-63 looked as good as anything likely to fly in the near future.

Then there were delays. For a time it may have seemed that the P-63 Kingcobra programme was never going to get off the ground. The first aircraft flew on 7 December 1942 but was lost in an accident a few weeks later. The second prototype flew on 5 February 1943 but crashed the following May.

Fortunately, a third prototype, the XP-63A, had been ordered in June 1942 and flew on 26 April 1943. The XP-63A (42-78015) had been conceived as a Merlin engine test-bed under the designation XP-63B but was never flown in that form. Powered by a 1,500hp Allison V-1710-93, it became an effective third prototype and test aircraft for the continuing development programme.

The XP-63A was actually the fastest Kingcobra built, attaining 426mph (686km/h) on military power at 20,000ft (6,096m), but air combat was not to be the Kingcobra's strong suit: the P-63 was intended for the ground-attack role. Its nose armament of one 37mm cannon and two 0.50in (12.7mm) machine-guns with a total of 900 rounds for all three guns, bolstered by additional wing guns in most models, was well suited for air-to-ground action. The Kingcobra also boasted 88lb (40kg) of armour, 100(US)gal of internal fuel, and provision for a 500lb (227kg) bomb or 75(US)gal drop-tank beneath the fuselage. Later machines were equipped to carry three 522lb (237kg) bombs.

The basic P-63A version is representative of the Kingcobra series. Dimensions of the P-63A included: wing span 38ft 4in (11.68m), length 32ft 8in (9.96m), height 12ft 7in (3.84m) and wing area 248sq ft (23.04m^2). The aircraft weighed 6,375lb (2,892kg) empty, a figure which rose to a maximum take-off weight of 10,500lb (4,763kg). This made it a light-weight as wartime fighters went, although the Kingcobra was a sturdy machine and could absorb considerable battle damage.

Performance figures for the P-63A Kingcobra included a maximum speed of 410mph (660km/h) at 25,000ft (7,620m), cruising speed of 378mph (608km/h), service ceiling of 43,000ft (13,110m) and range of 450 miles (724km).

P-63 Production

On 29 September 1942 the US Army ordered the Kingcobra into production, which began in October 1943. The production P-63A – 1,725 of which were built in numerous sub-variants with minor changes in armament, armour and ordnance – was followed in 1943 by the P-63C with a 1,800hp Allison V-1710-117 engine with water injection. One P-63A (42-68937) was tested by the RAF as the Kingcobra Mk I (FR408).

The first P-63C (42-70886) introduced a distinc-tive small ventral fin to improve longitudinal stability. 1,227 P-63Cs were built, with an internal fuel capacity of 107(US)gal and 201lb (91kg) of armour. 2,456 Kingcobras were delivered to Russia and 300 P-63Cs went to France's Armée de l'Air.

Minor improvements to the Kingcobra included a V-1710-109 and modified wings. The sole P-63D (43-11718) introduced not only increased wing span but a bubble canopy. The first P-63E (43-11720) had the improved wing but the standard canopy, and twelve aircraft in this series were built before contracts for 2,930 were cancelled at war's end. A sole P-63F (43-11719) introduced the V-1710-135 powerplant, taller vertical fin, and survived the war to become H. L. Pemberton's mount in the 1947 Cleveland Air Races; a second 'F' model was cancelled.

P-63s were ferried to Russia in seemingly endless numbers via Alaska and Iran. In Soviet hands, the P-63 Kingcobra proved to be a potent ground-attacker and tank-buster, although perhaps not the equal of the Ilyushin Il-2 Shturmovik. In Free French service, the P-63 seems to have had a more innocuous career. The relatively few Kingcobras retained by the US Army were used primarily for training. None ever reached the war zone or served in combat.

In 1945 and after, P-63 Kingcobras were used as flying targets, painted bright red, piloted, and shot at

The Bell P-63 Kingcobra represented a considerable advance over the earlier P-38 Airacobra. Introducing the taller tail evaluated on the XP-39E and a laminar-flow wing, the P-63 was faster and more powerful than its predecessor, although it never measured up to the best fighters of the war. (Bell)

Kingcobra 42-69417 was among 1,825 aircraft produced of the P-63A model, by far the most numerous version. It appears to be on a factory proving flight prior to delivery. The Kingcobra retained the nose-mounted 37mm cannon found on the earlier P-39 Airacobra. (Bell)

Bell RP-63C-2-BE was one of a number of Kingcobras which were reinforced with metal plating and used as manned, flying targets for fighters shooting with frangible bullets. This 1940s version of 'Top Gun' was a somewhat dubious practice. (via Roger Besecker)

The external lines of the Kingcobra are evident in this post-war view of Bell P-63F 43-11719 (the 'F' model having a non-standard vertical tail), registered NX1719 with race number 21 and flown by H. L. Pemberton in the Thompson Trophy race at Cleveland, Ohio, in 1947. (Clyde Gerdes)

by other fighters using frangible bullets. This was a most peculiar way to achieve some gunnery practice, but it seems to have worked. Combat equipment was removed and these 'robot' RP-63A and RP-63G aircraft were insulated with a 1,488lb (675kg) protective covering of duralumin alloy, bullet-proof windshield and canopy glass, a steel grille over the engine air intake, steel guards for the exhaust stubs, and thick-walled hollow propellers. When a hit was scored by another aircraft performing gunnery practice, a red light blinked to confirm impact, causing one RP-63A (42-69654) and the operation itself to be nicknamed 'Pinball'. For more than 35 years an RP-63G (45-57295) has been on outdoor display at Lackland AFB, Texas, where all enlisted airmen undergo basic training.

The sole XP-63H was converted from a P-63E to test new internal systems. Two P-63s without discrete designations were modified to test the V-shaped or 'butterfly' tail more familiarly associated with the Beechcraft Bonanza. A sole P-63 was rebuilt with swept-back wings and test-flown by the US Navy under the non-standard designation L-39. Total Kingcobra production reached 3,362. The type was Bell's last big success in the fighter field.

Reference was made in an earlier chapter to the North American P-64, which was the next Army fighter designation in numerical order. After that in this review of fighters which were not among the best of the war years comes a twin-engined design.

Although Grumman's first attempt at a twin-engined US Army fighter, the XP-50, was cut off prematurely by the loss of the aircraft, Grumman proceeded with the XP-50 programme and partly from the fascination with large 'convoy fighters' felt by Colonel Elliott Roosevelt and others at the outbreak of American participation in the war.

Following the loss of the only XP-50, Grumman managed to arouse Army interest in their company model G-46, a larger twin-engined fighter to be powered by 1,700hp Wright R-2600-22W Double Wasp 18-cylinder radials with either two-stage mechanical superchargers or turbo-superchargers. Design work on that concept, begun in October 1939, prompted Grumman engineers to pursue further efforts with the company model G-49, an export version proposed in February 1940, and with the company model G-51, a naval fighter which was submitted on 24 March 1941. Neither of these aircraft was built, but Army officers made known a strong interest in a twin-engined fighter with a pressurized cockpit and two 37mm cannon as well as four 0.50in (12.7mm) machine-guns.

The XP-65 was essentially a land-based version of the US Navy twin-engined fighter which became the post-war F7F Tigercat. The XP-65 would have lacked the folding wings, carrier-deck landing gear, and second crew member of the F7F, and would have been an outstanding performer, highly suited to long-range escort missions over Europe.

The XP-65 would have been a big aircraft with a wing span of 52ft 6in (16m), length of 46ft 5in (14.15m), height of 15ft 2in (4.62m) and wing area of 455sq ft (42.27m²). Armament was to comprise four 20mm cannon and four 0.50in (12.7mm) machine-guns. The XP-65 was to have had a maximum speed of 429mph (690km/h), service ceiling of 40,000ft (12,405m) and range of 825 miles (1,397km).

XP-65 Myth

It is not true, as has been widely reported, that the US Army tested an F7F Tigercat at Wright Field,

The author photographed this Kingcobra on static display while going through basic training at Lackland Air Force Base, Texas, in August 1957. RP-63G 45-57295, another flying target from the frangible bullet project, is still on outdoor display at Lackland. (A/3C Robert F. Dorr)

Ohio, and found the machine unsuited for its use. In fact, the F7F did not fly until more than two years after the Army's decision had been made. The Army ordered two XP-65 prototypes on 16 June 1941, two weeks before the Navy awarded a contract for two F7F prototypes. Subsequently both services agreed that a single design would not meet their very different requirements, and on 16 January 1942 the Army dropped out of the programme to enable Grumman to optimize the design for naval use.

The XP-65 would have outperformed all other US twin-engined fighters then being contemplated (XP-49, XP-58, Hughes XF-11) and could have been available much sooner. Furthermore, the Army could have made cost-effective use of another air-cooled fighter, the P-47 Thunderbolt being the only type employed in numbers during the war. Had Grumman not wanted the XP-65 to interfere with their prodigious outpouring of Hellcats, the pro-gramme could have been transferred to another builder such as Vultee or Vought. At the latter company, Charles Lindbergh was investigating the performance of twin-engined fighter designs.

Vultee was the company that made use of the next fighter designation in numerical order. Together with William Schwendler and Dick Hutton at Grum-man, Richard Palmer of Vultee was another aero-nautical engineer and ace designer of warplanes who received far too little credit. In 1938 Palmer's design team conceived Vultee's company Model 48 as an all-metal, low-wing monoplane fighter with retract-able undercarriage and a unique flush-fitting cowling

over its 1,200hp Pratt & Whitney R-1830-S3C4-G Twin Wasp 14-cylinder twin-row radial engine driv-ing a Hamilton Standard 23E50 three-bladed hydro-matic propeller. The design work marked the beginning of the saga of a fighter which came along too late to be of much use to anybody, spending its US Army career as a neglected orphan.

The full story of the Vultee 48, which became the P-66 Vanguard, includes an order from Sweden, tests by Britain, routine duties defending the western USA, and a cameo appearance in Chinese markings. The Vanguard was a major programme which evolved almost by accident, changing purpose as events themselves changed.

As with many other fighters, the Vanguard soon underwent a series of minor changes. The low-drag cowling design, fitted on the same P & W engine in the Curtiss XP-42, posed cooling problems and, although tested on Vultee's fourth prototype by Vance Breese in 1939, was discarded in favour of conventional open-air cooling.

The production prototype of the Vultee Model 48C Vanguard, as it became known, flew in September 1940. Sweden ordered 144 examples with the Flyg-vapen designation J 10. Although one Vanguard flew with Swedish markings, the 1940 embargo on export American sales – which also affected a number of Seversky P-35s – prevented delivery of any of the aircraft. Unwittingly the US forced Sweden to develop her own indigenous aircraft industry – a major investment for a country with a population of six million.

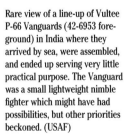

Rare view of a line-up of Vultee P-66 Vanguards (42-6953 fore-ground) in India where they arrived by sea, were assembled, and ended up serving very little practical purpose. The Vanguard was a small lightweight nimble fighter which might have had possibilities, but other priorities beckoned. (USAF)

With the Vultee fighter still in need of a home, Britain laid plans to purchase 100 Vanguards with serials BW208–BW307. This was during the troubled times when the ability of the Royal Air Force to equip with British-built fighters was not fully assured, and it turned out to be an unnecessary indulgence. Only three aircraft (BW208–BW210) actually flew with the RAF serials painted on before British plans were changed. It was apparently at this juncture that these machines acquired US serial numbers (42-6832 to 42-6975) and the out-of-sequence designation P-66.

While the Vultee fighter was still on the production line, fifteen Vanguards were earmarked for US Army operational training duties on the American west coast with the 14th Pursuit Group at Oakland, California. It was one of numerous occasions when the Army had to bear the expense of maintaining and operating an aircraft type in small, uneconomical numbers. The remaining 129 Vanguards were scheduled for delivery to China – the orphan still in search of adoption.

The P-66 Vanguard was a clean-looking fighter and had typical characteristics for a pre-war design, including a maximum speed of 340mph (558km/h), service ceiling of 28,200ft (8,595m) and range of 850 miles (1,360km). Dimensions were: wing span 35ft 10in (10.9m), length 28ft 5in (8.66m), height 13ft

(3.94m) and wing area 197sq ft (18.3m^2). Weight empty was 5,235lb (2,371kg) and maximum take-off weight 7,400lb (3,352kg). Armament of the P-66 Vanguard included four 0.50in (12.7mm) Colt synchronized machine-guns in the cowling and four 0.30in (7.62mm) Colt wing machine-guns.

The Chinese P-66 Vanguards were shipped by sea to Karachi, India. Plans called for them to be reassembled and flown to Chengtu, China. Some crashed during trial flights after reassembly, some were lost en route, and others were simply stored in and out of the Karachi aerodrome's massive dirigible hangar. Says technician Sam Timson, 'Some of them rotted there.' Indeed, if the P-66 is remembered as anything, it is as a collection of wrecked relics cluttering that giant hangar.

The P-66 should have been about equal to the Nakajima Ki-43 'Oscar' fighters the Japanese Army would throw against it in the south-west China theatre. Formidably armed with its eight guns, the P-66 was manoeuvrable and had good endurance. But Chinese pilots trained on the tricycle-gear Bell P-39 found it difficult to land this unforgiving 'tail-dragger' and cracked up many of them in trial flights at Karachi. A mid-air collision within eyesight of dozens of people near the runway's end snuffed out the lives of two Chinese pilots in an instant. Hydraulic problems and swollen rubber seals ham-

Although 100 RAF serials were allocated to prospective British versions of the Vultee P-66 Vanguard, only three flew in RAF colours, BW209 being shown here. The P-66 was too late to attain much of a production order with its pre-war technology, and was never a success in combat. (Vultee)

pered P-66s already weathered by their long sea voyage.

As few as 79 aircraft of the 129 shipped actually reached Chengtu. Flying the P-66 in combat was an experience, but scarcely an inspiring one, for beleaguered Chinese airmen. In a crosswind on the ground, the wide 13ft (3.96m) undercarriage track of the P-66 almost invited a catastrophic ground loop.

In most respects, the Vanguard handled well in the air but was unstable in a high-speed dive, and had poor spin and stall characteristics. It also had a superficial resemblance to its adversaries: in a confusing 21 November 1943 air battle, Chinese pilots shot down one Japanese Ki-43 but also despatched two friendly P-66s! In spite of all this, a few Chinese pilots scored air-to-air kills in the P-66 Vanguard and some may eventually have ended up in the hands of Chinese Communist forces.

McDonnell XP-67

Again, we return to the quest for a successful, large, twin-engined fighter, this time from a builder which had never turned out a fighter before, although the name was to become more familiar in post-war years.

The McDonnell XP-67 'Bomber Destroyer', or 'Moonbat', emanated from a little-known St Louis, Missouri, firm established by James S. McDonnell in 1939. The company picked up considerable wartime business, manufacturing Fairchild AT-13 advanced trainers, but the XP-67 was the first aircraft of McDonnell's own design. By the time it flew on 6 January 1944, the XP-67 was probably already too late to have any realistic hope of a production order.

The original design was for an engine located behind the pilot and driving a pair of pusher propellers through right-angle extension shafts, but this was rejected by the US Army Air Corps at the very time, in 1940, when it was ordering three machines of similar layout (Vultee XP-54, Curtiss XP-55, Northrop XP-56). McDonnell engineers then came up with a more conventional twin-engined fighter powered by two 1,150hp Continental XI-1430-17/19 engines with augmentor stacks providing additional thrust beyond that afforded by the four-bladed propellers.

The XP-67's sleek engine nacelles blended smoothly into the wings, as did the fuselage shape at the wing roots, thus offering minimal- drag although not providing additional lift. The company received a go-ahead to build two XP-67s (42-11677 and 42-11678) on 22 May 1941.

Rolled out at St Louis on 29 November 1943 – more than a year after the builder had originally hoped to fly it – the XP-67 was plagued by engine problems and, once, by a ground fire which very nearly destroyed the aircraft. In its early 1944 flight tests, it handled well but every measure of its performance fell short of expectations. It had been intended that the engines would provide 1,400hp and that a speed of 448mph (721km/h) at 20,000ft (6,192m) could be obtained. Actual top speed was around 405mph (652km/h) at that altitude. Service ceiling of the XP-67 was 37,000ft (11,278m), while range was 2,100 miles (3,380km).

Ferried to Wright Field, Ohio, the XP-67 was undergoing an official Army evaluation on 6 September 1944 when the starboard engine caught fire. The pilot landed safely but the blaze engulfed the

XP-67 fighter 42-11677 on roll-out at St Louis, 29 November 1943, displays the roomy cockpit and big twin engines which were to typify later fighters from its new manufacturer, McDonnell. The XP-67 was aerodynamically a very clean machine and might well have escorted Fortresses and Liberators to Berlin had the P-51D Mustang not proved up to the job. (McDonnell)

machine. A plan to complete the second prototype with an unusual four-engined configuration consisting of two 1,695hp Packard V-1650 licence-built Merlins and two 2,300lb (1,043kg) thrust jet engines proved too ambitious and the project had to be shelved. Although it was never among Colonel Elliott Roosevelt's candidates for a 'convoy fighter', had the XP-67 been available earlier it might well have escorted Fortresses and Liberators to Berlin. As had been the case with Grumman's XP-50, progress was halted in part because of the loss of the only prototype.

The XP-67 was 42ft (12.80m) long, with a wing span of 55ft (16.76m), height of 14ft 9in (4.50m) and wing area of 414sq ft (38.46m^2). It weighed 16,395lb (7,437kg) empty and had a maximum take-off weight of no less than 23,115lb (10,485kg). Plans existed to arm the aircraft with no fewer than six 37mm cannon – which almost certainly would have sharply reduced performance. As it turned out, the XP-67 was simply another interesting idea whose time had not yet come.

Almost no information has survived the war about the Vultee XP-68 Tornado, a 'might have been' fighter design that never got off the drawing-board. Apparently it was to have been powered by a huge 2,500hp Pratt & Whitney R-2160 in-line engine with large hollow-bladed, contra-rotating propellers. A number of post-war histories have ignored the XP-68 altogether, although the project apparently reached the stage where production was contemplated at Vultee's Nashville, Tennessee, plant.

The colossal R-2160 engine was also the proposed powerplant for the Republic XP-69, a planned conventional fighter of rather clean and graceful lines. The engine was a real behemoth, with no

fewer than 42 cylinders arrayed in six rows and displacing 21,670 cubic inches. Undaunted by this excess, the US Army ordered two prototypes of the XP-69, or company AP-18, in July 1941.

The busy design team headed by Alexander Kartveli at Republic undertook work on the XP-69 at about the same time as Kartveli was fashioning a 'Super Thunderbolt', which went through several conceptual stages before emerging as the XP-72. It seems likely that the latter project had a higher priority. Nevertheless, Republic completed a three-quarters-scale mock-up of the XP-69 in May 1942.

The XP-69 was configured with its engine mounted behind the pilot and fed by a bulged under-

Close-up of the cockpit of the McDonnell XP-67 fighter shows what this wartime fighter looked like on the inside. (McDonnell)

Somewhat retouched photo of the McDonnell XP-67 fighter in flight near the manufacturer's St Louis, Missouri, plant. (McDonnell)

Rare photo of the 9/10ths-scale model of the Republic XP-69 fighter in the National Advisory Committee for Aeronautics' wind tunnel at Langley Army Airfield, near Hampton, Virginia. Contra-rotating propellers were an important feature of the XP-69 design. (via George Cully)

fuselage air intake. It was to have contra-rotating propellers driven by an extension shaft passing beneath the pilot's feet. Engineering challenges posed by the airframe were formidable and Kartveli's team knew, early on, that the engine faced developmental problems as well.

The XP-69 was big. Dimensions included: wing span 51ft 8in (15.75m), length 51ft 6in (15.70m), height 17ft 3in (5.26m) and wing area 505sq ft (46.91m²). The XP-69 was to weight 15,250lb (7,074kg) empty, with a maximum take-off weight of 26,164lb (11,868kg).

There was considerable difficulty in developing the engine. Added to which, Kartveli's team seemed certain that the coming XP-72 held more promise. Although a nine-tenths-scale model of the XP-69 was tested at the National Advisory Committee for Aeronautics' wind tunnel at Langley Field, Virginia, the big fighter was never completed – another 'might have been' of war years which produced plenty of them.

Douglas P-70

Before the USA entered the war, Army officers in Washington were already searching for a short cut that would enable them to field a night interceptor quickly. RAF experience, coupled with the promise of the new invention known as radar, told them what was needed to cope with the threat of air attack at night. When an intruding enemy aircraft was detected, the night fighter would be guided to its target by a GCI (ground control interception) operator, who

watched the enemy on radar and passed directions to bring the night fighter to within 600ft (186m) of the enemy. By then, hopefully, the night fighter would be tracking the enemy with its own AI (airborne interception) radar. In the best of circumstances, the night fighter pilot would make visual contact and engage. The Douglas A-20 Havoc offered an ideal airframe with which to develop this idea, since it had the space for AI radar as well as enormous firepower. The night fighter required range and staying power, but did not need to 'yank and bank' in a dogfight, so it mattered little – or so it seemed – if the twin-engined Havoc was a little sluggish.

The designation P-70 was assigned by the Army to night fighter versions of the A-20 Havoc. Although they had a higher number, these aircraft were developed earlier than the Northrop P-61 Black Widow. The P-70 was at best an interim solution.

The first P-70 (39-735) was a conversion of the prototype A-20 Havoc fitted with two 1,600hp Pratt & Whitney R-2600-11 radial engines, a 'solid' nose containing British-designed AI radar, and an under-fuselage gun pack with four 20mm cannon.

The prototype was followed by 59 P-70s, converted from A-20 standard, 13 P-70A-1s converted from the A-20C with six nose-mounted 0.50in (12.7mm) machine-guns encircling the AI radar, and 26 P-70A-2s converted from A-20Gs. The sole P-70B was another A-20 conversion with the six-gun armament in blisters on the side of the fuselage, while the designation P-70B-2 went to A-20Gs and A-20Js used as night fighter trainers.

The P-70 aircraft was unchanged in size from the A-20 Havoc on which it was based. The crew of two sat in tandem, the pilot enjoying plenty of room and good visibility from his perch atop tricycle landing gear. Dimensions included: wing span 61ft 4in (15.57m), length 47ft 7in (14.50m), height 18ft 1in (5.51m) and wing area 465sq ft (43.20m²). Remarkably little heavier than some single-engined fighters, the P-70 weighed 15,730lb (7,135kg) empty and had a maximum take-off weight of 19,750lb (8,958kg). Maximum speed was 338mph (544km/h), service ceiling 28,250ft (7,188m) and range 1,090 miles (1,754km). The ceiling is important: for all its other qualities, the P-70 simply could not fly as high as some of the fighters and bombers it was designed to intercept.

Although the P-70 has a firm place among the lesser-known fighters of the war, it did at least get into service and into combat. The USAAF's 6th Night Fighter Squadron, the first unit given a true nocturnal mission, formed in Hawaii in September 1942 with P-70s. A detachment headed by Major Sydney F. Wharton deployed to Henderson Field on Guadalcanal, where besieged Marines were being battered by Japanese nocturnal air raids. There, P-70 crews and maintenance people lived and fought in abominably primitive conditions, which were not kind to the aeroplane or its radar.

On 18 April 1943 a P-70 shot down a Japanese 'Betty' bomber after a wild chase, pursuing its adversary through exploding friendly anti-aircraft fire in a weaving engagement witnessed by hundreds on the ground. Other air-to-air actions produced no aerial victories but may have had some impact in deterring nocturnal air raids. Wharton's P-70 detachment later fought in New Guinea.

The 418th Night Fighter Squadron also fought with P-70s at Guadalcanal. Its commander, Major Carroll C. Smith, later flew P-61 Black Widows and became one of the few aces to score five kills at night. The 419th and 421st squadrons, which followed, flew P-70s briefly.

The radar aboard most P-70s was primitive by any standard, and the Havoc never possessed the agility to tangle with 'Zeros' or other lightweight fighters. Throughout the P-70 programme attempts were made to refine and develop the night fighting capability of the 205 aircraft involved. The sole P-70B, however, was the only machine in the series equipped with fully working SCR-720 centimetric AI radar of the type later used on the P-61 Black Widow. In combat, pilots found the P-70 unable to climb rapidly enough for real effectiveness, and the number of kills scored at Guadalcanal and New Guinea remained small. Pilots in the 418th Night Fighter Squadron were so dissatisfied that they

When the decision was made to transform the Douglas A-20 Havoc attack bomber into a night fighter, the A-20 prototype (39-735) was converted for the role. Rare photo illustrates 39-735 in its original A-20 configuration before modifications were carried out. (Douglas)

The second Douglas A-20 Havoc (39-736) after partial conversion to P-70 night fighter configuration. The original P-70 which preceded P-70A-1 and A-2 models, as shown here, had a British radar in a solid nose and a cannon mounted in a ventral fairing. (USAF)

▷ Two P-70 night fighters packing ventral cannon in flight over the south-west American desert. Antenna for nose radar protrudes ahead of the aircraft while underfuselage cannon tray is also visible. Americans did not have as much success as the RAF with a night fighter based on the Havoc, and this type was quickly overshadowed by the Northrop P-61 Black Widow. (Douglas)

requested and obtained P-38H Lightnings with jury-rigged SCR-540 AI radar, long before the P-38M night fighter was developed. This marked the end of the P-70's significance as a combatant.

The designation XP-71 was given to a Curtiss design for a huge fighter, as large as a B-25 Mitchell, to have been powered by two turbo-supercharged 3,450hp Pratt & Whitney R-4360-13 Wasp Major pusher radials. This proposed fighter did not progress very far in the drawing-board stage and no likenesses of it seem to have survived.

'Super Thunderbolt'

A most impressive 'might have been' was the Republic XP-72, loosely based on the P-47 Thunderbolt airframe and designed by Alexander Kartveli and his design team around the same hefty, 28-cylinder, 3,000hp Pratt & Whitney R-4360-13 Wasp Major. As with its predecessor, the XP-72 was brute-sized. Its powerplant was, simply, the most powerful piston engine to reach production in any country during the war years.

Although its design was already well advanced before the threat appeared, the XP-72 was seen by USAAF officers as an antidote for the Germans' high-speed V-1 flying bomb. Plans were made to employ the XP-72 as an interceptor to catch these 'doodle-bugs' short of their targets, taking advantage of the fighter's ability to reach 20,000ft (6,096m) in just under five minutes.

When it was rolled out at Farmingdale, the XP-72 looked exactly like a Super Thunderbolt. It had a wing span of 40ft 11⅞in (12.49m), length of 36ft 7¹³/₁₆in (11.17m), height of 14ft 6in (4.41m) and wing area of 300sq ft (27.87m²). In fact, the XP-72 was only slightly heavier than late Thunderbolts,

thanks to intensive weight-paring efforts by Kartveli's staff, which among other things resulted in modest armament of six 0.50in (12.7mm) machine-guns. The XP-72 tipped the scales at 10,965lb (4,973kg) when empty and 14,750lb (6,690kg) fully loaded.

The first of two XP-72 prototypes (43-6598) flew at Farmingdale on 2 February 1944, using a large four-bladed propeller and a mechanical two-stage supercharger. The second prototype (43-6599) flew in July 1944 with the intended Aeroproducts six-bladed contra-rotating propeller. The second machine, however, was lost on an early test flight. The fuel consumption of its powerful engine limited the range of the XP-72, optimistically quoted at 1,200 miles (1,931km). While its service ceiling of 42,000ft (12,801m) was respectable enough, the arrival on the scene of jet-propelled fighters made the XP-72's top speed of 490mph (789km/h) inadequate. One hundred production P-72s were on order at one time and would probably have entered service and seen combat had the war lasted longer. The production aircraft were cancelled near the end of the conflict.

For reasons which have never been properly explained, the US Army did not assign the designations P-73 and P-74 to any aircraft. One possible explanation is that the builder of the XP-75 (see later) wanted an appealing designation number when it made a debut in the aircraft-manufacturing business. A better explanation is that aircraft designer Don Berlin was infatuated with the number 75. At Curtiss, the Berlin era of fighter projects had begun with the company's model 75, one version of which became the Army's P-36 Mohawk. When he left Curtiss in December 1941 and joined the Fisher Body Division of General Motors, Berlin may have, to quote speculation, 'put a bee in the Army's bonnet' about skipping to the P-75 designation.

Aircraft 43-9740 began life as a production A-20G Havoc but was converted to a P-70 night fighter. This aircraft is believed to be the only P-70B equipped with SCR-720 centimetric airborne interception radar of the type later employed with considerable success aboard the P-61 Black Widow. (via Norman Polmar)

The XP-75 Eagle was the only aircraft ever manufactured by the Fisher Body Division of General Motors. This little-known pursuit ship was built to a 1942 US Army requirement for a single-seat interceptor with a high rate of climb. A key requirement was to launch the project with minimal use of strategic materials needed in the mass production of other warplanes.

Don Berlin, whose work on early Curtiss fighters had contributed to the design of the P-51 Mustang, took charge of the engineering effort at Fisher on the XP-75 project. Berlin reckoned that components from other aeroplanes could be combined with the 2,885hp Allison V-3420-23 24-cylinder banked Vee liquid-cooled engine at greatly reduced cost, the result being a fighter easy to manufacture in a short time, needing few additional raw materials, to cope with the war's urgent demands.

This approach made the first of two XP-75 prototypes (43-46950 and 44-32162) a kind of hybrid, built with P-51 Mustang outer wing panels, F4U Corsair landing gear, and A-24 Dauntless tail unit. In the heady environment of the early war months, when the Army seemed willing to buy anything, an order was placed for 2,500 production P-75s. Had it reached fruition, the little-known P-75 Eagle would have become one of the very familiar aircraft types of the war years.

As the war developed, the Army was less interested in an interceptor and more inclined to want a long-range escort fighter. With the change in mission came a contract for six production XP-75As, no longer made from fragments of other aeroplanes. The XP-75A introduced a bubble canopy rather than the braced hood on the earlier machines. The XP-75A also introduced internal changes brought

The XP-72, sometimes referred to unofficially as the 'Super Thunderbolt', represented Republic's ultimate design for a wartime fighter and was powered by a massive 3,000hp Pratt & Whitney R-4360 Wasp Major radial engine. Had the war lasted longer, production P-72s might have reached the final fight against Japan. (Republic)

The second XP-72, 43-6599, was fitted with an Aero Products dual-rotation propeller. Wartime literature claimed that the aircraft reached a speed of 504mph (811km/h), although this figure was reached in actual flight only by the closely related XP-47J Thunderbolt. (Republic)

Viewed from any angle, the second Republic XP-72, with its six-bladed propeller, was a 'mean machine'. Originally designed as an interceptor, it was considered for the kind of long-range fighter missions which later became routine, but a production order was not forthcoming. (Republic)

about by the change in mission, with its greater fuel and range requirements. The XP-75A also had more components designed and built new from the outset.

The XP-75A was another large fighter. Dimensions included: wing span 49ft 4in (15.04m), length 40ft 5in (12.32m), height 15ft 6in (4.72m) and wing area 347sq ft (32.24m^2). Empty weight was 11,495lb (5,214kg) and maximum take-off weight 18,210lb (8,260kg). Performance figures indicate a maximum speed of about 400mph (644km/h), service ceiling of 36,000ft (10,975m) and range of 3,000 miles (4,828km). The XP-75A was to have been a veritable flying armada with ten 0.50in (12.7mm) forward-firing machine-guns, four in the fuselage and six in the wings.

The XP-75A Eagle had some basic aerodynamic

problems and even before the first aircraft (44-44550) flew in September 1944 it was apparent that the type was a disappointment. Long-delayed, the XP-75A could not even be fully evaluated until after P-51 Mustangs were already escorting bombers to Berlin. During its flight test programme, three Eagles were lost in crashes, two of them fatal, and on 27 October 1944 the Army cancelled the programme so abruptly that the sixth and final XP-75A never flew. One immaculate XP-75A (44-44553) has survived in non-flying condition and is displayed at the Air Force Museum in Dayton, Ohio.

The designation P-76 was assigned on 24 February 1942 to a variant of the Bell P-39 Airacobra. Apparently this was the same aircraft which emerged in production form as the P-39M.

The original configuration of the Fisher XP-75, seen here on the first prototype (43-46950), resembled cartoon creations of Rube Goldberg, who drew contraptions which purred, hissed, rattled and whined but did not accomplish much. This machine has P-51 Mustang outer wing panels, F4U Corsair landing gear and A-24 Dauntless empennage. (USAF)

Rare view at Wright Field, Ohio, of the second XP-75 (44-32162), a one-of-a-kind aircraft which must have been a real experience to fly. The later P-75A had a bubble canopy and squared-off tail, but even with improvements the Fisher fighter never found a practical role. (via Warren Bodie)

Bell XP-77

This review of 'might have been' fighters concludes with one of the most rakish of wartime machines, which took to the air on April Fools Day, 1944, at Niagara Falls, New York. The Bell XP-77 pursuit fighter was an all-wood lightweight made from Sitka spruce, patterned after racers of the 1930s and intended to operate from grass runways.

Partly because, once again, it posed little demand on strategic materials, the idea of a small, cheap, all-wood fighter had high appeal early in the war. In early 1941 the Bell firm began work on a machine at first called the 'Tri-4' – shorthand for an informal Army specification which demanded '400hp, 4,000lb and 400mph'.

On 16 May 1942 the Army ordered 25 'Tri-4' aircraft. 'It was a mistake,' says John J. Carr, engineer for Bell on the project. Delays, technical problems with sub-contracting on plywood construction, and disappointing wind-tunnel tests caused the manufacturer to suggest by early 1943 that the number of machines on order be reduced to six. In May 1943 the Army pared this number to two and serial numbers (43-34915 and 43-34916) were belatedly assigned.

The XP-77 was a single-seat aircraft with a tricycle undercarriage and a single Ranger SGV-770C-1B in-line engine developing up to 450hp. Empty weight was a mere 2,855lb (1,295kg), maximum take-off weight 4,029lb (1,827kg).

With a fuel capacity of 56(US)gal, the XP-77 had

a range of 550 miles (885km) and service ceiling of 30,100ft (9,175m). Dimensions of the aircraft reflected its bantam status: wing span 27ft 6in (8.38m), length 22ft 10½in (6.97m), height 8ft 2¼in (2.50m) and wing area 100sq ft (9.29m²).

Certainly the XP-77 (like the original Fisher XP-75 concept) might have served a purpose if the predicted shortage of critical aluminium alloy metals for aircraft had materialized. Plans existed to arm the sleek XP-77 with two synchronized 0.50in (12.7mm) machine-guns firing through the propeller disc and mounted atop the engine, or a cannon firing through the propeller hub.

By the beginning of July 1944, the second XP-77 was being tested at Eglin Field, Florida. On 2 October the aircraft fell out of an Immelmann turn into an inverted spin. The pilot recovered, but the aircraft then went into an upright flat spin, from which he could not recover and he was forced to jump. The pilot parachuted safely, but the aircraft was wrecked.

So, too, was the XP-77 programme. Plagued by noise and vibration, an unexpectedly long take-off run, and general performance 'inferior to present fighter aircraft' (according to an official report), the XP-77 was killed by administrative decision on 2 December 1944.

The prototype went to Wright Field, then Eglin, then back to Wright. It was seen at post-war displays wearing spurious markings, including stripes around the fuselage. Viewers might have admired its racy lines, never knowing that when it achieved its peak speed of 328mph (528km/h) at 12,000ft (3,715m), the disappointing XP-77 fell far short of the speed its designers had been charged with attaining. Described in cowboy terms as 'an engine with a saddle on it', the surviving XP-77 is thought to have been scrapped in the immediate post-war period.

The XP-78 designation was applied briefly to the Merlin-powered North American P-51 Mustang, and fortunately was changed to P-51B before any of these superb fighters were actually built.

The XP-79, which is next in numerical order but was conceived some years later, was a Northrop flying-wing fighter of all-magnesium construction. Early plans called for it to be powered by one 2,000lb (907kg) thrust Aerojet rocket engine. After development of the rocket powerplant had been delayed, Northrop built the XP-79B 'Flying Ram' (43-52437), powered by two 2,000lb (907kg) thrust Westinghouse J30 axial-flow turbojets. Not flown until 12 September 1945, this bizarre machine probably belongs to the category of post-war aeroplanes. It was not a success, although it continued an already long-standing Northrop association with the flying wing planform, which was to reappear in one design or another for the remainder of the century.

It is almost impossible to measure the contribution to knowledge – to say nothing of the impact on individual lives – of the 'might have beens' described here, the P-63, XP-65, P-66, XP-67, XP-68, XP-69, P-70, XP-71, XP-72, XP-75, XP-77 and XP-79. This round dozen of Army fighters in the war years could be left out of a brief account of the conflict with no serious loss to historical accuracy. So too, perhaps, could some of the Navy fighters be omitted from the following chapter, but it is impossible to avoid curiosity about these little-known aircraft. More, then, is the pity that most of the manufacturers either no longer exist, or have not kept historical records. It was a fascinating and exciting era, a time of new ideas and genuine invention, and every one of these aircraft had a place in it, as well as a small part, at least, in determining the outcome of the conflict.

Included in the category of 'also rans' was the Bell XP-77, an all-wood lightweight fighter made from Sitka spruce and patterned after small, nimbler racers of the 1930s. The XP-77 might have fared well in a fight but would not have been able to travel very far. It was one of the smallest fighters of the Second World War. (Bell)

Navy Fighters

Once the United States had recoiled and recovered from the shock of being hurled into a war for which few preparations had been made, engineers, industry and test pilots began developing and producing a succession of fighters which required no apology or explanation. The US Navy's Hellcats and Corsairs became the best of their kind. The pilots who flew them went through a series of incarnations – the highly experienced veteran of pre-war service, the inexperienced new product of a citizen armada, and finally the experienced wartime pilot who took on the best the enemy had to offer, and prevailed.

In the US Navy as elsewhere, for aircraft designs which succeeded, dozens failed to make the grade for one reason or another – often arbitrary reasons. Usually, if an aircraft failed to go into production, it had too many design problems or it came along too late. Had the timing been different, we might have seen squadrons of carrier-based, jet-prop Ryan Fireballs swarming down on the Japanese home islands, or circular-shaped 'Flying Flapjacks' fighting the final air duels of the war before VJ-Day. Timing was everything. As was the case with the all-white Curtiss XF14C-2 and so many othr Navy fighters, the only thing wrong with the aircraft was that it came along at the wrong time, after the Hellcat and Corsair had cemented their place in history.

It should be mentioned here that in this volume it has been decided to consider wartime fighters, rather loosely, in the order of the designations they received. In the US Army the designation was simple. Each fighter was a pursuit ship, and they came in number order, the P-47 following the P-46. A suffix letter indicated a variant, the P-47C being followed by the P-47D. An 'X' prefix indicated that the aeroplane was experimental, as in XP-47E.

The US Navy had a different system which was not readily apparent to all. In the Navy system of aircraft designations, the suffix letter was a quick reference to an aeroplane's manufacturer and could be handy, but only so long as the observer knew which letter went with which builder. Newcomers to the aviation scene needed time to learn that the Navy assigned the suffix 'A' (as in F2A Buffalo) not to a firm whose name began with 'A', but to Brewster. Other suffix letters in the Navy system included: 'B' for Boeing, 'C' Curtiss; 'F' Grumman, 'G' Goodyear, 'H' McDonnell, 'J' North American, 'L' Bell, 'M' General Motors (and Martin), 'N' Naval Aircraft Factory, 'R' Ryan, 'T' Northrop, 'U' Vought, 'V' Lockheed and 'Y' Consolidated (some being manufacturers which produced no fighters in the war).

In the Navy system, the prefix 'F' indicated a fighter and the number which followed indicated how many fighter designs had been developed by a builder (the F4U being Vought's fourth Navy fighter, the F6F being Grumman's sixth). A number added as a final suffix after a dash (the -3 in F6F-3, or the -4 in F4U-4) identified a variant of a major aircraft type. The F6F-3 was the third major variant of the Hellcat, the F4U-4 the fourth variant of the Corsair. A specialized mission could be added at the end with yet another letter, as in F6F-3N where the final 'N' indicated a night fighter mission.

So the reader may consider this presentation to be in no order at all or, if he chooses, may note that we begin with the 'A' suffix (Brewster), move on to 'B' (Boeing) and so on.

Portly Buffalo

In 1940 any naval aviator might have been forgiven for guessing that the standard American fighter of

the coming conflict would be the Brewster F2A
Buffalo. The portly Buffalo had won a production
order after a direct contest with Grumman's Wildcat
and was given great prominence in the Brewster
company's advertising. At the time, few realized that
the Brewster firm was suffering from terminal
management problems. Fewer still perhaps were
aware that the American standard for fighter performance, in those pre-war years, was strictly second-
rate. Before Americans were drawn into the war,
they had little glimpse of fighters from Messerschmitt
and Mitsubishi and might therefore have been
deluded into thinking that the Brewster Buffalo was
adequate.

The Buffalo traces its origin to a 1936 US Navy
requirement for a new generation of carrier-based
fighters. The aircraft-carrier itself was still a rather
new concept at this time, and naval planners were
only beginning to create the doctrine and tactics
which would mate a first-class fighting ship with its
aerial complement, the Carrier Air Group.

The Navy seemed not yet to have made up its
mind at this juncture whether the day of the biplane
fighter was near its end. The new fighter being
sought by the service was specified to be a monoplane (and to have wing flaps, arrester hook,
enclosed cockpit and retractable landing gear), but
one design actually submitted to the Navy retained
the established biplane configuration. This was the
Grumman XF4F-1, submitted along with the
Brewster XF2A-1 and the unsuccessful Seversky
XFN-1. So uncertain was the Navy that it seriously
considered the XF4F-1 as back-up insurance in case
a monoplane failed. In due course, however, the
XF2A-1 won an unqualified nod and Grumman went
back to the drawing-boards, later re-establishing
their dominance with the monoplane XF4F-2
Wildcat.

To launch the F2A series, a single prototype of the
Brewster XF2A-1 was ordered on 22 June 1936 and
made its maiden flight in December 1937. The
fighter has been described as both stubby and fat,
characteristics of earlier Brewster designs, although
a look at its dimensions shows that the aircraft was
actually very normal in size: wingspan 35ft (10.67m),
length 26ft 4in (8.03m), height 12ft 1in (3.68m) and
wing area 208.9sq ft (19.41m^2). Not a heavyweight
despite its impression of size, the XF2A-1 weighed
4,723lb (2,146kg) empty and had a maximum take-
off weight of 7,158lb (3,247kg).

Power for the new fighter was provided by a
950hp Wright XR-1820-22 Cyclone radial engine.
The XF2A-1 was a mid-wing monoplane of all-metal
construction except for fabric-covered control surfaces. The main units of the tailwheel undercarriage

A herculean effort went into filming these Brewster F2A-2 Buffalo fighters peeling off on 3 August 1942. An earlier version of this picture went into a Brewster advertisement at the start of December 1941 and proclaimed that 'fast, hard-hitting Brewster shipboard fighters' would 'guard the Pacific outposts of America's possessions'. The ad was focused on Hawaii (still, in those days, a 'possession' and not yet a state), but it was to be a few days longer before most people learned the name of the big Navy base there – Pearl Harbor. (USN)

Lieutenant Commander J. C. Clifton is the occupant of the very roomy cockpit in this Brewster F2A-2 Buffalo chugging along over American skies on 2 August 1942. His elaborate radio antenna and elongated gunsight probably work effectively, but Clifton is not flying the very best aircraft with which to confront a Mitsubishi 'Zero'. (USN)

retracted inwards to be housed in fuselage wells, and control surfaces included hydraulically operated split flaps.

Evaluation of the prototype began in January 1938, and on 11 June 1938 the Navy placed an order with Brewster for 54 production F2A-1s. Deliveries began in June 1939, and an early batch of nine fighters went to fighter squadron VF-3 operating aboard the USS *Saratoga*. Navy plans for further employment of the service's first monoplane fighter were interrupted when an unexpected need on the European continent resulted in 44 others being diverted to Finland, which was then locked in battle with the Soviet Union. These F2A-1s equipped the Finnish Air Force's premier fighter unit, HLeLv 24, and remained in front-line service, achieving remarkable results, until 1944. Finland's top air ace, Warrant Officer Juutilainen, scored 34 of his 92 aerial victories while flying the Buffalo.

Only eleven F2A-1s (BuNos 1386–1396) ended up in US Navy service. Eight were later upgraded to F2A-2 standard and assigned to squadron VS-201, flying from the escort carrier USS *Long Island* (CVE-1). As early as mid-1941, only one of these F2A-1s (1393) remained in inventory, assigned to a training unit.

Improved F2As

In early 1939 the Navy showed that it still felt confidence in the Buffalo. An order was placed for 43 improved F2A-2s, with a more powerful engine, improved propeller, and built-in flotation gear. The F2A-2 entered Navy service in September 1940. The 'Flying Chiefs' of squadron VF-2 made the transition from Grumman F2F biplanes to the F2A-1 Buffalo, and were pleased to have high-speed (by the standard of the time) monoplanes.

Based on a January 1941 order was the definitive F2A-3 version. The Brewster F2A-3 Buffalo introduced additional armour, a bullet-proof windshield and increased fuel capacity. The aircraft also had a redesigned nose section with a 10in extension to the forward fuselage between the wing and the cowling, which was to lead to problems with the centre of gravity. 108 were ordered (BuNos 01516 to 01623).

The F2A-3 version was delivered from August 1941 onwards to Navy squadrons VF-2, VF-3 and VS-201. Later, F2A-3s were replaced by the Wildcat in Navy colours and some were transferred to Marine Corps squadrons VMF-211 and VMF-221. In the Atlantic, VS-201 aboard *Long Island* operated the F2A-3 alongside Curtiss SOC Seagull observation

aircraft on Atlantic Neutrality Patrols. In the Pacific, VF-2 'Flying Chiefs' had the aircraft at the time of Pearl Harbor.

During the Battle of Midway, a four-aircraft flight headed by Captain Joseph Neefus intercepted a Japanese H8K 'Emily' flying-boat on a reconnaissance mission and shot it down, one of the first instances where the Brewster Buffalo shined. The 25 or so Buffaloes which teamed up with Wildcats to attempt a defence at Midway were massacred. One officer reported, 'It is my belief that any commander who orders a pilot out for combat in an F2A-3 should consider the pilot as lost before leaving the ground.'

It is almost impossible to describe the rage felt by Navy and Marine fliers when they found themselves totally outclassed in the cockpit of the F2A-3 Buffalo. Some of this was misguided – the anger over the Buffalo was a convenient way to ignore more deeply rooted reasons for failure and defeat in the early days of the Pacific war – but for whatever reason, the Buffalo went down in ignominy. One said that his Buffalo was 'meat on the table' for aggressive, experienced Japanese pilots in their formidable 'Zeros'. At Wake Island, where the Japanese military machine overran American defenders, some Buffaloes flew only one mission before being wiped out. The F2A-3 was overweight, unstable, and not very manoeuvrable. Its armament of four 0.50in (12.7mm) machine-guns was ineffective.

The XF2A-4 was the final effort to improve the Buffalo design. This was an experimental, pressurized-cockpit variant with a four-bladed propeller. One was built (being a conversion of an earlier Buffalo) and production was not contemplated.

Figures for the performance of the Buffalo indicate a maximum speed of 321mph (517km/h), service ceiling of 33,200ft (10,120m) and range of 965 miles (1,553km). No match for its adversaries, the Buffalo was quickly replaced in the Fleet by the Wildcat. There were a number of reasons for this apart from the aeroplane's lacklustre performance, including Navy displeasure with Brewster's continuing production problems, poor management and unpopular sales team. Apart from the Finns, foreign users fared little better. RAF, Australian, and Netherlands East Indies export versions of the Buffalo had little impact on the course of the conflict.

The F3A designation went to the Brewster-produced Vought F4U Corsair. F3A-1s served in the Fleet alongside Corsairs from the original builder.

Another Brewster design being considered by the Navy was a twin-boom aircraft, Proposal 33A, conceived by Dayton Brown, designer of the Buffalo. The twin-boom, shipboard fighter never received a Navy designation (which would have been F4A-1) and was never built.

Boeing Fighter

A generation apart from the Buffalo, the Boeing XF8B was the only wartime fighter produced by the Seattle, Washington, manufacturer which turned out tens of thousands of bombers. The XF8B-1 was a response to a perceived need for a long-range fighter-bomber able to extend the striking range of aircraft-carriers during the final offensive against Japan. Three XF8B-1s (BuNos 57984 to 57986), known to the manufacturer as the Model 400, were ordered on 4 May 1943.

First flown on 27 November 1944, the XF8B-1 was powered by a 2,500hp Pratt & Whitney R-4360-10 Wasp Major driving six-bladed contra-rotating propellers. Armament was six 0.50in (12.7mm) machine-guns plus 6,400lb (2,903kg) of bombs and torpedoes. Because Army fighters with the R-4360 were never completed, the XF8B-1 became the most powerful single-engined fighter developed by any nation during the war. Only the prototype flew before VJ-Day, however, and the XF8B-1 was not fully evaluated until long after the war. Boeing found themselves with other priorities, and the first jets appeared before the propeller-driven XF8B-1 could show its mettle.

The XF14C was one of two Navy fighters developed by Curtiss during the war years. Curtiss, who had not built a Navy fighter since the F13C of the 1930s, won a June 1941 contract for two examples of their Model 94, one (the XF14C-1) to be powered by an Avco Lycoming H-2470-4 engine and the other (XF14C-2) by a 2,300hp Wright XR-3350-16 radial. When development of the Lycoming powerplant ran into difficulty, only the XF14C-2 was completed. Basically, it was a navalized version of the Army's P-62 but without the latter's pressurized canopy.

Dimensions of the XF14C-2 included: wing span 46ft (14.02m), length 37ft 9in (11.51m), height 17ft (5.18m) and wing area 375sq ft (34.84m²). Somewhat lighter than its Army Air Corps counterpart but far from a featherweight, the XF14C-2 weighed 10,531lb (4,777kg) empty and 14,950lb (6,781kg) loaded.

It appears that the XF14C-2 was relatively successful in early flight tests. Performance statistics included: maximum speed 418mph (673km/h), service ceiling 39,800ft (12,130m) and range 1,530 miles (2,456km). The XF14C-2 was painted in an all-white finish which was non-standard and looked very impressive. It might have had a bright future had it appeared earlier, but by mid-1944 when flight testing

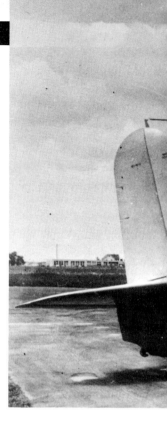

The US Navy developed a number of fighters which gained from technical lessons learned during the war years but were completed too late to have any effect on the outcome of the conflict. The Curtiss XF14C-1 was rolled out in 1943 but did not become well known until after VJ-Day. It was one of numerous aircraft with contra-rotating propellers, also manufactured by Curtiss. (USN)

got under way, the F4U Corsair and F6F Hellcat were well established on the production lines and in squadron service with the Navy. Whatever its merit, the XF14C-2 did not offer a significant improvement over the Hellcat and Corsair, so the programme was terminated after a few test flights.

There remained one further Second World War fighter to emerge from the Curtiss stable, one of the final products of a great aircraft manufacturer now experiencing a foundering of fortune.

This was the XF15C. The US Navy was looking at pure-jet power for its combat aircraft (although not as quickly or with as much enthusiasm as the Army), and had some doubts. Thus, in April 1944, the Navy ordered from Curtiss three prototypes of a single-seat fighter to be powered by a composite of reciprocating and turbojet engines.

Designated XF15C-1 and known to its manufacturer as the model 99, the final Curtiss fighter for the Navy had a 2,100hp Pratt & Whitney R-2800-34W radial piston engine and a 2,700lb (1,225kg) thrust Allis-Chalmers H-1B turbojet engine installed in the centre of the fuselage. The latter was a licence-built American adaptation of Britain's de Havilland Goblin turbojet. The jet-prop combination, also flown on the Ryan FR-1 Fireball (see later) and Convair XP-81, combined the proven capabilities of the old with the obvious advantages of the new. It was a compromise at a time when American industrial and technical genius needed no compromises – a time when the bold leap directly to jet power was being made with great success in other aircraft designs.

XF15C-1 Flight

The first of the trio of XF15C-1 prototypes made its maiden flight on 27 February 1945. It was an all-metal cantilever low-wing monoplane with retractable landing gear and by any measure it was big. The XF15C-1's wing spanned 48ft (14.63m) and its fuselage was 44ft (13.41m) in length; height was 15ft 3in (4.65m) and its squared-off wing had an area of 400sq ft (37.16m^2).

The XF15X-1 was both too large and too heavy to have become a successful carrier-based fighter. It weighed 12,648lb (5,737kg) empty, a figure which rose to 18,698lb (8,481kg) at maximum take-off weight.

The first prototype, flown with a conventional tail unit and at first without the jet engine installed, was lost in an accident in May 1945. Flight tests resumed with the second and third prototypes, these being fitted with a T-tail of the kind that came into vogue later. Just as the XF15C-1 project began to regain momentum lost by the crash, the war ended. In the dismantling of the military establishment which came with peace, funding for new aircraft was limited. The Navy – which never flew a pure jet during the war, except for a borrowed Army P-59 Airacomet – abandoned the Curtiss design and turned belatedly to pure jet designs.

If the XF15C-1 had appeared earlier or the war had lasted longer, the Navy might well have ironed out wrinkles in the fighter's hybrid configuration and ended up with a ship able to outperform Hellcats and

Corsairs: the XF15C-1 was able to reach a speed of 469mph (755km/h) with both engines operating, although its speed fell to a disappointing 373mph (600km/h) on piston power only. The XF15C-1 is said to have had a ceiling of 41,800ft (12,740m) and range of 1,385 miles (2,229km).

The Grumman F7F Tigercat, or company model G-51, traces its origins to work in 1941 on a new twin-engined fighter for operations from the planned larger carriers of the 'Midway' class. Although the Army dropped out of participation with the parallel XP-65, the Navy awarded Grumman a contract for two XF7F-1 prototypes on 30 June 1941.

The F7F was an all-metal, cantilever, shoulder-wing, twin-engined monoplane with wings designed to fold for carrier stowage. The aircraft had retractable tricycle landing gear and a carrier arresting hook. The aircraft achieved a certain grace with a very thin, teardrop-shaped fuselage and two rather fat engines, both 2,100hp Pratt & Whitney R-2800-22W Double Wasp radials driving three-bladed propellers.

Had it operated from carriers, the Tigercat would have been the largest piston-engined fighter ever to do so. Wing span was 51ft 6in (15.70m), length 45ft 4½in (13.83m), height 16ft 7in (5.05m) and wing area 455sq ft (42.27m²). In its production form, the aircraft weighed 16,270lb (7,380kg) empty and 25,720lb (11,666kg) fully loaded.

The first flight of an XF7F-1 Tigercat was made on 3 November 1943 by Grumman's ubiquitous Bob Hall, although Hall had inadvertently become airborne for a few seconds during taxi runs the previous day. Even before this, Grumman received a contract for 500 production aircraft under the designation F7F-1. These were intended for the Marine Corps which was then struggling through its island-hopping campaign against Japanese bastions in the Pacific. The intention was to station the F7F-1 Tigercats at Marine land bases, where they could support ground troops. In fact, by the time production Tigercats were available, the war had ended.

The first production F7F-1 was generally similar to the prototypes, as were the 33 aircraft which followed – all of these being single-seaters – and deliveries began in April 1944. The 35th aircraft was modified for use as a night fighter under the designation XF7F-2N, and 30 production F7F-2N aircraft followed in 1944. These differed from earlier machines by deletion of the aft fuselage fuel tank to provide space for the radar operator's position.

The F7F-3 version marked a return to the single-seat configuration; 189 of these were built, powered by R-2800-34 engines. This was the last version to

be in production during the war years, although the post-war era saw F7F-3N, F7F-3E, F7F-3P and F7F-4N versions. Outside the scope of this narrative, the Tigercat performed admirably with Marine Corps units during the Korean War and scored a number of night air-to-air kills.

The F7F-3 version was capable of a maximum speed of 435mph (700km/h), service ceiling of 40,700ft (12,405m) and had a range of 1,200 miles (1,931km). The Tigercat was armed with four 20mm cannon in the wing roots and four 0.50in (12.7mm) machine-guns in the nose. In the centre-line position under the fuselage, it could carry a fuel tank, bomb, or torpedo.

The Grumman F8F Bearcat was designed from wartime experience with the goal of achieving a lightweight, high-powered interceptor able to operate from small escort carrier decks as well as larger ships. Two XF8F-1 prototypes were ordered on 27 November 1943 and the first flew on 21 August 1944. The Bearcat was smaller than the Navy's famous Hellcat and 20 per cent lighter. Powered by a 2,100hp Pratt & Whitney R-2800-34W Double Wasp radial, it was capable of 421mph (678km/h).

Delivery of production F8F-1s began by VJ-Day. Eventually 1,266 aircraft were delivered, including 765 F8F-1, 100 F8F-1B, 36 F8F-1N, 293 F8F-2, 12 F8F-2N, and 60 F8F-2P fighters, and the Bearcat was still being used by the Vietnamese Air Force as late as 1962 – one of numerous aircraft which flew during the war years but made a mark in the post-war era.

The Eastern Aircraft division of General Motors, which manufactured the FM Wildcat (in FM-1 and FM-2 versions) received a Navy letter of intent in February 1945 to produce 1,876 Bearcats under the designation F3M. In fact, the war ended before a single F3M-1 could be produced, and the order was cancelled on VJ-Day.

Eastern Fighter

Meanwhile, Eastern were pursuing a fighter design of their own under the designation F2M. The F2M-1 may be the least-known American fighter of the war; its builder abandoned the aircraft business after VJ-Day and may have thrown out all historical records as early as 1945.

About all that is known about the F2M-1 is that it was to have been a low-wing, lightweight interceptor for operation from escort carriers. It would have been powered by a 1,200hp Wright R-1820-67/69 Cyclone 9-cylinder radial engine driving a three-bladed Curtiss constant-speed propeller. The requirement to be satisfied by the F2M-1 was either

The Grumman F7F Tigercat is only nominally a Second World War fighter. It was developed concurrently with the USAAF's unfinished XP-65 and was intended for carrier operations in the Pacific. However, it did not see combat until the Korean conflict which came five years later. This graceful, powerful, twin-engined machine served only in limited numbers, but was loved by the pilots who flew it. (via M. J. Kasiuba)

identical to, or similar to, that which produced the Bearcat, and the Navy may have felt enough confidence in Grumman not to need an alternative from another builder.

In 1942 the Navy drew up an unusual specification for a carrier-based fighter-bomber to be powered by one of the new turbojet engines in the rear fuselage and a piston engine mounted conventionally in the nose. This apparently was a separate requirement from the one which produced the Curtiss XF15C-1, although the combination of prop and jet power was the same. The Navy saw the piston engine as the ideal powerplant for landing and long-range cruise, or to supplement the turbojet in high-speed flight. The piston engine was also viewed as insurance against failure of the as yet unproven turbojet. Again, a compromise was being created and compromises have disadvantages.

The Ryan FR Fireball, the first fighter ever designed for the Navy by the San Diego, California, builder, was the result of this plan to mix jet and prop power. The Navy ordered three XFR-1 prototypes and 100 FR-1 production aircraft.

The first prototype made its maiden flight on 25 June 1944 without the turbojet, the first flight with both engines effective being made the following month. Deliveries of the production FR-1 began in March 1945, the type equipping US Navy squadron VF-66. Further production contracts raised the number of FR-1s on order to 1,300, but only 66 were actually built when the war ended. None saw combat service, although the FR-1 did serve aboard carriers briefly after the war.

The FR-1 was a low-wing, single-seater with tricycle landing gear which positioned the pilot very high for taxiing and take-off. Dimensions included: wing span 40ft (12.19m), length 32ft 4in (9.86m), height 13ft 7¼in (4.15m) and wing area 275sq ft (25.55m²). A relative lightweight, the FR-1 weighed 7,915lb (3,590kg) empty and 10,595lb (4,806kg) fully loaded. A post-war development was the F2R-1 Dark Shark with a 1,700shp General Electric TG-100

The first Ryan XFR-1 Fireball took to the air on 25 June 1944, while Allied armies were just beginning their drive into Europe. The aircraft was unusual in having both reciprocating and jet engines, and could sustain cruising flight with only the latter, as seen here. (Ryan)

A pair of Ryan FR-1 Fireball fighters over southern California near the maker's San Diego facility in about 1945. It is interesting to imagine how this very fast fighter might have performed in combat but the chance never arose, although the FR-1 had a modest career with the Fleet in post-war years. (Ryan)

The Ryan FR-1 Fireball was a clean functional design and those naval aviators who flew it always felt that they were a part of something special. The very straightforward and conventional piston engine up front was a real contrast to the newfangled jet in the tail. (Ryan)

The final embodiment of wartime technology in any aircraft having a propeller, the Ryan XF2R-1 Dark Shark looks as if it would have fared well against a 'Zero'. (Ryan)

(XT31-GE-2) turboprop engine in the nose and a 1,600lb (726kg) thrust General Electric J31-GE-2 turbojet in the tail.

The FR-1 Fireball attained a maximum speed on both engines of 426mph (686km/h), service ceiling of 43,100ft (13,135m) and range 1,030 miles (1,658km).

The Vought XF5U, or 'Flying Flapjack', was the next aircraft from this manufacturer to receive a fighter designation after the F4U Corsair. It was also one of the most unusual American aircraft of the war, although it probably should be viewed as a research aircraft rather than a fighter.

The idea behind the XF5U was to use a new aircraft configuration to produce a fighter capable of performing over an extreme of airspeeds ranging from 20 to 460mph (32 to 740km/h). The resulting 'flying saucer' had a wing of almost circular plan-

The Vought V-173 (BuNo 02978) was a 'proof of concept' aircraft for the XG5U-1 fighter which followed. Both were referred to as the 'flying pancake' (or 'flap-jack'), the term 'flying saucer' having not yet been invented. The largely fabric-covered V-173 was intended to lead to a successful naval fighter design, but it was not to be. (USN)

One of the most interesting aircraft developed during the war (although it did not begin taxi tests until after VJ-Day and, in fact, never flew at all), the Vought XF5U-1 (BuNo 33958) is seen with its original Hamilton Standard propellers. The pilot reached the cockpit by walking up steps on the back of the aircraft. (Vought)

form, which also comprised the primary structure of the aircraft. Control surfaces were confined to the rear of the wing, consisting of twin fins and rudders, with a swept tailplane on each side. The latter surfaces each had an elevator which could be used collectively for control in pitch or differentially for roll control.

The XF5U was to have retractable, tailwheel-type landing gear. It was to be powered by two 1,350hp Pratt & Whitney R-2800 Twin Wasp radials buried in the wing, one on each side of the fuselage. Via right-angle gearboxes, these engines were to drive specially developed propellers, one at the forward extremity of each wing. Apparently, the aircraft would have been impossible to fly in an asymmetrical condition, as clutches and shafting were provided to ensure that in an emergency both propellers could be driven by one engine.

During the war years, Vought flight-tested the lower-powered model V-173 aerodynamic test vehicle, which demonstrated that the XF5U configuration could work. Of wood and fabric construction, the V-173 made its first flight on 23 November 1942. The V-173 had some aerodynamic problems but was essentially stable with good handling characteristics, proof enough that the XF5U design was viable.

When the full-sized XF5U-1 was rolled out, it was a truly remarkable aircraft. Wing span, if it could be called that when one measured the breadth of the aeroplane across its 'ailevators', was 32ft 6in (9.91m). The saucer-like fuselage was 28ft 1in (8.56m) long. Height of the aircraft was 16ft 8in (5.08m) and the area of its lifting surface was some 475sq ft (44.13m^2). The XF5U-1 weighed 13,107lb (5,945kg) empty and 16,722lb (7,585kg) at maximum take-off weight.

Although it was transported by road to the desert at Muroc, California, and readied for flight, the XF5U-1 never flew. One can only wonder what this remarkable aircraft might have done. Estimated performance figures for the XF5U-1 included a maximum speed of 425mph (684km/h), service ceiling of 34,500ft (10,515m) and range of 710 miles (1,143km). The aircraft would have flown effectively at very low speeds and would have landed at 40mph (64km/h). Although armament was never installed, plans existed for either six 0.50in (12.7mm) machine-guns or four 20mm cannon, plus two 1,000lb (454kg) bombs. It can only be considered a loss that the XF5U-1 got as far as it did and never flew. Even when there was no longer a war going on, the aircraft would have had a valuable function contributing to research.

The XF5U-1 is depicted here with its second set of 'flapper' propeller blades, which were made of laminated wood. Painted on the nose is a likeness of cartoon character Bugs Bunny on a flying carpet. (Vought)

P-61 Black Widow

When Americans first spotted the Black Widow overhead, its existence had not been publicly announced; some feared that the unfamiliar aircraft was a German or Japanese invader. Wearing serial 42-39728 and crossing the California coast, this P-61 shows the dorsal barbette for four 20mm cannon fitted from the 201st P-61B onwards. (Northrop)

On a lazy summer afternoon in Washington in 1944, a government worker looked up to see two aeroplanes flying over. At first he thought he was seeing a pair of P-38 Lightnings. But though cloud cover above them was light, the mysterious duo never seemed to break out of the shade. The young man, an aviation buff, was jolted by the thought that the Luftwaffe must be overhead, for there existed no American aircraft which looked like this – twin booms, a sinister black colour overall, with multiple crew positions.

No one had released any details about the Northrop P-61 Black Widow. Many months were to elapse before the observer realized the identity of this new and exciting aircraft.

Fighting at night does not come naturally to man, and it took several decades for nocturnal air warfare

to become commonplace. Perhaps the night blitz on Britain in 1940 was the first sustained campaign to be carried out during the hours of darkness. The RAF fought during those hours with improvised equipment, hastily defined tactics, and aircraft which had been designed for day fighting. After the American entry into the war, night fighting continued to be the realm of equipment and aircraft which had never been intended for it. Indeed, by the time the Black Widow emerged as the first American aircraft ever to be designed specifically for nocturnal combat, Axis aircraft had mostly been removed from the skies and the need was not as great as in earlier years. This should not detract from the considerable achievement of the P-61 Black Widow, a remarkable warplane making use of radar and other electronics to ply its trade during the night hours.

The US Army Air Corps had had a night fighter as long ago as the Curtiss PN-1 of 1921, and some night training had been attempted during the years immediately preceding the war. After Britain introduced AI (airborne interception) radar with night fighter versions of the Douglas Havoc and Boston, American officers pushed for their own version – a need which became even more important after fighting started in the Pacific, and Japanese bombers paid visits during the hours of darkness.

As a stop-gap measure, the Douglas P-70 conversion of the Havoc was of some utility, but (except for one test aircraft) the P-70 lacked the kind of radar which became available as a result of a major scientific undertaking.

On 18 October 1940 the US Army decided to assign top priority to developing an AI radar which would exploit the cavity magnetron, a new device which simplified radars operating on centimetric wave lengths (rather than, as in the past, radars with wave lengths measured in metres). Development of a dramatic new AI radar was assigned to the Radiation Laboratory, a specially created subsidiary of the Massachusetts Institute of Technology (MIT). With British and American scientists co-operating in the effort on a crash basis, the first microwave radar developed in the US was being tested as early as 4 January 1941.

The new radar had the all-important British magnetron, a Westinghouse pulser, Sperry power-driven dish aerial, and a wholly new receiver set developed by Bell Telephone. Set up on a building rooftop at MIT (and later inside a flying Douglas B-18 Bolo bomber), the prototype centimetric radar showed viewers a stark image of the Boston skyline on the far side of the Charles River. A wholly new General Electric oscilloscope was devised to enable

The first Northrop XP-61 Black Widow (41-19509) with test pilot Vance Breese at the controls, heads aloft on its maiden flight at Hawthorne, California, on 26 May 1942. The canopy framework of this natural-metal aircraft is different from that of production machines, but the essential configuration of the Black Widow was well established from the start. (Northrop)

the operator to use it. Many months of work lay ahead, but this AI radar set eventually became the production SCR-720, the nerve centre of the successful P-61 Black Widow.

Northrop Fighter

On 21 October 1940, just after starting the scientific campaign which produced the radar, the Army requested Northrop's aircraft firm in Hawthorne, California, to begin work on an aircraft to carry the SCR-720.

Only recently on his own after an association with Douglas Aircraft, John K. (Jack) Northrop was a brilliant engineer and stern taskmaster. The P-61 Black Widow he eventually produced cannot be faulted. With hindsight some have argued, however, that none of it was really necessary, that the same

results might have been achieved by installing the revolutionary SCR-720 in a modified B-25 Mitchell or A-26 Invader. Indeed, one strong argument against the need for a dedicated airframe was the fine performance of RAF Mosquitoes and Beaufighters which were converted, not created, for the nocturnal role.

Jack Northrop, assisted by chief engineer Walt Cerny, met Army planners at Wright Field on 5 November 1940 and thrashed out details of the work ahead on the new aircraft. The Army foresaw a multi-place, twin-engined aircraft – perhaps similar to the abandoned Grumman XP-65 – with powerful twin R-2800 engines, cannon armament and, of course, the new radar. Northrop and the Army were in agreement on a twin-boom aircraft with a crew of three: pilot, radar operator and rear gunner. The radar operator/forward gunner would be located in

Close-up of a P-61 Black Widow with an apparent flight test being discussed. The aircraft may not have been aesthetically pleasing, but it had an appealing size and shape. (Northrop)

Northrop P-61 Black Widow on display at the original location of the US Air Force Museum at Dayton, Ohio, in July 1962. (Clyde Gerdes)

145

A Northrop P-61 Black Widow covered with a tarpaulin and, it appears, bearing the nickname 'No Love, No Nothing!' The location may be the Philippines. (via Jeff Ethell)

indicated that the big twin-boom fighter was a winner.

Big was, indeed, the word for the P-61. Northrop's night fighter was an imposing aircraft with an enormous wing spanning 66ft 0¾in (20.11m) with an area of 662sq ft (61.53m^2), possibly the largest wing ever to be flown on any fighter. The aircraft was 49ft 7in (15.11m) long and had a height of 14ft 8in (4.47m). The P-61 weighed a remarkable 23,450lb (10,637kg) empty and reached 36,200lb (16,420kg) at maximum all-up weight. The P-61 had a crew area more spacious than that of many medium bombers.

The second XP-61 took to the air on 18 November 1942 with a number of minor internal changes and painted from the beginning in the glossy black dope which gave the Black Widow its name. Early flight trials were promising, but not without difficulty.

The P-61's rectangular tailplane and elevators needed redesign to improve the Black Widow's pitch characteristics. The original fuel system, with a 270(US)gal flexible cell between the wing spars in the engine nacelles, was augmented by two further 120(US)gal internal tanks and provision for two 310(US)gal drop-tanks on underwing pylons. Tail booms on the prototype machines had been made of welded magnesium, but had to be replaced by booms of conventional flush-riveted light alloy. There were persistent problems with the performance of flaps, which had to be redesigned several times. The P-61 had been designed with enormous flaps which ran almost the full span of its wing trailing edge, making it exceedingly nimble for so large an aircraft; and once they were perfected the huge, twin-engined machine was truly a fighter, able to outmanoeuvre its adversaries at night.

Northrop moved ahead with thirteen YP-61 service-test aircraft (41-18876 to 41-18888). In April 1943 with flight testing far along and less capable P-70 night fighters already serving in combat units, the SCR-720 radar was installed in Black Widow number two. First indications were encouraging, but the Black Widow had another problem. The heavy dorsal gun turret was the culprit. It was equipped with four 0.50in (12.7mm) Colt-Browning M2 machine-guns with 560 rounds, supplementing the nose armament of four 20mm cannon with 200 rounds each. Flight testing showed that the turret, when slewed to the beam position, caused severe tail buffeting.

P-61A Model

Although not every US Army leader was enthusiastic about a dedicated aircraft for the night fighting role, 200 machines were ordered in the P-61A series (42-

Post-war view of a P-61B Black Widow (42-39600) on 23 June 1948 minus the turret which caused troublesome development problems and was left off many aircraft. The turret-less shape was the one used in combat in the China-Burma-India theatre. (USAF)

his own cockpit position above and behind the pilot with a gunsight view straight ahead, while the rear gunner would defend the aircraft's aft hemisphere.

There followed a considerable amount of argument between Northrop and the Army over issues ranging from the location of armament to structural components. In due course, the choice of power-plant was two 2,000hp Pratt & Whitney R-2800 Double Wasp 18-cylinder radials. On 11 January 1941 the Army placed a $1.1 million contract for two XP-61 prototypes (41-19509 and 41-19510).

In natural metal, the first XP-61 was rolled out in May 1942. This aircraft had a non-standard canopy design and a non-functioning mock-up of the intended dorsal gun barbette, which was to hold four 20mm cannon. Ballast filled the nose of the XP-61 in lieu of radar. Development of the radar was proceeding smoothly, in a situation where no expense was too high, but there was no need for it in early flight trials. On 26 May 1942 the first aircraft flew with Vance Breese as pilot, and early handling trials

5485 to 42-5634; 42-39398 to 42-39757). The war was continuing and time would not wait for the dorsal turret problem to be solved, so the gun barbette was fitted to only the first 37 P-61As. Eventually a solution was found and some of the 163 remaining aircraft had the turret retrofitted. An interesting sidelight is that presence or absence of the turret had no real effect on the Black Widow's maximum speed.

The production version of the Black Widow was credited with a maximum speed of 366mph (590km/h) when flying at 20,000ft (6,096m). Initial rate of climb was 2,090ft (637m) per minute. Service ceiling was as high as 41,100ft (12,725m) and range 1,350 miles (2,172km).

The P-61B was the second production version of the Black Widow. 450 were manufactured (42-39398 to 42-39757; 43-8231 to 43-8320) with 2,250hp R-2800-65 engines (actually introduced on the 46th P-61A). Most were equipped with the dorsal gun turret and had improvements in internal systems. Other features of the 'B' model included a slightly longer nose, 12ft 2in (3.71m) Curtiss Electric paddle-bladed hollow-steel propellers with more efficient blades, and four (rather than two) wing pylons for drop-tanks or 1,600lb (726kg) bombs.

The P-61C was the next production version of the Northrop night fighter. Power was provided by further improved 2,800hp R-2800-73 engines with CH-5 turbo-superchargers. This version introduced meshed wing airbrakes. The 'C' model was considerably faster than its predecessors, able to reach 430mph (692km/h) at high altitude where the Black Widow performed best. Forty-one were built (43-8321 to 43-8361) with orders for an additional 476 being cancelled on VJ-Day.

The XP-61D designation went to two P-61As (42-55559 and 42-5587) retrofitted with turbo-charged R-2800-77 engines for flight trials.

XP-61E referred to two P-61Bs (42-39549 and 42-39557) which were rebuilt with slender engine nacelles, four 0.50in (12.7mm) guns in the nose in place of radar, and a smaller crew of pilot and navigator located in tandem beneath a bubble canopy which was the largest piece of unmoulded Plexiglass ever attempted. The slimmer, slightly faster 'E' model with its tandem two-man crew was the inspiration for the Northrop FO-15 Reporter, the reconnaissance aircraft based on the Black Widow and based on part-complete P-61C airframes; 36 of these (45-59300 to 45-59335) served in the Air Force during post-war years. XF-15, XF-15A, and F-15A variants were built. These were the best performers in the series, capable of 440mph (708km/h) with a range of 4,000 miles (6,437km). Some of these aircraft remained in service in the Far East well into the 1950s and were redesignated RF-61Cs in 1948.

The XP-61F designation went to a single Black Widow (43-8338) which was to have been modified to a variation of the XP-61E configuration, but was never completed.

The P-61G was a weather-reconnaissance version of the Black Widow obtained by modifying a number of P-61B airframes in 1945.

Black Widow '317' of the 421st Night Fighter Squadron, 13th Air Force, makes a low pass over Puerto Princesa, Philippines, during the war. (via Jeff Ethell)

The 421st Night Fighter Squadron is depicted again in the form of P-61B Black Widow 42-39682 in a location with considerable precipitation. (via Jeff Ethell)

A 12th Air Force Black Widow over Italy. Aircraft 42-39684 is a late production P-61B. (via Jeff Ethell)

The F2T-1N was the naval version of the Black Widow, consisting of just a dozen surplus P-61As which were assigned bureau numbers (52750 to 52761) and were operated in a training capacity by the US Marine Corps.

The Army was anxious to get the Black Widow into service. The Douglas P-70 was proving inadequate in the night fighter role in the Pacific and the Lockheed P-38M Lightning night fighter was still a long way from being ready for service. The P-61 Black Widow was, to an unusual degree, a sophisticated and expensive aircraft which invited teething troubles and had plenty of them. Many early problems were solved – often the solution, as when removing the trouble-prone turret, was an urgent and 'dirty' fix which addressed the issue only indirectly – but the Black Widow was still trouble-prone as late as March 1944 when the 481st Night Fighter Group's 348th Night Fighter Squadron took delivery of the new fighter at Orlando, Florida.

Pilots were amazed at the size, power and strength of the Black Widow. Above all, they were impressed with the fact that such a large aircraft could be manoeuvred wildly in the heat of combat. The Army cautioned pilots not to engage in stalls, spins, flick rolls and sustained inverted flight, but the plain fact was that the P-61 was nearly as nimble as smaller, single-engined fighters. The pilot of a P-61 felt a little odd, knowing that his radar operator/forward gunner sat above, as well as behind him, and pilots were especially uncomfortable about the propellers being in line with their cockpit position. Another point of

discomfort, until it was rectified, was that the Black Widow was originally designed without handles or releases to extricate a crew trapped in the aircraft following a forced landing. Continuing difficulties in the basic Black Widow design were symbolized by 229 design changes in the fighter's cannon installation over two years of development.

Combat Action

By D-Day, 6 June 1944, deliveries of the Black Widow were proceeding at the rate of three a day to night fighter squadrons in Europe and the Pacific. The first air-to-air victory was credited on 6 July 1944 when the 6th Night Fighter Squadron shot down a Japanese Mitsubishi G4M 'Betty' bomber.

The 422nd and 425th Night Fighter Squadrons reached England as early as May 1944, but the Army confined crew members to a long programme of classroom study before any operational missions could be mounted. Meanwhile, Army leaders in the ETO (European Theatre of Operations) became enamoured of the idea that the de Havilland Mosquito could perform the nocturnal combat mission better than the big P-61. Lieutenant Colonel Oris B. Johnson of the 422nd and Major Leon G. Lewis of the 425th assembled their best crews and arranged for a showdown air engagement at Hurn. The Black Widow proved itself by a narrow margin (according to Mosquito pilots) or 'whipped the pants off' the other aircraft (if one believes P-61 pilots); and the trouble-prone P-61 was finally cleared for

combat over the European continent. Because of other priorities, however, the night fighter squadrons were relocated from Charmy Down to Scorton, 200 miles (322km) north of their original air base.

In August 1944 the 422nd and 425th went into action, flying night intruder missions against locomotives, supply convoys, even bridges, and getting into combat with Messerschmitt Bf 109s and 110s, Dornier Do 217s, and other Luftwaffe fighters which ventured out into the darkness. On the Italian front, the 414th Night Fighter Squadron converted from the Bristol Beaufighter to the P-61B Black Widow in time to score five aerial kills before the fighting ended. The 415th, 416th and 417th Squadrons also converted to the big Northrop night fighter, but did not see significant air-to-air action.

The Black Widow was one of several fighter types which in due course found themselves committed against the German V-1 flying bombs being hurled at the British Isles from mid-1944 onwards. P-61s caught and shot down nine of the flying bombs, one of them from a scant 100ft (30m) dead astern, which almost took the Black Widow with it.

The P-61 Black Widow really earned its spurs in the Pacific, with the 418th and 421st Night Fighter Squadrons, and in the vast CBI (China-Burma-India) theatre with the 426th and 427th Squadrons.

After its aircraft were transported by sea and assembled in India, the P-61A-equipped 426th arrived at Chengtu, China, on 6 October 1944, charged with providing security for B-29 bases in the region. The 427th arrived soon after, following a side trip to Italy. On 29 october 1944 a Black Widow crew headed by Captain Robert R. Scott shot down a Japanese twin-engined bomber to get the first night fighter kill ever scored in the CBI. It was hot at Chengtu and pilots sometimes flew barechested,

with helmet and parachute but no shirt. Some of the all-black P-61As in China carried lavish nose art and lengthy nicknames, ranging from 'Green-Eyed from Riverside' to 'Jing-Bow Joy Ride', although few photos have survived of these colourful touches of individuality.

A P-61 Black Widow of the 458th Night Fighter Squadron is one of a number of claimants to have scored the final air-to-air kill of the war.

Total P-61 production was 674 by the end of the war and 706 in all.

No P-61 Black Widow is flying today, much to the chagrin of enthusiasts who would like to see this very special and very rugged wartime fighter in action. We do not always remember our heritage as well as we might. A senior Northrop official in Washington was recently asked about reports that the current YF-23A Advanced Tactical Fighter would be nicknamed the 'Black Widow Two'. His response: 'I don't know about that. What was the Black Widow One?'

Salvage Effort

A diverse group of pilots and history buffs is working to salvage the wreckage of a P-61 Black Widow discovered in a remote corner of densely populated Okinawa, which is today part of Japan. The group hopes to return this Black Widow hulk to flying condition and present it at air shows.

Meanwhile, Black Widows are on static display in three locations around the United States. The US Air Force has aircraft 43-8353, a P-61C, restored to represent a different Black Widow, 42-39468. In its black paint scheme, guns pointing ahead from its resting spot on the museum floor, the P-61C retains some of the sinister look which is so characteristic of this unique warplane.

The extra lights on this deadly Northrop P-61 Black Widow in the Mediterranean area were put on for the photographer. Without the help of the lights, it would be difficult to create a likeness of the Black Widow in its natural, nocturnal environment. (via Jeff Ethell)

Of Mustangs and Jets

It is hard to believe that less than four years elapsed between the American entry into the Second World War and the victory achieved on VJ-Day. In the world of the fighter aircraft, the end of the conflict was also the end of an arduous journey from the poorly prepared fighter community of pre-war years to the aerial armada which reigned supreme as the Allies ruled the skies in the final weeks of the war. In less than four years, the operational American fighter aircraft progressed from the Seversky P-35 which was slaughtered en masse on 8 December 1941 to the North American P-51D Mustang which overcame all opposition by 15 August 1945. While Mustangs ruled the skies in the combat zone, the first jets were

flying. The American fighter had reached a peak – more powerful, faster, more heavily armed, than anyone could have imagined in the late 1930s. Air combat performance, which included speed, manoeuvrability and firepower, had improved almost beyond imagination.

Not that the Axis merely rolled over and played dead the moment Mustangs appeared on the scene. Germany had been first with jet aircraft and the Messerschmitt Me 262 was the world's first operational jet fighter. The Luftwaffe also fielded the Messerschmitt Me 163 rocket-propelled fighter, which was somewhat less practical but no less ominous. In the ETO, Eighth Air Force Chief General James E. Doolittle was seriously concerned about

German jets by late 1944 and had to admit that there was very little he could do about the problem, except to increase the number of escort fighters per long-range mission over the continent.

Returning from escorting a formation of Fortresses over Leuna on 8 November 1944, two P-51D Mustang pilots, Lieutenants James W. Kenney and Warren Corwin of the 357th Fighter Group, spotted a Luftwaffe aircraft moving towards the B-17s and identified it as an Me 262. The jets had been thrown into action and led by Major Walter Nowotny, an Austrian ace with 258 victories and holder of the Knight's Cross.

The Mustang pilots saw the jet make a firing pass from ten o'clock at the bomber formation. Next, the jet fighter made a surprisingly quick 180deg turn and prepared to come back for another pass from five o'clock. Kenney, with Corwin behind him, made a pass at the jet. Kenney began firing from about 400 yards and saw a puff of smoke belch forth from the Me 262.

The Luftwaffe pilot dived for the deck. Corwin flew a split-S to provide back-up support while Kenney rolled down on the Me 262 and got on his tail again. Kenney overshot twice, demonstrating that the Mustang was not to be underrated even in the presence of a jet, but the second time the Me 262 pilot went into a turn to the left, the American pilot was able to close in and score hits with his machine-guns. The German pilot, Captain Franz Schall, baled out, giving Kenney a memorable jet kill. A second Me 262 was claimed by another Mustang pilot in a separate action on the same day.

Thanks in no small measure to a series of blunders by the Germans, some of them caused by Hitler second-guessing his general staff, the Luftwaffe's growing fleet of jet fighters was not able to prevail over the persistent Allies and the Mustang continued to rule the air. On the other side of the world, Japan operated a few advanced propeller-driven fighters before the end of the conflict, but no operational jets, and there was no serious challenge to American supremacy. But things could have happened differently. And when it was all over, Americans were forced to admit to themselves that they might have moved more quickly in developing their own jets.

The saga of the American jet fighter begins with a young engineer whose schoolmates dubbed him 'Kelly' because he constantly wore green ties despite his Swedish ancestry. As early as 1939, Clarence L. (Kelly) Johnson had struggled to persuade his superiors to move ahead – with private investment, if necessary – to develop a prototype of a jet-powered fighter.

Jet Background

The idea was not new. A Greek named Hero invented a steam engine that operated on the jet principle before the coming of Christ. By 1939, metallurgy and the ability of science to confine fire within metal had advanced to a point where a true jet engine could be built. Frank Whittle in Britain was close behind Dr Hans-Joachim Pabst von Ohain in Germany in developing the jet engine, and it was an engine designed by the latter that produced the Heinkel He 178, the world's first jet aircraft, which made its first flight on 27 August 1939.

That year, under Kelly Johnson's direction, Lockheed produced at least three alternative design studies for a jet fighter known as the company model L-133 but never given a military designation. All these futuristic designs were twin-engined, incorporating unswept stainless steel wings.

In the Lockheed engineering group, Johnson had Nathan Price, an engineer with a record of accomplishment and considerable experience with industrial turbine powerplants. Johnson asked Price to try his hand at designing a turbojet engine. Price came up with a powerplant nearly a decade ahead of its time with such advanced features as 'two-spool' turbine stages and high compression ratio. The L-133 powered by Price's engine was estimated to be capable of 625mph (1,006km/h) at a startling altitude of 50,000ft (15,480m). But with wartime pressures building, Lockheed were unable to sell the L-133 to the Army Air Corps, possibly because it seemed a high-risk project – so important momentum was lost.

Bell Aircraft in Buffalo, New York, maintained their momentum from the beginning. First they proposed a jet concept which consisted of a P-39 Airacobra with two wing-mounted Westinghouse jet engines. The P-39 variant went nowhere, but the Bell XP-59A Airacomet became the first American jet aircraft, flying at Muroc Dry Lake, California, on 2 October 1942 with Robert M. Stanley as pilot. Taken by lorry to the test site with a fake propeller fixed to its nose to hide its true purpose, the XP-59A Airacomet was a mixture of American airframe technology and British gas turbine knowledge.

The XP-59 designation had originally been allocated to the Bell company model 16, a twin-boom, propeller-driven pusher fighter developed from the firm's unbuilt XP-52. When the project was cancelled at an early stage, reissuing the XP-59 designation seemed a prudent way to guard the secret that a jet fighter was under development. On 5 September 1941 Bell were asked to build three company model 27, or XP-59A, aircraft (42-108784 to 42-108786), each powered by two 2,000lb (907kg) thrust British

America's first jet fighter, lagging somewhat behind progress in jet propulsion attained in Germany and Britain, was developed under conditions of great secrecy until some numbers were flying and its existence had to be acknowledged. This Bell P-59A Airacomet is being evaluated at NAS Patuxent River, Maryland, in January 1944. (via M. J. Kasiuba)

I-A jet engines designed by Whittle and soon to be built in the USA as the General Electric I-16 (later J31-GE-5). Following Stanley's first flight in the XP-59A, the first military flight was made by Brigadier General Laurence C. Craigie on 2 October 1942.

The XP-59A Airacomet was about the size of larger, propeller-driven fighters. It was a mid-wing, tricycle-gear aircraft. Wing span was 45ft 6in (13.87m), length 38ft 1½in (11.62m), height 12ft (3.66m) and wing area 385.8sq ft (35.84m²). The first American jet fighter had an empty weight of 8,165lb (3,704kg) and maximum take-off weight of 13,700lb (6,214kg).

The XP-59A delivered only modest improvement in performance over the best propeller-driven fighters of the early 1940s, but Army planners were beginning to see, perhaps belatedly, that jet power was the wave of the future. Following the three test aircraft, thirteen service-test YP-59As (42-108771 to 42-108783) were evaluated, powered by American-built General Electric I-16s. These were followed by production orders for 20 P-59A Airacomets (44-22609 to 44-22628).

The P-59B designation went originally to a planned single-engined variant which was never built. The 30 P-59Bs completed (44-22629 to 44-22658) out of 80 originally ordered retained the twin-jet

layout and featured minor internal improvements. The designation XF2L-1 is sometimes quoted for US Navy Airacomets tested at Patuxent River, Maryland, and three of these did acquire Navy bureau numbers (44-22651, 44-22657 and 44-22658, becoming 64100, 64108 and 64109), but the XP-59A nomenclature was in fact retained.

It is unlikely that the US Army lost much by not getting the Bell P-59 Airacomet into combat. The P-59 was the first of the new wave, and it made an enormous contribution merely by proving that a jet fighter could be built and flown. In itself it was not much of a combat aeroplane and could easily have been defeated by a good pilot in a P-51 Mustang or an F4U Corsair. In fact, the Navy's tests showed that the P-59 was inferior to the Corsair in several respects.

Performance

Nor are performance figures for the P-59 Airacomet especially exciting. The first American jet fighter was credited with the rather unexceptional top speed of 409mph (658km/h) and normally cruised at 375mph (604km/h). Service ceiling was impressive, being 46,200ft (14,080m), but the Airacomet's range of 400 miles (644km) was far from remarkable. Sixty-six Airacomets of all versions were built. Armament was

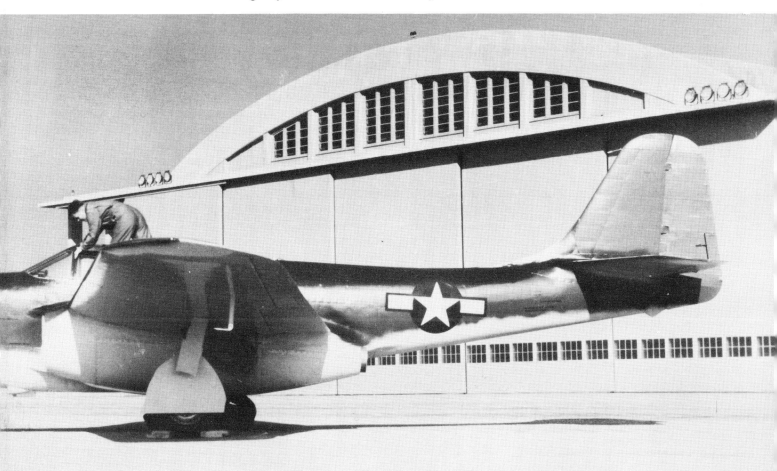

one 37mm M4 cannon and three 0.50in (12.7mm) machine-guns mounted in the nose.

A single YP-59A (42-108773) was shipped to the RAE test establishment at Farnborough in exchange for a Gloster Meteor, as flown by the RAF. This machine was given the British serial RJ362/G and was evaluated only briefly. It seems likely that British pilots found it inferior to the Meteor which, unlike the American jets, did get into combat before the war ended.

Late in its career, a number of P-59s served as drones and drone controllers, and at least one was built with an additional cockpit position in the nose.

Most of the other jet aircraft designed by Americans during the war years – among them the Northrop XP-79, Bell XP-83, Republic XP-84, McDonnell XFD and North American FJ – did not appear until long after VJ-Day and are not properly part of this account. The same cannot be said, however, of the Lockheed P-80 Shooting Star. Although the P-80 story begins nearly four years after Kelly Johnson's L-133 design was rejected, it remains very much a part of the events of that global war.

On 18 June 1943 Johnson took stairs two at a time, vaulting up to the office of Robert Gross, Lockheed's President. In the office were Gross and Hal Hibbard, the chief engineer.

'Wright Field wants us to submit a proposal for building a plane around a British jet engine,' Johnson told the two corporate leaders. 'I've worked out some figures. I think we can promise them 180-day delivery. What do you think?'

180 days! As we have seen, the story of the rapid design and development of the P-51 Mustang may have been largely a myth. If so, no one had ever developed a new aircraft in such a period, and certainly not an aircraft introducing revolutionary power. The time limit was brutal. But there could be only one outcome to the discussion. 'Okay, Kelly,' Gross concluded. 'It's your baby. We'll give you all the help we can.'

The USA was very much in arrears in jet aircraft development, however, and it was mostly because nobody had listened to Lockheed or to Johnson.

The Gloster E.28/39, Gloster Meteor, and Messerschmitt Me 262 all flew before the Bell XP-59A did. And, as previously noted, the XP-59A, unlike the Meteor or Me 262, was merely a test aircraft, never viewed as combat-capable. Belatedly, Bell forged ahead with studies for an 'XP-59B' version, intended as a functioning combat aircraft. Kelly Johnson's Lockheed design team at Burbank, California, may have had access to some of this material. In any event, in late 1943 Johnson and his staff made up for lost time.

The jet-powered Northrop XP-79 flying wing was designed to ram enemy bombers. It is only a small exaggeration to call it a suicide aircraft. In fact, it was dangerous to fly and did not fly very well. (Northrop)

Johnson travelled to Wright Field with a sketch of the proposed P-80 and a dozen pages of detailed specifications. He met General Henry H. (Hap) Arnold, Army Air Forces Chief of Staff, and reiterated the 180-day pledge. Johnson had in mind that the aircraft which would result from his labours would be simple – deceptively so. A straightforward, clean-lined aeroplane, it was to have only one real departure, other than its method of propulsion.

Johnson wanted what he called a 'wind-tunnel wing' on the new aircraft. This was a departure from proven aerofoil designs and could have been dangerous. The aerofoil Johnson picked was a laminar-flow type never tested on a propeller-driven aircraft, but wind-tunnel tests seemed to show that it would work.

Lockheed's letter contract was dated 23 June 1943. Hibbard and Johnson picked top people from throughout Lockheed and bought an entire machine shop to get tools which could not be spared from the production work on wartime aircraft then being built. To get a building, plant engineers slapped together a temporary structure near the wind tunnel at the Burbank facility known as B-1, made from old engine boxes and canvas in ten days.

Assistant project engineers with Johnson on the XP-80 were W. P. Ralston and Don Palmer, both of whom enjoyed long careers with Lockheed. At the peak of the development effort, the XP-80 project had only 128 men working on it – 23 engineers and 105 shop men. Art Viereck supervised the shop group.

Pressing Schedule

A calendar labelled 'Our Days Are Numbered' hung over the shop where the XP-80 took shape. Johnson enforced a schedule of 10 hours a day, six days a week. It was drafty and cold in the temporary building and the sickness rate was high. Nevertheless, Johnson had to force people not to come in on Sunday, telling them that without enough rest, they would not be able to make a contribution.

One problem that bothered XP-80 workers was the lack of the expected de Havilland jet engine. The men were working with only a blueprint. When the engine finally arrived, seven days before completion of the airframe, changes had to be made. These included the addition of 35lb (15.87kg) which put the XP-80 just 6lb (2.72kg) over the contracted weight of 8,600lb (3,900kg).

Put together ahead of the USAAF's demanding schedule – delivered not in 180 days but on the 143rd, 15 November 1943 – the prototype XP-80 (44-83020), nicknamed 'Lulu Belle', was powered by the belatedly delivered de Havilland H-1B Goblin

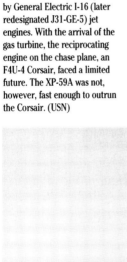

The old and the new. 42-108778 is the eighth of thirteen service-test Bell YP-59A Airacomets, powered by General Electric I-16 (later redesignated J31-GE-5) jet engines. With the arrival of the gas turbine, the reciprocating engine on the chase plane, an F4U-4 Corsair, faced a limited future. The XP-59A was not, however, fast enough to outrun the Corsair. (USN)

turbo-jet delivering a mere 3,000lb of thrust.

Late in the evening after the Army accepted the XP-80, Guy Bristow, the de Havilland engine expert, was giving the engine a final run-up before the scheduled flight the next morning. As the engine howled at full power, both intake ducts collapsed. Pieces of metal flew into the jet's hungry maw and vanished with a grinding noise. The Sunday rule was broken and Lockheed engineers put in a gruelling schedule to try to get the XP-80 back into flyable condition. In the end a new engine had to be installed.

The spinach-green prototype was finally ready to fly on 8 January 1944, with Milo Burcham at the controls. Johnson looked at Burcham and said, 'Just fly it, Milo. Find out if she's a lady or a witch. And if you have any trouble at all, bring her back.'

Burcham was later to say, 'You don't *fly* this aeroplane. You just hint to it where you want to go.' The first flight of the XP-80 built up to a peak when Burcham buzzed the crowd watching at Muroc Dry Lake.

The XP-80 was unique in having its green paint scheme and square-tipped wings and vertical fin. The original 'Lulu Belle' had a wing span of 37ft (11.45m), length of 32ft 10in (10.15m), height of 10ft (3.06m) and a maximum speed of 502mph (808km/h).

But the Goblin engine was not ideal for the aircraft. The Army wanted Lockheed to build a new version using a General Electric development of a Whittle engine called the I-40. Again, records were set and the first of two XP-80As with the new powerplant (44-83021 and 44-83022), called the 'Gray Ghost', was flown at Muroc on 10 June 1944 with Tony LeVier as pilot. The I-40 delivered 3,835lb

The kind of clean, clear static portrait which always excites the dyed-in-the-wool student of aviation history. P-59A Airacomet 44-22650 wears pre-1947 national insignia but a buzz number which suggests that the picture was taken after VJ-Day. The P-59 was not really ideal for military missions and never came close to being fielded in the combat zone. (Peter M. Bowers)

(1,740kg) of thrust. Lockheed received an immediate contract for thirteen service-test YP-80As (44-83023 to 44-83035).

By the war's end, two P-80s were in Italy getting ready for combat, two more had reached England, and no fewer than sixteen were flying in all. Taking the contingent to Italy was Lieutenant Colonel Jack Carter, who had been XP-80 project officer and was now on Lockheed's development planning staff. Just before the end of the fighting, P-80s flew in demonstrations and once or twice ventured out to look for German fighters – none of which were to be found.

As with any aircraft, especially one with a new concept in propulsion, the early P-80s had their problems. A turbine wheel disintegrated on the 'Gray Ghost', sawing off the tail of the plane and causing Tony LeVier to bale out and severely injure his back. Lockheed test pilot Ernie Claypool was killed

on a night flight in a P-80 when he went aloft to prove that the Lockheed fighter did not leave a comet-like trail as the German jets did. It was proved tragically – he collided with a B-25 Mitchell chase aircraft in the dark.

Early P-80 Shooting Star accidents claimed the lives of Burcham on 20 October 1944 (due to a fuel system failure) and of America's top air ace, Major Richard I. Bong, on 6 August 1945 (due to engine failure on take-off).

It was the highly successful J33, developed from British technology by General Electric but manufactured by Allison, which made the Shooting Star work. The J33-A-11 of 4,000lb thrust, the J33-A-19 of 5,200lb, and the J33-A-25 of 5,400lb powered postwar P-80A, 'B' and 'C' models.

The designation F-14A was assigned to the photo-reconnaissance version of the Lockheed fighter which became the FP-80A and later the RF-80A. The non-standard designation P-80R was used for a streamlined, one-off racing aircraft which set a speed record but was otherwise less than a full success.

The story of the Lockheed P-80 Shooting Star (which became the F-80 in 1947) goes well into the post-war era and includes valiant service in Korea, including a kill in history's first jet-versus-jet battle (against a MiG-15) on 8 November 1950. Some 1,714 examples of all versions of the P-80/F-80 were built. Perhaps even more important, the F-80 airframe became the basis of the F-94 interceptor which guarded the North American continent in the 1950s and of the R-33 trainer which was built in far larger numbers than any fighter variant.

P-80 Figures

A typical production P-80 Shooting Star had a wing span of 38ft 10½in (12.04m), length of 34ft 6in (10.68m) and height of 11ft 4in (3.50m). Empty weight was 8,240lb (3,738kg), while operational gross weight was about 15,000lb (6,800kg). Maximum speed at sea-level was 580mph (933km/h) and service ceiling 39,500ft (12,229m).

It was a long road from the Seversky P-35 to the Lockheed P-80. It was a long war. For every hero who survived and managed to excel, racking up kill marks on the canopy rails of a Mustang, Hellcat or Corsair, there were other men who did not get their names into print and who gave their lives, flying American fighters of the Second World War, in defence of freedom.

The story of American fighter aircraft in the Second World War ends with the Japanese Emperor's surrender to Allied forces on 15 August

1943. An F-5, photo-reconnaissance version of the P-38 Lightning, became the first Allied aircraft to land at a Japanese airfield after it was all over. On 7 September when the surrender document was signed aboard the battleship USS *Missouri* in Tokyo Bay, the US Navy put up what is believed to be the largest formation of military aircraft ever assembled – at least 1,400 aeroplanes in a low-level flyover, led by a brace of incomparable Hellcats.

What did not happen was a flyover by every type of fighter developed by the American industrial machine during the war years. By 1945 a number of aircraft types which had been in service in 1941 could no longer be found anywhere. Nor did anyone work very hard at salvaging wartime fighters for future museum-goers to enjoy. Half a century later, what survives for the entertainment and enlightenment of the student of history is a mishmash.

There were some wartime fighters – Lockheed XP-49, the lightweight XP-51G Mustang – which flew hundreds of hours, but of which no in-flight photograph has survived. At least one wartime fighter, the Hughes D-3, has never been depicted in any photo, while details of some fighter proposals, like the General Motors F2M-1, are virtually non-existent.

Some wartime manufacturers – Brewster and Republic – no longer exist. Others, such as Vought

and Martin, have been through restructuring on several occasions and no longer hold records or photos from the war. A few, such as Douglas and North American, have made an effort to preserve documents and pictures of their wartime role and can still be consulted today. The standard in the history field has long been in the hands of the Grumman Corporation at Bethpage, Long Island, with a history office peopled by Lois Lovisolo and Peter Kirkup – leagues ahead of other corporate historians.

The 'warbird' movement is now deeply rooted and has given millions of air show ticket-holders a chance to hear those Wright and Pratt & Whitney engines growling, those silver wings flashing in the sun, as restored pursuit ships hurtle overhead. But a festive air show is a time for fun and there must be other times, perforce, for contemplation. The men who flew American fighters to victory in the Second World War helped give us the freedom we enjoy today. But the sad truth remains, freedom does not survive for long without challenge and courage must be tested every generation. It has been said before and it will be said again: when we ponder what those fighter pilots achieved, we need to look very hard at ourselves and to ask ourselves whether we could do it again if we had to.

Two Lockheed P-80 Shooting Stars actually reached the European theatre before the end of hostilities. The prototype aircraft (44-83020), seen here, has survived and is being restored for display at the National Air and Space Museum. (Lockheed)

Index

159